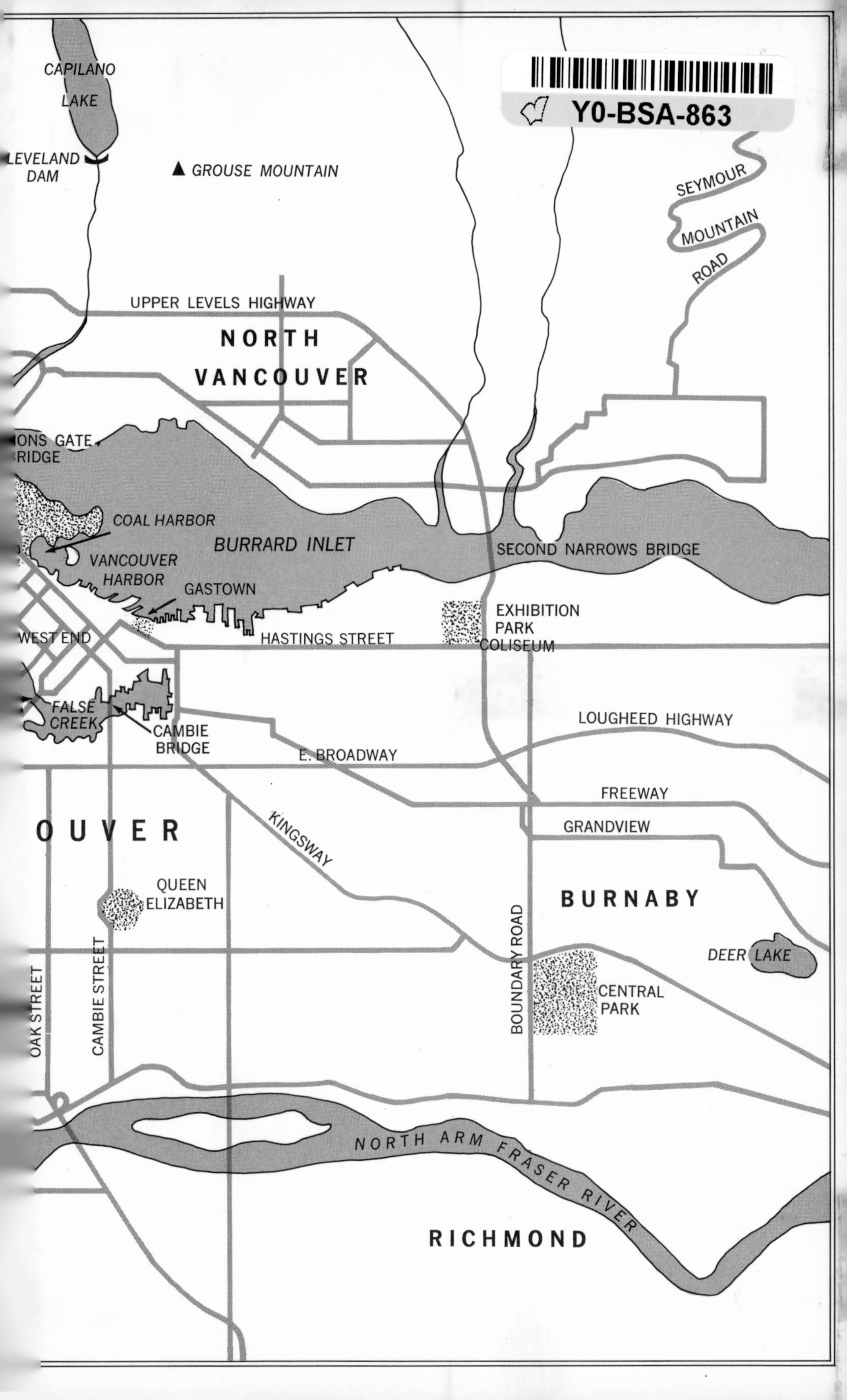
CAPILANO
LAKE
GROUSE MOUNTAIN
SEYMOUR
MOUNTAIN
ROAD
UPPER LEVELS HIGHWAY
NORTH
VANCOUVER
COAL HARBOR
BURRARD INLET
VANCOUVER
HARBOR
GASTOWN
SECOND NARROWS BRIDGE
EXHIBITION
PARK
COLISEUM
WEST END
HASTINGS STREET
FALSE
CREEK
CAMBIE
BRIDGE
LOUGHEED HIGHWAY
E. BROADWAY
FREEWAY
GRANDVIEW
KINGSWAY
BURNABY
QUEEN
ELIZABETH
BOUNDARY ROAD
DEER LAKE
CENTRAL
PARK
OAK STREET
CAMBIE STREET
NORTH ARM FRASER RIVER
RICHMOND

VANCOUVER

Eric Nicol

DOUBLEDAY CANADA, LIMITED TORONTO
DOUBLEDAY & COMPANY, INC. GARDEN CITY, NEW YORK
1970

LIBRARY OF CONGRESS CATALOG CARD NUMBER 74-132497

PRINTED IN THE UNITED STATES OF AMERICA

To my parents, William and Amelia Nicol,
who introduced me to the subject.

CONTENTS

THE VIEW FROM HERE

It has been called "the Riviera of Canada." It has also been called "the Liverpool of the Pacific." Because it lies almost halfway between Great Britain and the Antipodes, someone described it as "the City of Imperial Destiny." "The Pittsburgh of the West" and "the Glasgow of the Northwest" were two other designations intended to be flattering. An early-twentieth-century tourist perceived a physical resemblance between Burrard Inlet and the Sea of Marmora, and saw False Creek as a second Golden Horn. As both cities lay on a peninsula, he called the younger one "the Stamboul of the West," with all that this implied in the similitude of Stanley Park to Seraglio Point.

More commonly it has been called "the San Francisco of the North," "the Gateway to the Orient," "the Sunset Doorway of the Dominion" and any number of other exits to all points west. To the tourist bureau it is "Canada's Evergreen Playground," and to the less reverent, "Canada's Evergray Peeground." It has been called "the Terminal City," a name that only in later years gained the connotation of inoperable malignancy.

Most often it is called "Vancouver." The name should identify it best of all, but does not, for much of the world's population, because Vancouver shares its name with an island thirty miles to the west and larger than Belgium.

The confusion, and the spate of sobriquets derived of older

centers, were the price paid by a city that was not finally and officially named till 1886.

In 1886, when Vancouver was but a gaggle of shacks constituting little more than an impertinence to the surrounding wilderness, Halifax, its counterpart on the east coast, had been a recognizable city for more than a century. Toronto in 1886 was already enjoying the sybaritic comfort of central heating indoors, and outdoors the refinements of croquet and archery—at a time when an arrow shot in Vancouver was not yet classified as a leisure activity. As for Montreal, the year of Vancouver's incorporation as a city coincided with complaints from prominent citizens of the island city of the St. Lawrence that the rail approaches of the new and palatial Windsor Station would ruin their gardens.

Thus Vancouver is a story barely started. In 1969, the year in which the population of Greater Vancouver touched one million, Miss Margaret McNeil, the first white child born in Vancouver, was still very much alive at eighty-three and the recipient of a gift birthday cake from the city. In the perspective of history's eras, the ripples from the canoes of the Squamish villagers cleaving the inlet break against the bow wave of hovercraft on regular passenger service from the harbor.

In its short span of existence Vancouver has hardly had time to acquire glory, the military decoration of clusters of cannonballs such as ennoble the breastworks of Quebec and Louisburg. One of the city's most distinguished scholars, Dr. G. G. Sedgewick, voiced the opinion that Vancouver would never produce great human achievement: "A genius never arises," he said, "unless he comes from a soil potent with great happenings." Sedgewick himself came from the Maritimes, that cradle of wonders. His opinion has been shared by many other immigrants to the city, from Scots seeking the unholy grail of gold nuggets to young Americans dodging the draft. Having attained the shores of Vancouver, the world was their oyster, and they had no particular incentive to implant the irritant grain of sand that produces the pearl.

Despite the fact that the city was officially credited with siring, almost simultaneously, the most beautiful woman in the world and the strongest man in the world, the story of Vancouver does not lend itself to treatment as epic. Too many of the notable episodes of her short history have a strong element of the ludicrous—such as the fact that the only battle with the Indians was with East Indians, who won at least a moral victory before being shipped back to the Punjab. Nothing has been fired in anger, including the six head coaches expended by the professional football team during its sixteen years of struggle to appear contentious. In short, Vancouver's overture suggests not so much Wagner as Gilbert and Sullivan.

The story is of course by no means finished. One of the difficulties of writing the biography of a city is that, with exceptions such as Troy and Babylon, the subject outlives both the work and its author. A history of London or Paris or Rome, written less than a hundred years after their founding, would constitute no more than a preface. Vancouver has yet to know her Florentine Renaissance, let alone her Alexandrian Period. Moreover this early history is, of necessity, to a large degree anecdotal, possibly apocryphal. No sweep of grand armies, no Lady Hamilton entertaining the fleet attracted official historians to the scene of Vancouver's subjugation by an armada of realtors. To paraphrase Henry Ford slightly, of early Vancouver it may be said that history is bunkhouse.

A further hazard to historical accuracy is that there can be as many biographies of a city as there have been people who have lived their lives in it. This biography, certainly, carries no warranty of being objective. A man can no more be objective about the city that has been his home for most of his life than he could about a woman he had lived with for nearly fifty years. He cannot quote the statistics of change—the 36–24–34 that has become 36–36–36—without some intrusion of personal feeling.

My feeling about Vancouver is too personal for proper refrigeration of cold facts. I arrived in the city in August, 1920, at the age of eight months. My first impressions are therefore sketchy. Having been born into the middle of a Kingston winter, however, I am sure that the baby fat was grateful for its transfer to the milder climate. Except for a few years of absence dictated by World War II and post-graduate education, I made my home in Vancouver for the ensuing half-century. I married a Vancouver girl, my three children are natives, and our present house is only a five-minute stroll from the piece of Point Grey bush among whose uprooted stumps I played cowboys and Indians as a youngster. My children go to school with young members of the same Musqueam tribe that chased Simon Fraser back up the river, and needless to say we all share the same attitude toward easterners.

Many of my friends moved away to more exhilarating climates, where the exhilaration earned them $5,000 a year more, on the average, than they would have made doing the same job in Vancouver, handicapped by an atmosphere compulsively relaxing. A New York stage director who flew to Vancouver to discuss a play with me was able to stand the atmosphere for only forty-eight hours before fleeing to the United Airlines terminal with the strangled cry: "It's debilitating!"

To choose to remain in Vancouver all one's life, aware that no organism flourishes here in more spectacular variety than the fungus, is to forswear some of the blessings of materialism. The most intense drama played out, again and again, in this city has been the private agony of the company executive who, after being posted to Vancouver from Winnipeg as a regional manager, learns that he is being promoted to president of the company—and moved to Toronto. Such breast-beating, soul-searching and eventual abjuration of worldly splendor are nowhere else to be observed in the immediate vicinity of a $70,000 home.

Although I cannot claim impartiality, therefore, I do give notice to the reader that, within the limitations imposed by consumption of the lotus, I have tried to get the facts straight. I freely confess sins of omission, but none intentional. If I praise my love, I refuse to flatter. For instance let me cite right here the fact that on July 19, 1921, a drowned woman picked up by Japanese fishermen at Brockton Point was found to have webbed feet. She was promptly identified as a resident.

My honesty thus demonstrated, and after several hundred hours of research and keening over microfilm, I shall be deeply hurt if this history of Vancouver is read as a work of fiction. The facts speak for themselves, when I let them (which is quite often, actually), and perhaps they will be useful to historians, whether professional or dilettante, curious to pinpoint the moment when this painfully young, beautiful, publican's brat of a city reached the age of discretion.

ERIC NICOL

ACKNOWLEDGMENTS

Without the help of a small legion of librarians, all charming and prodigal with patience, this book would lack such substance as is to its credit. In particular I am grateful to Mrs. Anne Yandle and her staff in Special Collections at the University of British Columbia, and to Miss Shirley Mooney and her associates in the Pacific Press Library.

Mr. Ron D'Altroy, curator of the photo archives of the Vancouver Public Library, has been helpful well beyond the call of bureaucracy, as has been the staff of the Vancouver Visitors Bureau.

As research assistants Miss Patricia Roy and Mr. John Lees have granted me a portion of their valuable time. Finally, it would be difficult to exaggerate my dependence on the pioneer work of Major J. S. Matthews in recording and preserving the early history of Vancouver. Were it not for the loving care of this man, city archivist for a generous lifetime, very little lore would be available to those of us who bumble into the historical journals. Needless to say, the errors in fact are all my own work.

E.N.

VANCOUVER

CHAPTER 1

The Setting

Geological child of the last ice age • Intimations of humidity and other climate • The rain forest, the gentle predators

THE CITY clings to the coast, a crustacean that has found just enough foothold at the tide line a latitudinal minute before the continent plunges into the sea. The two parallel mountain chains extending from California to Alaska, abruptly, breath-takingly, commit to the deep the valley between them. The broad plain that from the south stretches a giant Chinese checkerboard of orange groves, vineyards, lettuce farms and forest, narrows under the fearsome compression of rock upheaved, is bade a heroic farewell by the outriding peaks of Mount Baker and the Olympic Peninsula, and vanishes beneath the waters of Puget Sound.

From this point northward the coast is a Switzerland whose most impressive valleys lie under green fathoms of sea. The outer range of the cordilleran family of mountains surfaces as innumerable islands, alpine peaks on whose lower slopes graze not goats but rock cod. Largest of these is the leviathan of Vancouver Island, whose huge bulk buffers the fury of the Pacific and moderates nature's fierce determination to limit the terrain to a verticality lashed by surf.

Yet the mainland coast of the Strait of Georgia is tortured by another violence of the geological past: deep fiords transversing the Coast Range, twisting inlets gouged by immense bulldozers of glacial ice. Here are Howe Sound, and the Indian Arm of Burrard Inlet, brooding in mist or fog or even simple twilight, their islands dorsal-finned killer whales frozen forever in the act of cresting the shadowed depths. These are the enigmas that gave the early explorers a *frisson* of trepidation. Even so hardened a sailor as Captain George Vancouver was moved to record, in *A Voyage of Discovery:*

> The low fertile shores we had been accustomed to see, though lately with some interruption, here no longer existed; their place was now occupied by the base of the stupendous snowy barrier, thinly wooded, and rising from the sea abruptly to the clouds; from whose frigid summit, the dissolving snow in foaming torrents rushed down the sides and chasms of its rugged surface, exhibiting altogether a sublime, though gloomy spectacle, which animated nature seemed to have deserted. . . .

This "unfathomable sea" the early visitors willingly put behind them: a nice place to visit, but they wouldn't want to live here, "entrapped," as Captain Vancouver wrote home from Nootka Sound in 1794, "in this infernal ocean."

The captain failed to notice the one gentling factor in the situation of the city that was to be named after him, that boded a setting hospitable to man, namely the delta of the Fraser River.

The great river made the city possible. As its first highway to the interior. As provider of the lush valley to victual it. As a creator of the Burrard Peninsula itself on which the city was to bloom, literally. Sixty million years ago, during the age of mammals, the granddaddy of the Fraser flowed through the lower mainland area and out to sea. From the super-delta of this river was hardened the sandstone of Stanley Park and Kitsilano Beach, in whose beds lie fossils of semitropical plant life—palms, sequoias, giant ferns. Across this exemplary foundation flowed the glaciers of the ice ages, glacial till layering with sands, marine clays enriched with the bones of whales and shellfish. During the last ice age, fifteen thousand years ago, the Fraser Valley lay under ice a mile thick, while only a few hundred miles to the south men continued to live in unglaciated flatlands. The terrestrial heavings of the period include the small volcano that is part of Little Mountain.

The ultimate mix of the eons' geological blender was glacial drift and sand or sandy loam, and delta clay, fine-grained and containing an abundance of organic matter. Exceptionally fertile, combining good water-holding capacity with drainage, here lay a garden waiting for the gardener. Before he came it was already covered by some of the largest plants on earth—magnificent stands of Douglas fir, a forest whose individuals stood hundreds of feet tall, with skin thicker than most fully-grown trees. Eden grew disguised by its own prodigiousness.

Thus Vancouver lies at the exact junction of the inevitable with the impossible. From the shallow ridge of Burrard Peninsula the view to the south is placid, extrovert; the view to the north eruptive in barriers of mountain. Merely to turn around is to be reminded that, though man may be infinitely perfectible, a certain humility is imposed by nature.

The two ridges of Burrard Peninsula, separated by False Creek, are bounded on the south by the Fraser, on the north by Burrard Inlet, the peninsula having as its western extremity Point Grey, its eastern limit the Pitt River. North to south the peninsula measures about 8½ miles; east to west, 22½ miles. The spine of land humps here and there, but it is generally low, rarely more than 400 feet above sea level, though the northern edge drops off at heights up to 1,300 feet. An early visitor to Vancouver, Bernard McEvoy, describing the attractions of the young city, wrote: "One of the minor ones is that their city is not on a dead level, but exhibits a pleasing diversity of grade, so that everywhere you get views of sea and mountains by walking an inconsiderable distance."

Between Point Grey and the North Shore mountains lies Burrard Inlet. The outer harbor, English Bay, measures 4½ miles north-south and 5½ miles west-east, being 360 feet deep at the mouth and providing safe anchorage for ships waiting their turn to enter the inner harbor.

The inner harbor of the inlet is a dazzling feat of illusion, Providence performing sleight of hand on a grand scale. So narrow—1,200 feet—is the strait between the North Shore and Stanley Park's Prospect Point that the Spanish navigator Narváez looked hard and saw no break between the dense fringes of forest. He called the promontory Punta de la Bodega, an example of seeing the point yet missing the meaning.

Since that error of 1791 tens of thousands of explorers have passed through the First Narrows, most of them gripping the rail of their ocean liner a shade more tightly than necessary at the closeness of the great cliffs, then experiencing the marvelous moment when the inner harbor expands before their eyes into the port of Vancouver.

From that protective entranceway the inlet extends thirteen and a half miles to the head of the inlet, broadening into bays of deep, safe mooring, whose only problem to shipping is the erratic currents of the tides in a harbor that drains as furiously as a Scottish bathtub.

The harbor fulfills all the natural requirements of a great port, and provides a backdrop of spectacular beauty to solace sailors denied shore leave. The outer pool of English Bay, with an area of about twenty square miles, has its shallow end on the south shore, the deep along the north. The south shore consists of sandy beaches eroded by tide and wind from the high clay banks that reach eastward nearly three miles from Point Grey. In-shore here the water is too shallow for bottoms other than those plying the bikini.

The North Shore, in contrast, rugged and rocky with many small, deep coves—"where the surf tramps musically ashore," as one admirer put it—affords shelter for fish boats and tugs, as well as berths for ocean-going freighters in the stretch east of the First Narrows. This inner harbor of the inlet inherits its virtues from the ancient outlet of the Fraser River, deepened by glaciation, but without the precipitous shoring of the fiord that makes dock installation difficult.

One anomaly should, however, be mentioned. Usually the great port cities—Naples for instance—face outward to the sea. The situation of Vancouver's harbor caused her to face inward. It is interesting to speculate that this introversion has convoluted the character of the city's inhabitants. Introspection comes naturally to those whose horizon is one day foreshortened by mountain range, the next day by even more circumambient mist.

The Coast Range mountains visible from Vancouver on a clear day include the Lions (5,800 feet) and Grouse Mountain (4,200 feet) as well as Hollyburn Ridge and Seymour Mountain. The Lions, so named because of the resemblance of the two peaks, vis-à-vis, to Landseer's cats couchant in Trafalgar Square, are to Vancouver what Sugar Loaf Mountain is to Rio, Diamond Head to Honolulu. They guard the entrance to the harbor in the spirit of general admission that is essential to a city largely supported by tourism.

The Lions are visible only to the arrived. Vancouver is covert about such vistas. It is possible to live in the city for many years without having discovered all the perspectives that open to the eye only from specific viewpoints, most of them unmapped.

Among these secretive glories are the deep canyons that valley both shores, particularly those of the North Shore mountains, where they cleave to depths of more than four thousand feet and shelter the dark turbulence of Capilano, Lynn and Seymour creeks.

Deception laid upon deception is False Creek, a tidal inlet once snaking four and a half miles between the ridges on which the city grew, and Lost Lagoon, so named by the Indian poetess Pauline Johnson, who in canoeing about her favorite haunt of Coal Harbour one evening found that the tide had gone out from the pretty cove, leaving a mud flat. The Indian name for the lagoon, Chul-wah-ulch, meaning "dry when the tide goes out," suggests that there is nothing like sound engineering for making illusion more attractive than reality.

Trompe l'oeil, the French call it, the tableau in which objects are reproduced so faithfully that they become illusive. Most often it is the light that collaborates with the topography of Vancouver to deceive the eye. Rare are the days when the light is sharply declarative, as in Calgary, or Winnipeg, or (the edges rubbed off somewhat) Toronto or Montreal. More commonly Vancouver light is gently diffused, a composite of grays or a pastel water color. The Vancouver sky looks ever ready to be washed away, as it invariably is. As a magazine writer of 1911 put it, with the zesty metaphor of the time: "Of course, this is only when the light is on a high key, but whether the light key is high or low, whether fuming mist or quilted clouds improvise variations, whether the whimpering breeze brushes the zinc-blue water into a thousand silver mirrors or the rough, round salty sea-wind chases the little ships home, English Bay has wonderful beauty."

The situation of Vancouver demonstrates, with a conclusiveness at times overwhelming, the effect on precipitation of a mountain range intercepting moisture-laden winds from the ocean. As one geographer has described it in print: "The rugged slops with precipitous walls descend into the water." A Freudian slop, this, understandable in view of the 130 inches of precipitation that is the annual average for the moister North Shore slops.

Just across the inlet, removed from the full impact of soggy air condensing against the mountainside, Vancouver has an annual precipitation of 60.24 inches, diminishing as the recipient moves southward through the city. South Vancouver receives 49.40 inches, and on Sea Island the International Airport is, relatively speaking, a desert.

Mother of all this humidity is the Pacific Ocean. The earth does not offer a broader bosom from which to draw liquid sustenance. From the Gulf of Alaska that yields the cold rain, from the area of the Hawaiian Islands to which the coast gives suck for its monsoons, Vancouver enjoys the mammary plenitude that makes it the wettest of all the major cities of Canada. In Vancouver the rainy season, like the courting period of Robert Benchley's newts, opens in March and extends through the following February. The driest month is July, provided one's holidays fall in June or August.

Just as the northern Indians are said to have forty different names for snow, Vancouver people have a variety of names for rain, of which the most printable is "Scotch mist." Snow is not a factor in the mystique of Vancouver, whose inhabitants are the exception to the rule that designates Canadians as "God's frozen people." The coast Indians have their own prognosis of a snowstorm: "Big snow, little snow. Little snow, big snow." The big, fat flakes that more usually constitute snowfall on the city swirl down like demented doilies, dainty-looking to none but strangers who do not recognize them for what they are: prospective slush.

Yet in winter there is always the chance of a dry snow born of the cold front that has crept down the interior valleys of British Columbia and broken through to salt water, via the inlets, in a diminished reprise of the ice age. The snow that squeaks beneath the boot, that decorates the tree branch without bowing it, is never out of the question for Christmas Eve, though the more common state of climatic affairs has roses budded, and the lawns looking greenly lush and accusing to him who has given his mower a holiday. Among other abnormalities it must be noted that on June 23, 1901, snow flurries struck the southern outskirts of the city, turning to hail that subdued a Methodist tent meeting on Mount Pleasant with the drums of the Lord. And on December 28, 1968, Vancouver shivered in the grip of the only sub-zero temperature (—.2 degree) recorded to that time.

This capacity for the unexpected relieves the rain monotony which, for those who lose faith in small miracles, no doubt contributes to Vancouver's having the highest rate of suicides in the country. Rather than dwell on the exceptional, however, boosters of the city's climate extol the prevailing characteristics of mildness and equability. This elemental restraint is exercised by the Pacific. Besides being an inexhaustible source of moisture the ocean is latent heat. The warm Japan Current curls along the coast to bring vast quantities of warm water into contact with latitude 49° 17′, a combination that makes for temperance so far unmatched by the W.C.T.U.

Besides providing radiant heat, the same ocean currents that take the chill off winter moderate the warmth of summer—an air conditioner whose moving parts are serviced by Jehovah. The mean annual temperature at Vancouver is 49.1 degrees, the mean annual range of temperature being 27.9 degrees as compared with Toronto's 46 degrees, Edmonton's 55.2 degrees, and Winnipeg's 69.3 degrees.

The same conduction system reduces the daily range (twenty-four-hour interval) to less than 15 degrees, against the 35 degrees that on the central plains make the difference between day and night a matter of putting on something besides the lights. Similarly the mean diurnal variability is small. Vancouver has nothing to compare with the chinook that defrosts Calgary so quickly that the thinner people spoil.

In fact strong winds of any kind are unusual in Vancouver. Typhoon Frieda, which swept up the coast in October, 1962, was a unique experience for the city. Normally the prevailing winds, from the southeast in winter, from the southwest in summer, expend any gale force over the Gulf and enter the city tractably, often as breezes sweet and light as a butterfly kiss. (The average hourly velocity is 4.4 mph; Toronto, 10.9 mph; Montreal, 13.6 mph; Winnipeg, 12.9 mph.)

Often there is no breeze at all. Then into the clear, cool dusk of autumn the fog funnels through the inlet, up the Fraser, with the weird velocity of the motionless, rolling over the city, submerging its shallows, leaving its hills and tops of buildings as islets in a sea of cotton wool, stilling the rumble of the metropolis and making its people captive to that doleful contralto, the foghorn. With the maximum fog frequency of Canada's larger cities, Vancouver looks very much like San Francisco at those times when it cannot be seen at all.

Vancouver shades its nearest rival, the Great Lakes, as Canada's cloudiest area. The diversity of types of cloud observable by those enterprising enough to lie on their backs, in a buttercupped field, is *sans pareil.* Billowing cumulo-nimbus turns mountain into a sundae for the gods. Or Vancouver's clouds can drift in strata of opposite direction, can lower the sky to the height of a tall Swede, can reproduce the shirred texture of the tidal sand bar, with all the colors of a child's paintbox.

Inevitably, such atmospheric profusion has its exception: Vancouver has the least amount of sunshine of Canada's major cities. The percentage of sunshine is approximately the same as at London or Antwerp, though it is sometimes difficult to convince the immigrant from the Old World. Because of British Columbia's liquor laws, the homeland often seems sunnier to settlers. Vancouver has been slow to permit drinking outdoors, as in the sidewalk cafes that have made Paris the city of eternal sunshine.

The coastal Indians, unlike those farther south, have not been disposed to worship the sun, possibly because they never saw enough of it to be convinced of divinity. But the diffidence of the solar body to expose itself makes its appearance all the more precious. Some people appreciate Vancouver's sunshine so much that they spend the winter in Palm Springs just to be near it.

In Vancouver a heat wave is defined as a warm, sunny morning followed by a warm, sunny afternoon. In some years, summer falls on a Thursday. If the moss grows only on the north side of the trunk, the person is from out of town. So run the articles of faith in Vancouver's sunshine. "The summer climate of Vancouver, and of all the lower mainland of British Columbia, can be described with no other word than perfect," summarized a Vancouver Tourist Bureau brochure published in 1906, adding that from the middle of June, "and at all events with the first of July, there is an unbroken spell of fine weather until late in September and often into October." Climatic data such as these make the west coast Indian legends look as factual as a ferry schedule.

Vancouver people also live something of a lie when they quote as official the weather observations made at Vancouver International Airport, several miles to the south, in sunny Richmond. For example, the average January precipitation at the airport is 5.24 inches; at City Hall, 8.28 inches. The closer the proximity to the inlet and the North Shore mountains, the greater the risk, for the sedentary, of breaking out in mushrooms.

If the sun is a fickle presence, however, even more so are thunder and lightning. High drama is not part of the repertory played within the proscenium of Vancouver's sky. Climatically, the Vancouverite is perhaps closer to the Tahitian than to the Torontonian. The off-shore breeze lulls him. He is mildly marinated in salt air. His sea-level intake of ozone is so considerable that visiting motorists doze off at traffic lights. Easterners in town become excessively relaxed, suffer twinges of Calvinist guilt and go to church for the first time in years to purge themselves of languor. Vancouver has had the largest number of drug addicts in Canada, not counting those on the nod from the psychedelic experience of simply inhaling, exhaling.

Does moderation of climate encourage extremes of behavior? The history of Vancouver, with some exceptions, indicates the contrary. The temperance of conduct nurtured by the mother country, with its very similar climatic temper, has by and large been transplanted successfully into the forest soil. A more ingenuous generation might even assume that Vancouver's climate was decreed by Queen Victoria, whom excesses in performance of whatever kind did not amuse.

The flora of Vancouver, immigrants that settled in following the glacial period, are no more flamboyant than the human cohabitants. Of trees, the evergreen arbutus is perhaps the most exotic dancer, stripping its bark with some mildly sensational bumps, if no grinds. More common are the alder and yew, the dogwood and the willow, and particularly the broad-leafed maple impressing with sheer amplitude, a totality of greenness that makes the red patches of the flicker woodpecker a color accent almost too bold.

Some of the smaller growth is subtropical and unique in Canada —grasses, wild hyacinth, paintbrush—and there is an overlap of southern fauna in the residency of the wood thrush, the towhee, and the cuckoo which, at the northern limit of its range, has been heard commenting on the various levels of government. Bluebirds and bobolink are no longer observed with any frequency, but the Stellar's jaybird has willingly picked up the slack of conversation, shifting through the fir trees with a blue-black, crest-erect scolding of all other species that have persisted in his precinct.

Nothing in this green corner of creation is sinister. The shark that attacked diver John Bruce, January 8, 1925, while he was repairing a water main ninety feet below the surface of Second Narrows, would have qualified as another fish story had not Bruce stunned the seven-foot man-eater with an iron bar and landed it on a wharf. More regular proprietors of the purlieus are the black bear and the cinnamon bear, barging through the underbrush with the subtlety of a landslide, button eyes set to savage nothing more sensate than the salmonberry. Ferocity finds an advocate only in the cougar, and the cat clings closely to its assignment of thinning out the coast deer whose fertility would otherwise compromise the breed's reputation for shyness.

The great bald eagle soars effortlessly over the inlet, describing on the unlined page of the sky the spiraled circles of the McLean system of penmanship. The voices of the avian chorus are rather coarse—crows, gulls, ducks, the inharmonious heron—or sadly piping killdeer, mosquito hawks soughing. Vancouver has been the natural environment for Scottish Presbyterian ministers. It has engendered fewer fine singers than radio hot-line commentators.

Vancouver has always, however, been close to the silent voices of the sea, to the salmon and the herring and the killer whale whose amazing intelligence was respected by the Indian and has been discovered by the white man in the due time with which he observes creatures other than himself.

Monarch of all this primordial splendor, the largest living thing in the northern latitudes, was the rain forest itself, the stand of cedar, hemlock and, above all, what came to be known as the Douglas fir. Beneath these giants lay a jungle society dependent on their presence: graceful ferns and mosses, fungi, the skunk cabbage—sensationally phallic but unwise in choice of scent—and that slow-motion stalker, the leopard slug.

This was the truly virgin forest, preserved till recent times not only by the absence of white men but by bough-dripping dampness that sponged out the lightning strikes that elsewhere decimated the mammoth evergreens. At the time of the discovery of Burrard Inlet in the eighteenth century, the peninsula on the south and the lower mountain slopes to the north were covered completely by the finest timber of its kind in the world. Soil, climate and history had conjoined to present to the new men from Europe the treasure that was to buy Vancouver from the wilderness and sustain it as the main source of wealth. It is therefore embarrassing to have to record that, having cast their gaze on these riches immediately accessible, the white masters of the intellect chose as their first attempt at resource development: coal mining.

The *opéra bouffe* that is the history of Vancouver opened with a rousing rendition of "Can't See the Forest for the Trees."

CHAPTER 2 1791–1862

Exploration: A Saga of Inadvertence

The Spanish but not the main • Captain Vancouver investigates the inlet for Northwest Passage • Moody and the Royal Engineers • The Plumper finds coal • The Three Greenhorns buy some property

AMERICA's experience of discovery has been largely that of being blundered upon by explorers who were looking for something else. Vancouver lives under an even thicker historical cloud—after it was found the search went on for more desirable property.

The same two nations whose ships battled and plundered one another to gain possession of Aztec gold and the coasts of South American waters, in the waters off Burrard Inlet cooperated, made accommodations, and peaceably completed the transaction of the bartered bride who is too homely to fight over. Captain George Vancouver's account of his encounter off Point Grey with the Spanish ships of Galiano and Valdéz is enough to sicken the lover of lively action and blood-stained contention. True, Vancouver does criticize the Spaniards for their cramped quarters aboard ship, but he concedes: "in point of living, they possessed many more comforts than could reasonably have been expected."

The tone is that of a suburban matron getting a peek at the inside of the house of someone earlier moved into the neighborhood. Today, a stone cairn on Point Grey's Marine Drive draws attention to the spot where representatives of the two rival powers met and compared menus.

From the beginning, the explorers dispatched from Europe were concerned not with acquiring real estate but with finding the Strait of Anian, the Northwest Passage that would facilitate trade with the lands of silk and spices. It was to establish the truth or falsity of Juan de Fuca's locating the elusive strait, at the same latitude as the vicinity of the future Vancouver city, that Captain Cook was detoured from the more agreeable scene of the South Pacific.

To the eye of the sailor looking for a seaway to the Atlantic, anything less was a dead-end street. Thus it was not till very nearly the nineteenth century that the great powers bestirred themselves to explore for its own sake the coastline whose sea otter were to provide such a valuable item of trade.

The first European to venture into the Gulf of Georgia and view the future site of Vancouver was Pilot Commander José María Narváez, in the *Santa Saturnina.* The year was 1791. Narváez charted the area and named its headlands, but did not penetrate beyond the Isla de Langara that is today's Point Grey. The white water of the flooding Fraser River, curling into English Bay, caused Narváez to interpret Point Grey as an island lying between two arms of the river.

The year following, two Spanish ships, the *Sutil* and *Mexicana,* under the command of Dionisio Alcalá Galiano and Cayento Valdéz, arrived to chart the Gulf more accurately. Spanish names abound both in the islands and in Vancouver, where they mingle with the very English and the very Indian. (Three successive streets in Point Grey are called Sasamat, Trimble and Blanca.) It is amusing if idle to speculate on what the city would be like today had the imperial vigor of Spain been waxing instead of waning. The wedding of Spanish custom with west coat air would have bred the world's longest siesta.

However, it was an Englishman who first subjected to thorough scrutiny the locus of the city that was to bear his name. Captain George Vancouver, a veteran of voyages with the incomparable Cook, had already toured the Antipodes and the South Pacific when his two ships, *Discovery* and *Chatham,* entered the Strait of Juan de Fuca, and took the measure of the sound that Vancouver named after one of his officers, Mr. Puget. With typical thoroughness, the kind of dogged British adherence to regulations that bowed the backs of his oarsmen and made them pray for deliverance to a less scrupulous command, the captain cast anchor in the sound and continued his research northward through "the Gulph" in a yawl, which he skippered, accompanied by a launch commanded by Mr. Puget. These smaller craft were navigable in the tortuous inlets where the larger ships of sail could come to several kinds of grief. If they were commensurately small comfort to the rowers that powered them, they were less intimidating than the Spanish sloop that the Indians saw as a supernatural apparition—a floating island from which hung giant cobwebs.

In *A Voyage of Discovery* Vancouver describes the arrival of the first European tourists officially welcomed by the indigenes:

> From point Grey we proceeded first up the eastern branch of the sound, where, about a league from its entrance, we passed to the northward of an island which nearly terminated its extent, forming a passage from ten to seven fathoms deep, not more than a cable's length in width. The island lying exactly across the channel, appeared to form a similar passage to the south of it, with a smaller island lying before it. From these islands, the channel, in width about half a mile, continued its direction about east. Here we were met by about fifty Indians, in their canoes, who conducted themselves with the greatest decorum and civility [the "island" was Stanley Park, the Indians the port's first welcoming committee] presenting us with several fish cooked, and undressed, of the sort already mentioned as resembling smelt.

According to the Indians' account of the reception, as Vancouver's two boats passed inward through the First Narrows the Indians of the village of Whoi-whoi, near the present Lumberman's Arch in Stanley Park, paddled forth in their canoes and showered the visitors with handfuls of soft white feathers plucked from waterfowl. The picture of the snowy down fluttering over the newcomers, escorted by natives conducting themselves with the greatest decorum, hardly fulfills the conventional tableau of ambush by redskins.

The feathers were in fact the opening salvo of what has come to be known as the soft sell. Vancouver continues his account: "These good people, finding we were inclined to make some return for their hospitality, showed much understanding in preferring iron to copper. . . ." Thus were the city's roots as a trading port firmly set in the original inhabitants. Captain Vancouver found these Indians second only to those up Howe Sound in their "ardent desire for commercial transactions." The Howe Sound villagers excelled "not only in bartering amongst themselves the different valuables they had obtained from us, but when that trade became slack, in exchanging those articles again with our people; in which traffic they always took care to gain some advantage, and would frequently exult on the occasion." If General Custer had made his last stand against the Squamish it appears that there would have been no massacre in the usual sense, but he would have gone home without his watch, his horse and his pants, and blowing feathers out of his nose.

Captain Vancouver accommodated the new friends met in the inlet by proceeding "under an easy sail" deeper into "this channel, which, after Sir Harry Burrard of the navy I have distinguished by the name of Burrard's Channel." Encouraged to keep pace in their canoes, the Indians repeatedly assembled for conferences, on which Vancouver comments: "In our short intercourse with the people of this country, we have generally found these consultations take place." This natural disposition toward jaw-jaw instead of war-war spared the city the background of bloodshed that is glamorous only to the generation that never felt a wound.

So tranquil was the entrance that, on reaching the head of the inlet, the crews of the two boats elected to spend the night ashore. The steep banks affording no convenient space for pitching a tent, some slept in the boats.

> Some of the young gentlemen, however, preferring the stony beach for their couch, without considering the line of high water mark, found themselves incommoded by the flood tide, of which they were not apprized until they were nearly afloat; and one of them slept so sound, that I believe he might have been conveyed to some distance, had he not been awakened by his companions.

This was the first but by no means the last tribute paid to the sedative effect of the site. Any brave hearts asleep in the deep were outnumbered by those that dozed off on the surface.

Retracing their route, the following morning, Captain Vancouver and his crews noted the southern shore: "of a moderate height, and though rocky, well covered with trees of large growth, especially of the pine tribe." This was the heartland of Vancouver-to-be. Had the good captain known that he was gazing upon the main conservatory of his name's renown, he might have spared it a longer paragraph.

His more immediate interest, however, was completion of the exploration of the gulf and the sudden congestion of traffic around Point Grey: the ships of Galiano and Valdéz. Having passed the time of day with the Spaniards, and sensibly accepted with good grace—though "no small degree of mortifications"—the news that the Spaniards had explored the gulf a year earlier, and more completely, Vancouver declined the invitation of a lift back to his mother ships, and rowed doughtily southward.

His last commercial contact with the Indians of the area cost him a wicked amount of reputation. Off what is now called Sturgeon Bank, and what he described as "swampy flat," the captain "purchased of the natives some excellent fish of that kind, weighing from fourteen to two hundred pounds each." The sturgeon is a river fish, yet the explorer continued on his way, beyond the muddied waters of the estuary, oblivious of the presence of the great river that the Spaniards had dubbed Rio Biancho and that later would bear the name of Simon Fraser.

Captain Vancouver had entered Burrard Inlet June 13, 1792. In due course he circumnavigated Vancouver Island, finished his painstaking survey of the coast and sailed home to write his account of a prodigious feat of seamanship. But for almost seventy years after his visit, Burrard Inlet seems to have remained undisturbed by white men. It was as if he had never come. The Indian villages drowsed in the sun or by the smoke of the longhouse fires. The children played among the canoes drawn up on the pebbly beaches, and shouted to children of other villages close enough to be within earshot. For almost seven decades, while literary Europe responded to the romantic revival and the mysticism of untrammeled wilds, the inlet remained more chastely primitive than the most romantic visions of Chateaubriand and Shelley. While men discussed the desirability of return to the state of Rousseau's happy savage, the real thing speared salmon in these quiet waters.

The Squamish tribal history does record, however, that about the time of the Crimean War the Indians made an agreement with British naval officers whereby, in the event of enemy invasion of Burrard Inlet, the British would defend the south shore, the Squamish the north shore. It is beguiling to think that the Charge of the Light Brigade, whatever its other tactical deficiencies, was in no danger of being outflanked at Whoi-whoi.

Apocryphal or not, the story presages the historical fact that the quiet inlet was to draw next notice as a convenience to the military.

The event that stirred new interest in the whole area of the lower mainland was the discovery of gold along the Fraser River in 1858. As the prospectors poured up the valley to the strands that yielded yellow wealth, the need for control of a wilderness complicated by human greed led the British government to create the crown colony of British Columbia. James Douglas, governor of Vancouver Island, became also governor of the new colony. In addition, a company of Royal Engineers under Colonel R. C. Moody was dispatched from England to make surveys, build roads and enforce the Queen's law.

Moody was responsible for choosing the village of Queensborough, later New Westminster, as the capital of the colony. Burrard Inlet was the back door to the capital and to the golden arterial highway of the Fraser. To establish the inlet as an alternative route of access to New Westminster, Moody's men in 1859 built a pack trail to the inlet. In 1861 the trail was widened to take wagons and was named North Road. This was to be the supply line in the event of blockade of the Fraser mouth, either by military foe or the ice of winter. Needless to say, the *hubris* of present-day Vancouver has been moderated not a whit by the fact that its development began as a facility to be used in case of emergency only.

The Royal Engineers charted the coastline of the inlet and designated the future Stanley Park as a military reserve, the natural parapet in the defense of New Westminster against hostile action from the rear. Moody's men were in fact a remarkable body of troops—150 officers and other ranks—not only planning military redoubts but also building houses and churches, making maps and preparing the first postage stamps. Their versatility alone was enough to bewilder lawlessness into submission. When Colonel Moody slung lead it was as a plumb line.

By 1863 his engineers had completed the survey of lots 181–185, townsite of Granville, and on the disbanding of his force each man received a grant of 150 acres. Moody and most of his men returned to England, the rest remaining to make their homes in the colony, but all were on the ground floor of the land speculation that has been the guiding light of Vancouver from the moment that the site was but a gleam in the surveyor's eye.

Meantime, Burrard Inlet had been charted by the naval arm. In 1859, Her Majesty's Surveying Ship *Plumper*—one of the most happily named vessels in maritime annals—nosed along the shoreline so productively that on June 14 Captain George Henry Richards was able to report to Governor Douglas the discovery of coal seams on the southern side of the inner harbor, about a mile and a half within the First Narrows.

> Having visited the spot and satisfied myself that sufficient [coal] could be procured with facility to test practically in our furnaces under steam, I dispatched a boat and procured in the course of a few hours over two tons, it has been used in the ship's galley (Grant's patent distilling apparatus) with success, and I shall shortly take an opportunity of giving it a further trial in the steam furnaces.

Richards was excited enough about his find to send off samples to Colonel Moody.

> . . . as it appears to me that it may exercise a considerable and possibly an immediate influence on the prosperity of the new town of Queensborough, on the Fraser, within such an easy distance both by land and sea of this fine Port; I have thought it right to apprise your Excellency of the facts without delay, and I send the "Shark" to Esquimalt for this purpose; she will also carry to you specimens of the coal, with the fossiliferous sandstone in which it is embedded.

A supplementary report by Dr. C. B. Wood, the ship's surgeon with a flair for geology, concluded:

> Selected samples of coal taken from the second seam presented all the outward character of English Newcastle, it burns freely in a common furnace, and produces little smoke. In the overlying sandstone or roof a considerable number of beautiful vegetable fossils are found, mostly leaves of exogens belonging to the orders of Mastworts and Willow-worts. In conclusion I may observe that indica-

> tions of coal are likewise observed about 100 yards from the line of cropping I have described in the sandstone cliff, which are here 7 or 8 feet in thickness covered by a deep vegetable mould, in the shape of small seams of coal firmly embedded between layers of sandstone.

By the same remarkable kind of coincidence that marked Captain Vancouver's meeting the Spanish ships off Point Grey, another party of coal seekers shared time and place with the *Plumper*. Walter Moberly, an explorer and surveyor of some fame, and one of the cofounders of the village of Queensborough, had joined up with Robert Burnaby, the Secretary of the Department of Lands and Works, to bring a party of men to Burrard Inlet to prospect for coal. The story goes that, having made camp at the foot of what is now Bute Street, the prospectors were startled to see H.M.S.S. *Plumper* steam around Brockton Point. By one account, the two exploring groups had a merry beach party around the roaring fire, which may or may not have benefited from lumps of the coal of little smoke.

If so, it was one of the last social affairs so heated. Contrary to Dr. Wood's expectation, the coal seam proved to be of no commercial value. This failure was entirely merciful, sparing the capacious inlet the fate of a coal-mining town, with Stanley Park a pitted blot on creation. Of the first industrial promise nothing remains but the name Coal Harbour, a nominative companion piece for False Creek.

One lump of the coal was, however, destined to play a further part in Vancouver's history. This morsel, displayed in a New Westminster shop window, caught the eye of a young prospector named John Morton. A Yorkshire potter whose venture into the Cariboo gold fields had proved sterile, Morton was reminded that in England he and his father had always found the best clay in the neighborhood of veins of coal. Morton hired an Indian guide to take him to the mother lode. The safari down the newly cut trail to the inlet, the canoe trip to Coal Harbour and around Stanley Park, the night spent under the stars, appear to have been something of an idyll in that late summer of 1862. So much so, that when Morton found the coal to be embedded in sandstone instead of clay, his disappointment was offset by his being enamored of the wild place. He was the first white man sufficiently smitten to want to live here.

More than this, Morton was able to convey his enthusiasm to the two other Englishmen who were his cronies. One, Sam Brighouse, was a cousin that he had persuaded to accompany him from England to the land of opportunity—the United States. Aboard the paddle-wheel steamer *Great Eastern,* outward bound for New York, the two had befriended William Hailstone, who joined them on their trek to San Francisco via the route of the forty-niners. Subsequently the trio sailed north to Esquimalt, moving up the Fraser on June 25, 1862, in search of the elusive gold dust and nugget.

A man whose persuasiveness clearly outshone his talent for practical industry, Morton convinced Brighouse and Hailstone that they should try farming his new-found paradise. The phantasy in which they took equal shares was that working this land could be more profitable than washing river silt. The three partners thus bought 550 acres of lot 185, lying between the two government reserves set by Colonely Moody; that is, between the future Stanley Park on the west and what is now Burrard Street on the east. On the north their property line was the inlet; on the south, English Bay. In short, they pre-empted the entire area of today's West End, acre for acre probably the most valuable piece of real estate west of Toronto's Golden Mile.

The land cost them $1.01 an acre.

The general feeling at the time among their acquaintances was that the "three greenhorn Englishmen" had squandered their grub-stake. It was said that the government polished up the chunk of coal in the New Westminster shop window in hopes of bagging another clay pigeon.

Subject to some misgivings of their own, John, Sam and Willie cleared a patch of their land and became the first settlers in what was to be Vancouver—a distinction whose significance escaped them at the time. During the winter of 1862–63 they built a shack on the bluff overlooking the inlet, just west of the present site of the Marine Building. They cut a trail southward to False Creek, by which they could link up with the military trail to New Westminster. Simple enough to say, but a work of such monumental drudgery, through more than a mile of chilled jungle, that the three pioneers must have asked themselves more than once whether they were compelled by method or bush madness.

The unhallowed trinity, drawing on resources of strength peculiar to the servants of Britain's imperial destiny, also built a brickyard and put in a vegetable plot. In addition to living in the midst of somewhat unpredictable Indians, and having a tenuous line of communication with the outside world, the partners could not all go off to town together for an extended holiday. One of them had always to be in residence to conform with the legal requirement of pre-emption.

Pre-emption, by authority of Governor Douglas, was a method of land acquisition permitting a British subject to obtain a grant of land not yet surveyed. Until the land was surveyed, no payment was required. Emboldened by this budget plan, the three men in a hut had taken very nearly the full pre-emption limit of 160 acres to a customer. The suspicion that they had bitten off more than they could comfortably chew was sharpened by the arrival, in the winter of 1863, of the party of Royal Engineers to make the first property survey of the peninsula, supplementing the already existing bloc, which was to become Hastings Townsite, with four lots and a townsite reserve—the future village of Granville.

Facing the bleak facts of bill collection, Morton & Co. returned to the Cariboo, presumably in shifts. They established a toehold on reality, however, in that instead of panning for gold they dug ditches and built roads. They were not trying to find their fortune up-river. They sought to make enough money to hang onto the soggy Eldorado of real estate fronting on Coal Harbour.

According to one chronicler (J. H. Grant, "Burrard Inlet in Early Times," *British Columbia Magazine*, June, 1911) their periods of residency were not altogether grim.

> They had plenty to eat and were not lonely. Among other things they had brought to the shack a grindstone. This implement proved a veritable gold mine. The Indians had never seen a grindstone, and when they learned to use it they were overjoyed. Morton and his *tillicums* told them to use it whenever they wished. In return for this privilege the grateful natives kept the shack well supplied with fish and *mowich*. For their groceries the pioneers walked to New Westminster and packed them on their backs over "Maxie's trail."

This legend of the merry millers does not anticipate the more stark circumstances of 1864, when the partners were obliged to lease their farm to tenants while they set out to find a livelihood. Morton and Hailstone returned to California, and Brighouse became the first white settler on Lulu Island, which was genuine farmland. Sam eventually bought 697 acres there, to prosper mightily as a dairyman, become the squire of the delta and later re-enter Vancouver's story as a character of substance.

Meanwhile, back at the ranch, the tenants disappeared, and the Indians solved the maintenance problem by burning the barn and stable. Morton returned from California, still scratching for the means to keep body and soul integrated, to work on a farm at Mission, up the Fraser Valley. The turning point of his fortunes, and those of his colleagues, came in 1884 with the negotiations between the colony and the Canadian Pacific Railway regarding the terminus of the railway. The three stalwarts helped to satisfy the railway's demand for compensatory property by donating part of their acreage. They then sat on their remaining real estate with the expectancy of the spider who has grown very lean spinning out his silk but has the comfort of knowing that his web is placed exactly where the flies will swarm.

A map filed in the land registry office in 1884 shows the West End designated as "City of Liverpool." Behind this large concept lay the active imaginations of Morton, Brighouse and Hailstone, aided by some real-estate associates who knew the value of thinking big, when hawking property to speculators. Their creative thinking was duly rewarded, and only the fickleness of Fate, which is a subsidiary of Canadian Pacific, saved the future inhabitants from being known as neo-Liverpudlians.

John Morton did not abandon the place where his bonanza was so dearly bought. As an old man he lived on Denman Street, near the roller rink, on a fractional remainder of his pre-emption. Neither hardship nor ill health had diminished his ability to laugh at the circuitous ways of success and failure. Asked by Grant if he had much land left after his donation to the railway, the old pioneer chuckled and replied without bitterness: "Ay, lad, ay, I had. Then I fell among forty thieves. . . ."

John Morton was the first but not the last to be waylaid in Baghdad-on-the-Bay.

CHAPTER 3

The Oldest Families

The Squamish and their ancestry • Experience with the white explorer • Way of life and vitality born of the potlatch

JOHN MORTON'S circumnavigation of what was to be Stanley Park, in a canoe paddled by the Indian who had brought him to the source of the lump of coal, included a visit to one of the Indian villages on the promontory. Here he noticed that some of the Indians had an odd kind of limp. He later learned from Chief Capilano that the cripples were members of the Squamish tribe who had been returned home after years of slavery among hostile nations. Their captors had cut the tendon above the knee, dislocating the kneecap so that it was impossible for the slave to run away.

Return of the slaves had been ordered by Colonel Moody, a great emancipator in addition to his other manifold duties. But the hobbled villagers were grim evidence that social life was almost as savage, in some respects, as that of the white man.

Undeterred, Morton took a fancy to Deadman's Island, the islet in Coal Harbour. His attempt to acquire it was thwarted by objections from Chief Capilano, who pointed out that the island was "dead ground." According to one Indian story, the Island of the Dead Men was the scene of a great battle between northern and southern tribes, which culminated in two hundred warriors' volunteering to be exchanged for captured women and children. To a man, the warriors were put to death. Fire-flower at once sprang up where they fell, frightening the foe into retreat. (In keeping with its military history, Deadman's Island later became home to the naval training station H.M.C.S. *Discovery.*) Morton paddled across to the islet on his own and found hundreds of cedar boxes lashed to the upper boughs of the trees. One of the boxes had fallen, the lid broken open to reveal a jumble of bones, a tassel of black hair.

The Squamish custom of burying the dead aloft was a tribute not only to the swiftness of rot in this cooperative climate but also to the paucity of open ground in which to inter the deceased. The Indian village lived on the beach, constantly crowded by the dense growth to the rear, and had better sense than to pollute its property with cadavers.

Who were these people who gave the departed a leg-up to the Happy Hunting Ground? Not the original inhabitants. The generally accepted anthropological belief is that, several tens of thousands of years ago, Mongolians crossed Bering Strait and drifted down the coast. Ancestors of the Eskimo, these people are also thought to have engendered the longheaded Indian of British Columbia. The latter left a monument to their appetite for shellfish: the Great Fraser Midden at Marpole, more than four acres of shell refuse heap, five to fifteen feet in depth, that must have been at least a thousand years in the making and which was once topped by trees equally old. A similar deposit of shell lay below the village of Whoi-whoi at Lumberman's Arch in Stanley Park, moraine of mollusk enough to surface the first road around the park with shimmering white shell.

The Longheads were subsequently displaced by migratory tribes from the southeast, of which the Squamish tribe was one. It is estimated that at the time of Captain Vancouver's visit three to five thousand Squamish peopled the villages of the vicinity.

The Squamish story of the coming of the first white man—legend by the time Morton showed up—relates not to Captain Vancouver but probably to a Spanish vessel seen on Howe Sound. Not only the ship's spectral appearance of a floating island but also the white faces of the crew convinced the Indians that the ship was from the spirit world. Curiosity getting the better of trepidation, some of the villagers paddled out to the ghost ship and were welcomed aboard, the tour including the gift of a bag of flour. The Indians looked at the mountaintops—as usual crested with snow—and concluded that only a spirit people could produce snow, in a sack, at sea-level, in the summertime.

As a parting present, the Indians also received what they took to be a bag full of buttons. Returned to the village, the Indians discovered these to be low-grade buttons: no holes for sewing onto blankets. They tried to return the defective buttons, but the ship had gone, leaving the Indians with a useless sack of coins.

The Squamish have since yielded ground to flour-faces who have a sharp awareness of the value of coins but sometimes wonder whether they have all their buttons.

Indeed, the more the white man studies the social life of the earlier inhabitants of the inlet, the more impressed he has become with their culture. The buttons were mostly ornamental, as the Squamish dressed in smocks of cedar cloth, or wore blankets of dogs' hair or goats' wool. Their conical hats served as built-in umbrellas. In summer, the Indians dispensed with clothing as temperature allowed, and to this extent would have blended with the beach crowd of today.

The Squamish lived in cedar plank houses, several families to a house, each with its own fire. These condominiums, dark and smoky of interior, had much of the ambiance of the contemporary steak house, but the menu was more varied: clams and other shellfish, fish in variety, edible roots and berries. Smoked salmon was not a delicacy but the staple of diet.

Besides sharing the west coastal Indians' reputation of being the greatest natural carpenters of the North American nations, the Squamish practiced a highly evolved method of displaying status: the potlatch. The rivalry of chiefs, their immediate families, and their villages, making lavish gifts to invited guests from other villages, establishes a line of descent for the status-seeking of today's Vancouverite, who commonly establishes his superiority by complaining in public of how high his city taxes are.

The potlatch too was a public occasion for acquiring higher status. So important were its proceedings that witnesses were invited, and paid, to confirm that no corners were cut—an early form of tax accountant. All the guests, who might number several hundred and might stay for weeks, had to be entertained and presented with gifts, the extravagance of the presentation being the index of the wealth and resources of the host. To anyone whose impression of the social life of the west coast Indian, before the white man, is based on the simple values of the Hollywood western—scalp or be scalped—the complexity of potlatch economies comes as something of a shock. As explained in *People of the Potlatch* (Vancouver Art Gallery and University of British Columbia):

> Gifts were ranked in importance: to rival chiefs would be given the valuable canoes, carved chests, slaves and fine clothing, while at the other end of the social scale, small strips of blanket were a token payment. A careful accounting was kept of each gift and to whom it went, for these potlatch distributions were at the basis of Northwest Coast economy. Each gift or its equivalent was *owed* back to the giver and was to be paid back within a stated interval, plus a definite rate of interest. In some cases the value to be returned was a 100% increase. This made for a system of circulating credit on which a man could count, calling back his wealth in due time. It was also an insurance system, for payment was owed to the heirs of a deceased man in his stead, or conversely owed by the heirs of a debtor. For a man to fail in his obligations was unthinkable.

Inevitably, this highly competitive, capitalist society stimulated all the arts—the canoe had to be the finest in its decorative hues, the carved chests the most exquisite, the blankets the most cleverly woven. Oratory, songs and dances embellished the occasion's entertainment, the dramatic production having to be up to professional standard.

When the British banned the potlatch, the creative impetus was stilled. There was no longer any motivation for even the industry and enterprise to acquire wealth. It has taken Vancouver's white population a century to involve status with a comparable subsidization of the creative arts. It is debatable whether it has yet produced anything to compete, in brilliance and originality, with the arts of the Raven.

The secret may have been that the Squamish society blended with the environment instead of being imposed upon it. The Indians believed, for instance, that man was totally dependent on the goodwill of the creatures he killed for food or clothing, that he was obliged to propitiate them. They spoke of the Salmon people, the Deer people, as beings of equal rank, spiritually interchangeable with man, outward appearance notwithstanding. The white man has been slow to attain the camaraderie of this anthropomorphic view of life. The annual salmon derbies, for example, in which thousands of fish are boated in the interest of winning a prize of cash value, would seem to be offensive to those Salmon people who, say the Squamish, were once tormented by small boys and became so grieved and indignant that they swam upstream, never again to return to the fishing ground.

For the Squamish, ecology lay at the center of their being, and they did not suffer pollution of the spirit till the white man came.

They also displayed a rather charming modesty in not creating God in their own image. According to legend, the creator of the world was the Great Raven. His son, the Younger Raven, was so spoiled that his father had to give him a box of stars to play with. Younger Raven threw the stars up the smoke hole of the lodge, and they stuck in the sky. The moon and sun were lofted into being via the same sooty route, and Vancouver's sky has retained something of this smoke-hole genesis, the drift from forest fires, or logging site burn-off, often paling the sun and transforming the moon into a shield of burnished copper.

The raven, wily enough to be kin to First Cause, survives in the forested fringes of Vancouver, though turned to thieving and mischief like other demoted divinities.

The Squamish villages, too, have become peripheral. According to August Jack Khahtsahlano, a Squamish born about 1870 to the family whose name was adopted for the Kitsilano district of Vancouver, there were ten villages on Burrard Inlet and Point Grey at the time of the white man's coming. When the white man did come, many of the Indians were simply absorbed, temporarily at least, into a community that from the start was gloriously polyglot. Assimilation was no problem. White men took Indian women for their wives, churched or otherwise, and the women by no means disgraced the name of motherhood. The group to which the white newcomer related was that of the total environment. One such, Ronald Campbell Campbell-Johnston—whose derivation was scarcely an enigma—wrote in his *The Story of the Totem:* "Like a stricken deer, or wounded bird, in his anguish of heart, the Gael seeks the wild solitude of the moor, the better to commune alone with the Greater Power, that sustains and comforts all living creatures." As a refugee from the "dimeasach sasunnach," the author gives poignant utterance to the Call of the Wild that made so many highlanders feel at home with the aborigine, bringing with them "their particular lofty ideals about Nature, their mystic, ancient songs connected with Fingal and Ossian, wraiths in every stick and stone. . . ."

They also brought with them a sharp sense of the worth of the holeless button, these "large-hearted Gaels," as did the luckless prospectors, the Englishmen slipped below the salt, the Chinese laborers, the sailors of every nationality who jumped ship. But the spirit of accommodation to nature, and to one another, was inherent in this place. It was entirely appropriate that its first poetess should have Indian blood, and that Pauline Johnson should preserve the legend of the Two Sisters.

The legend tells that when a great chief who was at war with northern tribes held a feast to celebrate the coming of age of his two beautiful daughters, they begged him to invite these same enemies. And the war canoes came, empty of weapons, full of presents, and women and children, and there was the greatest celebration ever seen. Whereupon the Lord Tyee was so pleased that "in the cup of his hands he lifted the chief's daughters and set them forever in a high place, for they had borne two offspring—Peace and Brotherhood—each of which is now a great Tyee ruling this land."

The Two Sisters are known today as the Lions. Whether seen as kings of the jungle or Indian princesses, however, the peaks suggest the proud repose of a people at peace with their world.

CHAPTER 4 1862–1875

Placenta of Sawdust

Sue Moody's mill, and Captain Stamp's • The "aggregation of filth" that was Gastown • Gassy and the Deighton House • The town of Granville welcomes the lumber ships

THE prognosis of anybody's choosing to live on the west coast of Canada was, till modern times, unfavorable. Jonathan Swift was said to have chosen the situation of British Columbia for Brobdingnag, the land of the giants in *Gulliver's Travels.* He did not picture it as the ideal place for retirement.

Later, when the Canadian Pacific Railway first put bonds on the market for completion of the transcontinental railway, the English journal *London Truth* peered into its murky crystal ball and predicted:

> This railway . . . will connect with the eastern part of the Dominion a province which embraces about as forbidding country as any on the face of the earth. British Columbia is a barren, cold mountain country that is not worth keeping. It would never have been inhabited at all unless by trappers of the Hudson's Bay Company, had the "gold fever" not taken a party of mining adventurers there. Fifty railroads would not galvanize it into prosperity.

John Morton may have been afflicted by a residue of the gold fever, but those who followed him as residents of the inlet had temperature normal. In the same season in which he located himself on the south shore there were stirrings on the north. The North Shore was in fact destined to be senior in development of industry. It was there, in 1862–63, that the firm of Hicks and Baker built a small sawmill powered by the engine of a navy sloop that had come to grief up the coast. The company had to borrow heavily. After the first day of operation, when the mill cut ten thousand feet of lumber, the creditors foreclosed. Faith was harder to harvest than fir.

In 1862 T. W. Graham and Company acquired 480 acres of timber on the North Shore at the spot later known as Moodyville. The loggers built a water-power mill, cutting timber in the adjoining forest and hauling it to the mill with oxen. Pioneer Mills, as the operation was called, shipped the first cargo of lumber from Burrard Inlet to New Westminster aboard *The Flying Dutchman.* In August, 1863, the *Dutchman* left New Westminster for the Pioneer Mills with a party of excursionists, whose mission was to celebrate the birth of this infant commerce on the inlet. It was typical of the pioneers hereabouts to seize upon any occasion as excuse for an outing. No sooner was the wharf built than ladies with picnic baskets bustled onto it, and the stump barely logged became seating for the festive farthingale.

This was the first of many pleasure parties to sail from New Westminster to the inlet and spend the day on shore while the ship was being loaded with lumber. For variety, the trippers crossed to the south shore by small boat and returned to New Westminster via the North Road—the west coast version of the Grand Tour.

The mill was bought by Sewell ("Sue") Moody, no relation to the intrepid Colonel but an American from Maine who had been rafting lumber between the inlet and Victoria. Moody expanded the mill and its lumber trade to include foreign markets, and fathered the nearby settlement of Moodyville that was the first white community on the inlet.

He also locked horns, over a land lease, with the man who was to be paterfamilias of industrial growth on the opposite shore of the inlet—Captain Edward Stamp. Owner of a sawmill at Port Alberni on Vancouver Island, Stamp had been a sea captain who diversified by gathering spars in Puget Sound. In 1864 he arrived on Burrard Inlet and determined to build a sawmill on the south shore. He returned to England where by April, 1865, he had organized and incorporated the British Columbia and Vancouver Island Spar, Lumber and Sawmill Company, with a capitalization of £100,000. Captain Stamp was the kind of man who inspired confidence by sheer strength of character.

Returned to the inlet, his first plan was to build his mill at Brockton Point, in what was to become Stanley Park. Captain Tom Pamphlet, a sidekick with whom Stamp later fell out in a typical excess of choler, dissuaded Stamp by pointing out that the tide rip off the point was so severe that several of Pamphlet's ships had dragged anchor at that station. Stamp retreated to calmer waters farther up the inlet, and for the second time the future park was saved from the ravages of primary industry.

Stamp's requirements for investing in the new site were only slightly less rough than the rip of the tide. As presented to the colonial secretary, they were:

1. That Burrard Inlet be made a port of entry.
2. That we be allowed to purchase 100 acres at $1.00 per acre, adjacent to the mill site.
3. That we may select 15,000 acres on Fraser River, Burrard Inlet, Howe Sound and adjacent coast and 1000 acres spar land at Port Neville to lease for 21 years at one cent per acre.
4. That we may purchase 12,000 acres (if it can be found) where we may pasture our oxen when from hard work they require rest.
5. That we have the free right of way for our fresh water from lake to mill.
6. That all mill machinery be admitted free of duty.

Governor Seymour, newly arrived in British Columbia and anxious to encourage industrial development in whatever unlikely places of the colony, approved the demands, which were acceded to in full. This coup alone was enough to win for Captain Stamp a place of envy in the esteem of later generations of Vancouver businessmen dealing with government. The hard-bargaining skipper had boxed the compass of the ship of state. He had his mill. He had his port. All he needed was a smile from the gods. They laughed out loud.

Stamp's mill was sawing lumber by the summer of '67. His technical experts consisted of Lockhart, a master mechanic, and Damm, the saw-straightener. The remainder of the crew was made up of Indians and ship-jumping sailors—ideal conditions, in fact, for rapid turnover in ownership.

Stamp chartered vessels to transport to the mill spars cut by his woods foreman, Jerry Rogers. Rogers, also seasoned in Alberni, had in '65 set up a spar-cutting camp on the south shore of English

Bay, west of what is now Kitsilano. Jerry's Cove has endured as Jericho Beach, the biblical connotation becoming relevant only in later years when the area enclosed a federal government military depot against whose walls the Vancouver park commissioners trumpeted for years, before they at last tumbled before the host of sun worshipers.

By 1866–67 the future city thus had four loci of habitation: Stamp's mill and store with four or five acres of clearing; the shack on Coal Harbour where John Morton and his colleagues had tested their pastoral phantasy; Rogers' camp across the bay; and the Indian rancherie on False Creek that provided ferry service (a canoe and paddler sometimes disposed to be hailed from the opposite shore) as well as other amenities for lusty loggers.

Between these patches of humanity still lay the forest, fir mingling with the more slender hemlock, and salal thickly green where the great boughs admitted sunlight. Most of this land still stood for sale at one dollar an acre. But it was to the little settlement abutting Stamp's mill that the loggers moved in for the winter. Tradesmen appeared, with local industry in the form of the shoemaker's and the blacksmith shop. The larger village until about 1875 was Moodyville across the inlet, boasting the first library, the first school and the first electric lights (1882) north of San Francisco. But the mulch of sawdust around Stamp's mill was encouraging a scrub growth of hovels fated for bigger things than the prim company town on the North Shore. This motley community lay just west of the enclave of Stamp's mill, on government land. Captain J. A. Raymur, who assumed management of the mill after Captain Stamp decided that life was too short for contention with industrial problems, was reported to have prefaced his first visit to the shantytown with the remark: "What is the meaning of this aggregation of filth?" On being informed that he was observing a by-product of the mill he added: "Aye, aye, and I'll make the beggars mind me. I'll not permit a running sore to fasten itself on an industry entrusted to my care."

Clearly the auspices were somewhat less classic than those associated with Romulus and Remus.

Captain Raymur did indeed run a tight mill, if not the contiguous eyesore, on the property of what he had renamed Hastings Mill in honor of Admiral Hastings, commander of the British naval squadron in Esquimalt. The trails that linked it with the filthy aggregation had colorful names: Kanaka Row (Kanakas being natives of the South

Pacific who failed to leave with their ships), Canary Row, Nob Hill, Frenchtown and the Rookeries. The social tone was, however, definitely earthy, so much so that it is difficult to believe that on Nob Hill only ten years later the wife of a mill manager would have a tennis court on which would be photographed ladies in broad-brimmed hats, ruffled blouses and long skirts playing tennis—Victorian genteelness triumphing over neighborhood.

More immediately, however, the purlieu beyond the pale developed from serving something less wholesome than tennis balls. Gastown, as it was to be known, was born of a saloon. Montreal and Ottawa had their genesis at the junction of great rivers, but Vancouver's was the confluence of beer and whisky.

The man responsible for establishing this spa of healing beverages was one John Deighton, better known to his friends—who were legion —as Gassy Jack.

Nicknamed in tribute to his lack of verbal reticence, Gassy Jack does not fit the mold of the western hero, tall, silent and upright. He was rotund, garrulous and a testament to the weaknesses of the flesh. A fellow pioneer of Gastown, whose observations may or may not be colored by his opening a rival saloon, Joseph Manion described Deighton's arrival on the scene of alcoholic drought:

> He was a man of broad, ready humor, spicy and crisp and everflowing of grotesque, Falstaffian dimensions, with a green, muddy, deep purple complexion that told its own story. He had the gift of grouping words, which he flung from him with the volubility of a fake doctor. These words, shot at random, always hit a mark; unlucky would be the man whom Jack would nickname, for he would carry it as long as he lived.
>
> Jack arrived at Burrard Inlet late one drizzling afternoon, having paddled his way by water from New Westminster. He was accompanied by his family, consisting of his "leman" or squaw, her mother, her cousin, a big Indian who was the motive power and upon whom Jack often cast green-eyed looks, a yellow dog, two chickens, two weak-backed chairs and a barrel of whisky. Lookers-on remarked it was a doubtful-looking acquisition for the population.
>
> Gassy, with the craft of a Machiavelli, began to pass the loving cup with an unstinted hand, telling he had come

> to start a little business, that his means were limited and he would be glad to accept any assistance in the way of building a house. Saws and hammers instantly appeared, and the populace, led by a carpenter named Mike McNamara, rushed to the work of construction, and in twenty-four hours the Deighton House flung its doors open to the public.
>
> Deighton pulled himself to the roof of the building, loosened out the Union Jack, and in a homely speech, pointing to the flag, told his hearers that it represented all that was good, "the blood and guts" of England. It bobbed on every sea, had been his chum for forty years, he pinned his faith to it and would stay with it. He thanked everyone for their generous help and regretted that he would have to postpone the christening for a few days. He anticipated a shortage of drinks and dispatched the Indian cousin with an order to New Westminster, the answer to which read "Cannot deliver your order to Indian, particularly the fireworks part. Risk too great."

Born in Hull, Yorkshire, in 1830 and gone to sea as a youth favoring Yankee ships, whose rum ration was superior, John Deighton had hit the forty-niner trail to California and drifted north, trying his luck in the Fraser and Cariboo gold fields and returning unrequited to New Westminster, where he worked as a river pilot and gained local repute as a Canadian Mark Twain. Deighton opened a pub in New Westminster and had built up a literally roaring trade when he fell ill. He took a brief sabbatical in the Interior, long enough for an American friend, in whose charge he had left the saloon, to empty the till to buy fireworks with which to celebrate the Glorious Fourth. Harsh words were exchanged on Jack's return, and as a courtesy to his creditors the loquacious Yorkshireman jumped town, canoeing his entourage to the less hostile shores of Burrard Inlet.

The first Deighton House, which initially bore the less stately name of Globe Saloon, was a mere shack set among the cluster of companion shanties near the foot of Carrall Street. Deighton chose the site for its proximity (a few feet) to the boundary of the Hastings Mill property, a situation that combined evasion of the company's prohibition of sale of drink with accessibility for thirsty mill hands. With the nearest licensed premises in New Westminster—a three-mile row to Second Narrows and a nine-mile hike along the North Road, not considering the return trip—the oasis palmed by Gassy Jack was fallen upon gratefully by millworkers and visiting sailors, by loggers overwintering, and whatever human flotsam the tide of progress cast upon the beach.

On September 30, 1867, Deighton sold his first shot of liquor under license, over a bar whose beauty lay entirely in the eye of the beholder. It is unfortunate that the hallowed plank was not preserved for posterity, as symbol of the many blessings of forest products. But the Globe Saloon did seed something less perishable and more impressive: the new civilization. The shacks that grew up around it were drawn by the two vital elements of the cultural center: a Demosthenes whose flow gave wings to the spirit, and the agora extending beyond the rude Bacchic temple to the great maple tree nearby, the tree whose ample boughs shaded both discussion and a cool ale from the summer sun, or from dilution by shower.

For three years Gassy Jack rode out the turbulence of a frontier saloon, built in a jurisdictional no-man's land, by virtue of being the fastest tongue in the West. Then, in 1870, when Gastown consisted of nine small wooden buildings in a twenty-acre clearing shelving soggily down to the inlet, the government concluded its survey of the townsite—named Granville after a colonial secretary of appropriately liberal tendencies—and offered the first lots for sale. An early buyer was Captain Jack Deighton, proprietor of the Deighton House and sudden good citizen. He paid $67.50 for Lot 1, Block 2, a tremendous act of faith in the continuity of thirst. He reported the event to his brother Tom in Hull, in a letter dated June 28, 1870, and reproduced below without disturbance of the pioneer spelling.

> I was the first settler here three years ago I have purchased the largest land and it proves by luck to be the best but I can assure you it was a loansome place when I came here first surrounded by Indians I dare not look outdoors after dark. There was a friend of mine about a mile distant found with his head cut in two. The Indian was caught and hung. This place is a lumber country we have two Saw Mills here but only one is running at present—owing to the lumber market being low but both mills will run shortly. I have done well since I came here and I have seen hard times too. I find a man has few friends when he

> is sick and has no means. . . . I was here one year and a half before anyone found out I was making money finally it was found out and then a rush. Hotels, Saloons, Stores & everybody was going to make a pile and run me out but they did not succeed for I had done the most of the buisness all the time. I have got a good house and garden plenty of chickens and have an Indian boy to cook. I paid all my debts do not owe a cent and have a little cash beside. . . . These are the countries to try a man where he gets nothing but what he works for no windfalls no marriage dourys.

The dowry brought to him by Deighton's common-law wife was that of a remarkable fortitude in the presence of calamitous scenes of drinking. She also bore, without understanding, the speeches delivered by her husband at the banquets held at Deighton House. Other women guests wore European finery, while Mrs. Deighton held to her Indian garb of homemade jacket, skirt and shawl, her hair in braids and her tongue equally bonded.

Her husband's liberal views regarding the sale of spirituous beverages to Indians did nothing to alleviate the numerous brawls and several stabbings. Deighton and the two mill owners applied to Governor Seymour for an agent of law and order. The governor overcompensated, however, by setting up a customs office part-time with the jail. This was a blow to Gassy Jack, who had been operating as a free port. He expanded his Deighton House into a hotel, but it failed to prosper. He was the first but by no means the last of beer parlor operators to hold their license by offering hotel accommodation —a kind of curse laid upon the innkeeper by the first Christmas.

In addition to the strictures of the law Deighton had to cope with competition. When these saloonkeepers tried to remove a stump that blocked the path leading past his place to theirs—a menace to navigation to which the thoughtful drunk would show due respect by stopping at the Deighton House—Jack threatened them with a shotgun.

To this era belongs the brief commercial life of the Georgia Seagull Company. When a guest complained about the absence of feather pillows in the Deighton House, Gassy Jack and a pickup group of entrepreneurs planned to set up a long trough on the beach at Lulu Island, fill it with fish offal and quicklime to trap gulls, and pluck the birds, releasing them to grow a new set of down on a sustained yield basis. The company had to be abandoned when capital assets proved to consist of a box of cigars and a half-empty bottle of whisky.

Aggravating the blight of urbanization, Deighton's Indian woman died, and the younger one he bought to replace her developed the habit of running away at intervals, taking the furnishings of their home with her. Recovering the inanimate chattels took a lot out of the publican, and may have had something to do with his reappearance briefly as a Fraser River pilot, an event noted in an article published in the *Mainland Guardian* (New Westminster) of April 15, 1874. Captain John Deighton is reported to be in charge of the steamer *Onward*, but the same issue of the paper carries an advertisement extolling the comforts of "Deighton's Hotel, Granville," John Deighton, proprietor.

Gassy Jack died a year later, in 1875, and was buried in a new white shirt that cost $3.50, underdrawers at $1.75 and a $0.50 necktie, total funeral costs being $136.68. To go first-class was, after all, only fitting for the man who had introduced irrigation to hundreds, possibly thousands, of arid throats in his adopted home.

To his bastard son, a handsome lad known locally as the "Earl of Granville," Jack left his entire estate, which after payment of claims for $5,573.00 amounted to $304.89. The son died before the will was probated, but the "first lady of Vancouver" lived on, after returning to Squamish society at the Stawamus Indian Reserve, earning her living by making and selling baskets, almost till her death August 10, 1948.

Latterly some local historians have questioned that Granville was ever called "Gastown." The skepticism is unworthy of the man whom the city has honored as its most voluble citizen. In addition, an Admiralty chart drawn in 1876, and redrawn in 1877, includes a sketch of the harbor clearly designated "Gastown." That the name never had legal status was part of the Deighton heritage.

When the townsite became Granville in 1870, only two other lots were sold besides the one to Jack Deighton, one to Gregorio Fernandez and one to Ebenezer Brown, each of whom parted with fifty dollars. But gradually the warmth of human habitation drew more and more people to the shores of Burrard Inlet. In 1868 one Joseph Spratt introduced the first industrial addition to the lumber trade: a machine to press the oil from herring. Whether or not he had been driven into exile by the derisive implications of a Spratt set to catch a herring, Spratt hoped to profit from the millions of little fish that swarmed through the inlet. To this purpose he later built a barge only somewhat less memorable than Cleopatra's, 140 feet long, 33½-foot beam, 9-foot hold, and equipped with engines to pursue the herring. To handle the salmon that found their way aboard in error, "Spratt's Ark," as it was called, became a floating cannery. When the herring stopped coming to Burrard Inlet, the Indians blamed Spratt, whose method of fishing was to throw dynamite into the water to stun the fish. The Herring people are by nature fickle, and this treatment was more than sufficient to discourage, possibly forever, their entering the First Narrows in numbers.

Before long, Spratt's Ark was stationary, moored at a wharf which Spratt built just west of the present Marine Building and which was to play a heroic role in the Great Fire. Later still the ark became a bathing house, Spratt's oileries retiring to the North Shore and the processing of imported fish.

Meantime the decorous company town of Moodyville, across the inlet, from whose precincts the demon rum was firmly exorcised, attracted the more proper type of man and his family. Its first social organization (1868) was the Mechanics Institute of Burrard Inlet, with reading room and library. Part of the library was donated to form the nucleus of the Vancouver Public Library, when Vancouver was incorporated eighteen years later. Despite the presence in Moodyville of "Maiden Lane"—so named because it wasn't—"Sue" Moody successfully resisted attempts to open a saloon in his nice Victorian village till 1874, when the "Terminus" became the one and only, the lesser of the evils for the man tempted by the siren song, drifting from the south shore, of Gassy Jack ejecting a drunk.

On that same hedonist shore, but several miles up-inlet, Hastings Townsite developed as a bathing resort for folk from New Westminster. First named "Brighton," the clearing at the end of what was now Douglas Road satisfied the English expatriate's longing for immersion in salt water under conditions of acute physical discomfort. So popular became the wagon ride down the overblown trail to the seaside that the Brighton Hotel was built, and picturesque walks laid out, as well as provisions for bathing and boating. The watering place gained a few houses and a stage service to New Westminster that connected with a ferry to Moodyville that sometimes triangulated via Stamp's Mill, no road existing along the south shore. For a time the ferry service consisted of a rowboat operated by big John Thomas ("Navvy

Jack"), whose schedule was subject to change without notice. Later the steamer *Sea Foam* made the run between the mill towns and the hotel whose Saturday night dances were, by all accounts, unalloyed delight such as the inlet has not known since. Possibly infected by the sheer ebullience of the festivities, the *Sea Foam* blew up while at the Brighton wharf.

In May, 1869, Brighton was officially gazetted as Hastings Townsite, but only seven lots were sold at the first auction. Again, free land had been at least half the charm of the site. The renaming of Stamp's Mill as Hastings Mill, though the townsite was a distance apart, created confusion, but the townsite had no larger future for the name than that of a district in the East End of Vancouver. Fortune's child had neither the substance of the company mill town nor the gracious airs of the resort. It was a ragamuffin.

Granville drew its bumptious vigor from logging. As early as 1868 the mills were paying four dollars per thousand feet for logs, which meant that a hand logger could earn as much as a thousand dollars in a month or six weeks. Most of the bonanza found its way across the bar of the Deighton House and its proliferating competitors. The pattern was for loggers to make it in the summer at Jerry Rogers' logging operation, and lose it in the winter as residents—when not being thrown out—of the saloons. In the spring the loggers turned up broke at the logging camps, as welcome as the cyclic return of the fish they drank like.

In spite of periods of recession in the market for lumber, the number of vessels loading in Burrard Inlet steadily increased: in 1864, one ship: '65, six; '67, fifteen; '68, thirty-three; '69, forty-five. Most of the lumber carriers were bound for Australia. Because the means of loading lumber were gratifyingly slow, the ships' crews had plenty of time to spend all their wages in the village, compensating for the off-season when the loggers were away at camp. To be viable a saloon requires diversification of industry.

Aside from the lumber ships, communication between Burrard Inlet and the outside world remained for some time tenuous. Regular passenger ships did not appear till the eighties. The only link with the larger scene was the telegraph line built from New Westminster to Brighton in 1869, and extended by underwater cable to Moody's Mill. "Sue" Moody, who spent a fair amount of time in New Westminster, underwrote the cost of the telegraph.

In 1873, the violently expired *Sea Foam* was replaced by the

Chinaman, so called because she was imported from China on the deck of a lumber vessel. Skippered by Captain Van Bremmer, the flying *Chinaman* was joined by the *Lillie*, the *Leonora*, the *Senator* and the tug *Skidegate* in plying the coastal waters and forming the nucleus of what was to be the Union Steamship fleet.

The early steamers were a potpourri of craft including side-wheelers. Most celebrated of these pioneers, but by no means too exceptional, was the tug *Union*, more often known as "Sudden Jerks." Because of slippage in the transmission, her method of slowing progress —in the emergency that doubled for standard procedure—was for the captain to stuff sacking into the gears. The power train consisted of an engine lashed to the side of a threshing machine boiler. Yet the *Union* towed logs from False Creek to Moody's Mill till she reached such an advanced state of infirmity that it became customary to tie a line and buoy to the engine so that it could be salvaged in the likely event of the tug's sinking.

Most of the regular sailings were between the inlet and west coast ports of the U.S., particularly California. From 1866 to 1871 the population gained from frustrated forty-niners, while the mail was delivered by American express companies and paid for with U.S. postage. Connections with eastern Canada were virtually nil, and it was not till 1887 that the steamer *Maude* inaugurated the first regular ferry service between the inlet and Victoria, a twelve-hour trip under favorable conditions.

More quickly improved were the means of access to the inlet overland. By 1861 the McRobert's Trail from New Westminster to Musqueam, on the south slope of Point Grey, provided farmers of the flats with a means other than river boat of reaching the market town on the Fraser. The trail later became Marine Drive, the more pleasant for being sinuous. Also from New Westminster, the Douglas Road to Hastings Townsite bustled with traffic, the stage line being owned by W. R. Lewis, described by Joseph Manion as "an American citizen, a man of enterprise, somewhat brusque, but of sterling uprightness, whose word could always be relied upon. There were no reserved seats, peasants and peers being treated alike. He never deviated from his schedule for anybody; money or notes entrusted to his care were as safe as the registered mail. He was ably assisted by his chief whip and stable manager, James O'Halloran."

As the beginning of a second route southward, in 1872 a bridge was built across False Creek, which at that time seeped a marshy mile deeper inland than today. The bridge had no obvious connection with anything but a logging skid road, but it did lead to a public demand for a link with the Fraser and its valley. The North Arm Road (Fraser Street) was completed by 1875, enabling the logging companies to bring in, from the valley, feed for their oxen, instead of importing it by water from fabled Saanich. In the same year, a road was built to join Granville with Hastings Townsite, previously accessible only by water and Indian trail.

Thanks to these developments, Granville was gradually becoming the hub of various spindly spokes. The saloons reverberated with the laughter of rough men, with the rasp of accordion or fiddle, with occasional outbreaks of hymn on the advent of an itinerant "sky pilot," a preacher holding service at the bar. Besides the mill men and Jack Deighton, those beginning to profit from the growing forest of tall spars of ships loading in the harbor included George Black, the handsome butcher who drove beef cattle up from Oregon and also had a hotel in Hastings. There was Portuguese Joe (Gregorio Fernandez) who ran the first store—a long frame shack on the beach stocked with groceries, nets, whisky, knives and trinkets to beguile the Indian—and who was not to be confused with Portuguese Joe (Joseph Silvia Simmons), whose blue eyes betrayed the Scots ancestor said to have strayed from his Highland regiment during the Peninsular War, and whose marriage to a Musqueam princess, with Indian pomp and ceremony, produced numerous descendants. A third Portuguese Joe came to Granville in 1874 but mercifully moved to Pender Harbour.

There was also Hog Ned, who looked after the pigs at Hastings Sawmill, and Dumps Baker, who kept dogs in quantity, saying that he was running short if fewer than thirteen were on the premises. There was Hans the Boatman, a one-armed Hollander who ran a ferry across the inlet, rowing with his hook. There was Andrew Rusta, whose hut outlived all the other original structures of the West End, and had its photo taken with the neighboring Marine Building before finally succumbing.

There was the Kanaka mill hand whose Hawaiian name, Kee-am-oh, having been judged an offense against pronunciation, became "Campbell." This Polynesian branch of the clan flourished, and another generation of dusky Scots joined those of Portuguese extraction.

There was, too, "Leaping Louis" Gold, who opened his store in 1872 and imported his wife and son, Edward, a year later. Anti-

Semitism being as rampant as any Christian sentiment evoked by a few drinks of forty-rod, the loggers invariably headed for Gold's store when moved by the spirit of conversion. Louis was therefore obliged to develop a combative technique in keeping with his small stature, namely to leap into the air, swinging his fist in a mighty uppercut which, when conditions were propitious, reached a logger's chin. This apparition of launching usually fazed the already befuddled foe long enough for Leaping Louis to score a knockout.

In addition there was Henry Harvey, salesman at Hastings Mill who also performed as postmaster, and Jonathan Miller, teamster, merchant, tax collector and policeman. There was William Henry Soule, who captained the bark *Robert Kerr* that was to gain fame as a mercy ship. There were Gassy Jack's Boswell and rival hotelier, Joe Manion, and Jack Fannin the shoemaker who was always late with orders because he preferred shooting hides to sewing them. (He later became curator of the provincial museum.) There was the fair-skinned black man, Arthur Sullivan, whose good looks were lost in his grocery store but shone seraphically at the organ of the Methodist Hall. And there was the minister himself, who dedicated (1876) the Methodist Church on the shoreline. Reverend Thomas Derrick, "Old Hoisting Gear" to the irreverent, earned a name in keeping with the task of levitating the ballasted souls of his flock.

Derrick later shared the pastoral task with "The Merry Priest," Reverend Father Patrick Foy, first chaplain of the Holy Rosary Cathedral who baptized Margaret McNeil, the first white child born in Vancouver (April 27, 1886).

Besides the lords spiritual Granville had its lords temporal. The "Earl of Granville," the chubby little half-breed who was Gassy Jack's natural son, by no means lacked competition as gentry. Black the butcher was elevated to "the Laird of Hastings," and Joe Manion to "Mayor of Granville." The "Prince of Wales" was one of the last hereditary chiefs of the aboriginal incumbents.

"Sweet William," however, was no relation to the House of Orange. This sobriquet was born of the woman shortage in Granville. When Captain Calvin Patterson was lost at sea, two other sea captains appeared as suitors for the hand of the widow Patterson. One of these, Captain William Henry Soule, arrived on the inlet in 1869 and became shipping master of Hastings Sawmill. His rival, Captain William Rogers, was the brother of Jerry Rogers, the logger. As described by Vancouver *Province* writer Ernest Walter: "The desirable widow was invited to sail through life under the flag of Captain Rogers, and on alternate evenings to voyage under the banner of Captain Soule." This equitable arrangement was vetoed by the prize herself, who chose to sign on with Captain Soule, Captain Rogers winning the consolation prize of the title of "Sweet William."

But from Gassy Jack down, or up, none was as grateful for dubbing, or as ready to express his appreciation to his adopted community with a lifetime of public service, as "Old Black Joe" Fortes. If it is difficult today to understand why a black man would welcome this appellation, it is necessary to know that when Fortes came to Granville, in 1885, as an able seaman aboard Captain Soule's *Robert Kerr,* he was officially registered as Seraphim Fortes. The old sailing ship had a crew as patchy as her canvas, and anybody named "Seraphim," let alone a large colored man, had to defend his christening with his fists. In any event, Fortes took to the town that cheerfully called him "Joe." He worked as roustabout and shoeshine at the Sunnyside Hotel, a chunky outcropping of good humor whose coal hue proved out as better treasure than the ore assayed by the *Plumper.*

Because these more or less permanent residents were easier to count than the floating population docked at the saloons, accurate census figures for the settlement were hard to come by. The first Victoria Directory, 1871, lists 126 names for Burrard Inlet, but this enumeration, like that of later directories, excluded the non-Anglo-Saxon ethnic groups such as the Chinese and the mixed breeds who were largely responsible for keeping several sizable lumber mills working full blast. In November, 1873, Granville was given a population of sixty-five, including transients, with three licensed public houses: the Deighton House, Brown's Saloon—owned by Manion and Jones—and Alex McCrimmon's Sunnyside Hotel.

For these few dozen folk the true center of social life remained the Hastings Mill Store, built by Captain Stamp in 1865 to supply the workers and their families. From 1872 it was also the post office for Granville. It was here, among the country-store fragrances of bulk goods and candy, muslins, pipes, cigars and rounds of cheese, that the international news was thoroughly and soberly aired, Confederation discussed, the Fenian Raid of 1866 analyzed, and the U. S. Civil War brought to a satisfactory conclusion. The customer's credit was always good, at the mill store, the only freeloaders being the rats that flourished below the flooring, as they did under the other wooden structures built on pilings and skirted by plank sidewalk.

"The Cradle of Vancouver" the store has been called, but although the relationship to the Fathers of Confederation was not at once apparent, the future of the little town was being determined in a center of power remote from the aromatic crib.

CHAPTER 5 1876–1886

Umbilicus of Steel

The G.G. drops in • Confederation and plans for the railway • Cinderella Vancouver and the two ugly stepsisters, Port Moody and Victoria • Incorporation • Election of the first city council

JUST about the same time that Jack Deighton was selling the first drink of whisky to the volunteers that clapped together his saloon, a more reputable Canadian was toasting, with the same appreciation of good booze, the passing of the Act of Confederation. The year 1867 was *annus mirabilis* for both men, as it was for the Dominion and the dramshop that the eloquence of each had helped to create. Although it was not till 1871 that the colony of British Columbia joined Confederation, her main condition of union with the distant Canadas and Maritime Provinces—the building of a transcontinental railroad to the west coast—had vast import for Granville.

The relevance was not immediately apparent to the residents. At first the main effect of joining Confederation was the celebration of July 1 with the annual sports day, held on the flat portion of the sawdust pile at Hastings Mill. The Indians competed, and it was protocol that all the Indians won something. Otherwise their wives set up a wailing lament that took the edge off the occasion.

The meaning of Confederation was measurably enhanced, however, by the visit to Burrard Inlet in 1876 of the governor general and his wife, the Marquess and Marchioness of Dufferin. The party of dignitaries arrived from Vancouver Island aboard the H.M.S.

Amethyst, landing in small boats at Hastings Mill. The good people on hand to welcome them, to say nothing of the rough-and-readies who bulked out the crowd, were unsure how to express their respect for the Queen's representative. Some who were present swore that there was a salute fired from guns. Others denied this. Major J. S. Matthews, city archivist, declared that if there was a gun salute it was fired by shotguns. More general is agreement that "God Save the Queen" was played on a small hand organ borrowed from the school. With the inexorable completion of duty that characterized the Crown's deputies, the Marchioness expressed the wish to see some west coast Indians in natural surroundings. She was conveyed to the False Creek Indian rancherie where she democratically shook hands with an old squaw popularly known as "Virgin Mary"—to the consternation of the decent folk present and the delight of the majority.

The school whose hand organ provided the musical accompaniment for this ballet of *faux pas* was built in 1872. Moodyville had a school two years earlier, but the people of Granville elected a board of school trustees and hired Miss Georgina Sweeney as teacher at the very competitive salary of forty dollars a month. Even so, the turnover in teachers was brisk, marriageability being of somewhat lower standard than in more established communities. Average tenure of a teacher during the seventies was six months.

Having provisioned for the mind as well as the body, Granville attended to the spirit, in 1876, with construction on Water Street (*the* street) near Abbott (the next street and only intersection) of the Indian Methodist Church whose pastor was "Old Hoisting Gear." St. James Anglican Church rose (1881) slightly above the tide line and halfway between Granville and Hastings Mill, the third estate equidistant from industry and the lively arts.

The fourth estate was represented fitfully on Burrard Inlet during the seventies. The first newspaper, the Moodyville *Tickler,* tickled too hard and exhausted itself after three or four issues. The *Tickler* cost fifty cents a copy. Its editor, William Colbeck, was so forthright in his intent to milk the market that potential subscribers took offense. Typically aggressive was Colbeck's notice in the *Tickler* regarding placement in the paper of obituary notices:

> Notices of deaths, unless accompanied by a special fee, will be restricted to two lines and a half, but an enclosed five dollar bill (silver taken at a discount) will

> ensure a double-leaded, double black-edged column, devoted to praises of the deceased, and enumerating his peculiar vices (if he had any). His pedigree will be traced back to the Conquest, and his whole career will be "done up" so brown that his dearest relative, not even his mother-in-law, would be able to recognize the picture.
>
> For a gratuity, however, of twenty dollars, the editor guarantees to indite a delightfully sublime and pathetic obituary notice in blank verse, to put in a personal appearance, if requested, at the wake, and ere morning dawns amidst the ruin of broken heads and broken bottles, so customary at these mournful family gatherings, to pronounce such a eulogy over the dear remains as would bring tears to the eyes of a Dromedary!

While Editor Colbeck was leaning a little too hard on his classified section, newspapers elsewhere reported the upshot of British Columbia's joining Confederation: the failure of the Macdonald government to fulfill its promise of a railway to the west coast, eliciting the threat of separatism before the weld had fairly cooled. But by 1878 the Canadian Pacific Railway completed surveys that narrowed down to three the possible routes of rail through the mountains, one reaching tidewater at Bute Inlet, the second at the mouth of the Skeena, the third at Burrard Inlet.

The route taken for granted by Vancouver Islanders, and the premise on which they had voted in favor of joining the union of provinces, was that to Bute Inlet. An order-in-council of 1873 actually designated the Bute Inlet route, the Strait of Georgia to be bridged to Nanaimo or thereabouts, and Esquimalt made the rail terminus.

The concept of bridging the gulf, even in its northern straits, would shake the aplomb of today's engineer. But from the beginning it was characteristic of the coastal breed to think big. The bubble of the Paul Bunyan bridge popped only under the pressure of financing. Surveyors found that the Burrard Inlet route for rail was both shorter and cheaper than the Bute Inlet, with no gradient exceeding fifty feet.

The decision was a hard blow to Victoria. Lord Dufferin, the governor general, during his placatory visit to the province to assure the restless natives that the railroad would be built, had told Victorians that the Bute Inlet route had been approved, as indeed it had.

When Burrard Inlet was finally chosen, Victoria member of parliament Amor de Cosmos telegraphed his brother in Victoria to call a meeting of protest. Amor de Cosmos ("Universal Love") was one of British Columbia's several bizarre premiers. His urging of minor insurrection was stillborn, however, as most of Victoria's leading citizens were too busy negotiating purchase of property on Burrard Inlet.

With the myopia that was chronic among those viewing Burrard Inlet from a distant station, the Victoria *Daily Colonist* of October 21, 1884, murmured: "The policy of the C.P.R. cannot harm any of these three cities [Victoria, New Westminster and Nanaimo], and there will be no other cities on the coast in our time." Within ten years all three had been eclipsed by the unruly satellite that was Granville.

In fairness, it should be noted that the three cities had good reason to believe that they would retain their monopoly on metropolis. New Westminster, which enjoyed self-government by 1860, had by 1886 a population of three thousand, three public schools, a hotel of considerable elegance, and two newspapers. It was the natural center for a number of thriving valley municipalities: Richmond, whose three hundred residents almost doubled during the canning season; Delta, on the south arm of the Fraser, with its thriving trade in fish and farm produce via Ladner's Landing; Surrey, Maple Ridge, Fort Langley, Chilliwack and other farm centers. New Westminster was the hub with every expectation of becoming the big wheel.

Victoria, whose population of seven thousand in 1881 had boomed to eleven thousand by 1886, was well past the frontier stage, a mature commercial city that looked down its British nose at the damp squatters' roost across the gulf, an unsightly growth with no past, little present and less future, once the trees were logged off.

Even Nanaimo had greater presence as an industrial center, coal, in its very nature, being senior to wood.

The aspirations of all three cities were hamstrung by the economics of building a railroad. The locus of self-delusion thus shifted to Port Moody, at the head of Burrard Inlet, the apparent terminus. What the C.P.R. did to Port Moody was traumatic. The town has never recovered. From the sudden vision of real-estate riches to the falling of scales from the eyes, the transition of absentee landlords from hand-rubbing to hand-wringing, here was one of the great tragedies of the fast buck.

As early as 1859 an official report of exploration of the prairies included a projected wagon road to the coast, terminating at the head of Burrard Inlet and a settlement that the cartographer dubbed "Albert City." Once again, however, the promise held out by the federal government was to be thwarted by the railway company. In October, 1882, men were grading tracks eastward from Port Moody. In May, 1883, the *Duke of Abercorn* unloaded the first shipment of rails, and by October the first locomotive, also delivered by ship, was running on the rails and ready to aid construction farther east. To the eye—and especially the eye that glinted with land speculation—the designation of Port Moody as the rail terminus was a *fait accompli.*

In that same year, however, Premier Smithe of the provincial government was negotiating with the C.P.R. to have the terminus relocated at Granville. The provincial government was anxious to develop its holdings of land on Point Grey and adjacent areas. The C.P.R. was disposed to listen to the premier's request because at Port Moody the railway faced the prospect of lack of sufficient room to operate, owning not an acre outside the limited rail yard. In addition the Second Narrows was considered to be a perilous passage for ships required to navigate the inlet to its end.

In August, 1884, William Van Horne, general manager of the C.P.R., came to the coast to examine for himself the alternative site. What he saw convinced him that Port Moody was unsuitable as the terminus, though he at first ignored Granville as the best choice. He wrote to the minister of the interior: "Owing to the extreme force of the tide at the First Narrows, the entrance to Burrard Inlet for large steamships will be almost impracticable, except at low tide, and from investigations recently made it seems that English Bay must be utilized as the main harbour; and that the railway must be extended to run along that bay." Van Horne's apprehensions about the First Narrows stemmed from a healthy company concern for the future of the railway as a link in the All-Red Route, spanning the hemispheres.

All that remained was the dickering and the iron-horse trading, with the final result being that the provincial government obtained optimum terms for the railway's acceding to the choice that it would have made anyway. While the federal government was confirming the intention of terminating the railway at Port Moody, Van Horne was writing from Montreal to Premier Smithe:

> In as much as a comprehensive plan for a terminus, providing reasonably for the future as well as the present, will involve a large immediate outlay of money, and as the present available resources of the Company are required for the completion of their undertaking with the Government, they do not see their way clear to the extension of their line of railway beyond Port Moody, and the provision of the necessary docks and other facilities at a new point, unless they can acquire sufficient property so situated as to be made immediately saleable for sufficient amount to recoup the outlay mentioned.

The big "unless" involved acquisition by the C.P.R. of eleven thousand acres of prime property, including all of Granville Townsite Reserve and much of Point Grey. The steel snake was disposed to swallow a whole region and digest it later. The provincial government's counter offer of six thousand acres, which was accepted, was still a mother lode for the company, which was to remain Vancouver's wealthiest landlord for the ensuing century.

Meanwhile, ministered by the Port Moody *Gazette,* the badly burned speculators were receiving the medication of editorials such as that of October 11, 1884: "It is well known at Lloyd's that Port Moody is perfectly safe in every respect, but that in stormy weather none of the other places is safe for ships. How anyone in his senses could believe that an extension would be made, or if made, would be of any use, appears very droll to us." Madness is, however, all in the mind. Port Moody and its *Gazette* were doomed to lose their taste for drollery. Spurred by the special anguish of Vancouver Island speculators who had been stung twice, in two different places, Port Moody sought a court injunction to forestall extension of the railway beyond the promised land. The injunction was granted by Chief Justice Begbie, the colorful jurist whose bench was a saddle and whose justice was homespun. After lengthy litigation, however, the Supreme Court of Canada overruled the local agencies of law, order and a little quiet profit. Port Moody was dead, though it took some time to lie down.

February 13, 1886, the contract was formally signed between the provincial government and the C.P.R. The government made an outright gift to the company of District Lot 541—much of Vancouver's present business district. The company gained the entire waterfront, no city street reaching tidewater except on sufferance. The story is told that during the nineties a Vancouver longshoreman, asked by an American traveler "What's the government here?" replied: "C.P.R.'s the government here."

Premier Smithe had no way of knowing that Van Horne was so determined to put tracks through all the way to Coal Harbour that he had readied plans for bypassing Port Moody, if necessary, by building a trestle bridge nearly three miles long around the disputed right-of-way. In addition to the substantial grant of land from Smithe's government, the company secured appreciable holdings from a private syndicate, including original residents Morton, Brighouse and Hailstone. Some of these owners of small lots made what they thought was a killing, till the rapid increase of land values proved the corpus delicti to be their own.

Months before the C.P.R. got the government's signature on the contract, the main-chancers were settling around Granville like expectant sparrows in a livery stable. Thirty-nine unsold lots were given to the railway company on the understanding that the bona fide resident of a lot could buy it for two hundred dollars. This drew a claim-rush of squatters, vying to look Established Since 1870. One of these, a man named Orr who squatted on a lot in the old townsite, constructed an office that was betrayed by built-in obsolescence. When company employees moved it into the middle of the street, Orr quickly rebuilt on the lot. The next time, the company removed the office board by board, and he was out of residency.

An ascension lacking in grace and dignity, Vancouver did in fact rise from the squatting position. The birth of interest in the terminal town was a nativity somewhat less than immaculate, and in the view of every other coastal settlement was a miscarriage—of justice if nothing else. Three months before the first train arrived in Vancouver the Port Moody *Gazette* editorialized:

> The company have no right to make the branch and they cannot hold land; as soon as a verdict is rendered for the Port Moody lot holders, the rails now forming the "branch" will be thrown in the bay. Some Vancouverites who are ready to cling to a straw will assume to believe that a boom is coming; those who have land to sell will pretend to believe that Vancouver is sure to be the terminus, but every man of sense must know that this will never be the case.

Although "Vancouver" was already a hateful name to the town's neighbors on all sides, the name engaged the privileges that only the godfather, the C.P.R., could bestow. The story of how Vancouver got its name smacks of the fanciful, but its joyous and bucolic tone is too refreshing to be muted. The tale is that when Van Horne visited the terminal site in August, 1884, he discussed its future with Lauchlan Alexander Hamilton, C.P.R. land commissioner. The two men conversed in the village of Granville, which comprised a street one block long—Water Street from Carrall to Abbott—one side of which was raw beach. A single row of whitewashed buildings gazed upon the mountains. To the rear lay six blocks of logged-off forest landscaped by blackberry bushes and skunk cabbage, ornamentally pooled by swamp, and providing accommodation for large conventions of mosquitoes. Beyond this *jardin sauvage* lay the forest, in a line along what became Hastings Street from Carrall to Victory Square. Casting an eye across the unpromising vista, Van Horne cried: "Hamilton! Hamilton! This is destined to be a great city, perhaps the greatest in Canada, and we must see to it that it has a name commensurate with its dignity and importance, and Vancouver it shall be, if I have the ultimate decision."

The utterance sounds a bit contrived for the extempore. Van Horne was undoubtedly a man of enthusiasms, but in naming Vancouver his hallelujah appears to have been keyed to future travel-ticket sales of the C.P.R. He reasoned that travelers bound for North America, as well as many eastern Canadians, would have a hazy notion of the location of a place named Granville, but Vancouver Island was well enough known as a geographical feature to provide a rough fix. Vancouver has been in a rough fix ever since, people in other parts continuing to expect to find the city to be situated on the island namesake.

Naturally the choice of name pleased no one except the head office in Montreal. Victoria, in particular, fumed. To the injury of being done out of the rail terminus was added the insult of losing part of the island's means of identification. As late as April, 1887, the M.L.A. (member of the legislative assembly) for Victoria, David Higgins, was rising in the legislature to object to the name "Vancouver" for the city. Higgins charged that the name was an attempt "to snatch from the Island of Vancouver the name it had attained as a shipping point," reported the Vancouver *News*. "He proposed to make an amendment to change the name back to Granville." Another member rose to suggest that the name "Higginsville" be substituted for both "Vancouver" and "Granville," and the motion was defeated on a note of levity.

The final blow to regional pride was, as historian Tom MacInnes pointed out, that Vancouver was named by an American of Dutch descent after an Englishman of Dutch descent.

It did not take long, however, for the name to catch on with those to whom a rose would smell as sweet provided they had the nursery for sale. Only a month after Van Horne's dubbing the town, in September, 1884, a magazine called *The West Shore* published in Portland, Oregon, ran an article on Coal Harbour, over the signature of the enterprising realty firm of Gravely and Innes: "It is only once in a lifetime that the public have such a chance as the present, and we would recommend those who have money to investigate the merits of Vancouver on Coal Harbour before making other investments."

The December 5, 1884, edition of the Victoria *Times* reported laconically: "In a letter to a friend in this city, the General Manager of the Canadian Pacific Railway says that private improvements can be proceeded with now as the selection has been made, and it is a final one, both as to locality and name of city—that is Vancouver, which is received with favor in Montreal, Ottawa, Toronto and London, England." Victoria's wholesale merchants signed a manifesto threatening eastern traders with boycott of their goods if they appointed agents elsewhere in British Columbia. They informed the traders that the entrance to Vancouver harbor was unsafe for shipping, and hinted that the harbor was terrorized by everything short of a giant octopus with a taste for eastern maple syrup.

What kind of place was this hateful Vancouver of the mid-eighties? The Burrard Inlet Directory of Granville, 1882–83, listed 145 names: forty-four loggers, the rest mill men, stevedores, fishermen and merchants, plus one physician and surgeon, one constable, and one clerk (Hastings Mill Store). Photographs of these early days of Vancouver reveal an almost entirely male population, to whom decency was wearing a hat, a vested suit and stout boots. At work, the coat and vest were removed to reveal indefatigable braces and the upper portion of long underwear. Mustaches were both *de rigueur* and droopy. Equally bristly were the dogs that constituted companionship, big brutes of somber hue and resolute countenance. Man and beast, they radiate purpose.

By this female-starved fellowship the North Shore mountain peaks known today as the Lions were seen—in the polite version—as "Sheba's Breasts," a vicarious and certainly uplifted kind of eroticism.

Gradually, however, the women accrued. To more and more fast-beating hearts of ladies aboard the ships swinging around Prospect Point, the refuse burner at Hastings Mill glowed as a beacon of welcome. The gentler hand began to make itself felt in Granville society. The first social group outside the saloons, the Hastings Literary Institute, was presided over by mill manager R. H. Alexander, with active support of the company wives. The Burrard Inlet Boat Club raced its crews against boatmen from New Westminster as one way of escaping the social evenings organized in Granville by the Women's Christian Temperance League. And during the eighties a Moodyville-Granville social group of young people calling themselves the Midnight Adieu Club held dances fortnightly in Blair's Hall. At midnight the ball disbanded into couples walking the beach-side boardwalk to Hastings Mill wharf, where the Moodyville members were seen aboard the ferry home. (Granville's docking facilities consisted of a more hazardous public float at the foot of Carrall, about three feet wide—two cedar logs lashed together and running out beyond the shallows. On a wet, slippery night, the midnight adieu here could be permanent farewell.)

For the married women of the town, the premier social event was arrival of a new sailing vessel in the harbor, as it was customary for ships' captains to be accompanied by their wives. The visitors were entertained at tea, or invited to join a picnic. The picnic tradition was established early and endured long in Vancouver, as did that of extending hospitality to visiting crews. As for the masters of the ships, they sometimes returned the social favor with a ball held aboard ship, and a harbor still largely locked in wilderness would shimmer with the lights of a windjammer *en fête*, and carry the ripple of feminine laughter to the dark clam beds.

Highlight of the social season of 1882 was the visit to the inlet of the governor general, the Marquess of Lorne. Anticipating that he would be accompanied by the Queen's daughter, Princess Louise, the people of Granville selected a prominent Douglas fir standing near the beach west of the mill, with the intention of presenting the tree, so to speak, to Her Highness. Regrettably the governor general arrived without his wife. He was shown the Princess Louise tree, but having had a surfeit of demonstrations of wood-chopping he declined to witness the scheduled felling of a nearby spruce in his honor. Instead the marquess accepted the invitation of "Protestant Bill" Macdonald to wash down the sawdust in his throat, both repairing to a bar where a retinue of gawkers watched the Queen's representative order a sherry—a historic event in itself.

While the womenfolk of Granville were nurturing hospitality, on the shore of False Creek was sown the seed of another Vancouver tradition: the English garden. The Maddams ranch stood at the fringe of the Mount Pleasant forest, habitat of bear, deer, cougar and wildcat. Maddams, formerly a messenger in Queen Victoria's household, brought with him his countrymen's love of gardening. When in later years a plaque was unveiled to commemorate the ranch, city archivist Matthews said in his speech of dedication: "He [Maddams] imported bulbs from Holland, shrubs from Japan, grew roses, rhododendrons, azaleas about a terraced lawn. In the spring time the Queen Anne cherry trees, in bloom in the orchard, were beautiful to see. He kept pigeons and poultry, grew rhubarb and made rhubarb wine, clear, amber and sparkling. It was potent, too—there was no Liquor Control Board in those days—and the up-coast loggers loved it."

Vancouver's pioneer farm, McCleery's, lay along the north bank of the Fraser. Built in 1873, the big farmhouse served as a way station where dignitaries traveling from Victoria to New Westminster could stop off and refresh themselves, where Sunday service was held, the washbasin doubling as collection plate, and where Mrs. Harry Logan for years held out as protectress of Vancouver's oldest remaining domicile.

Penetration by thoroughfare south from Granville was in the transition stage in the early eighties. Crude trails developed into the only slightly more refined corduroy road, the skid road whose name was to fall on semantically evil days, but whose logs laid crosswise made all the difference for oxen straining at a load of logs or a stoneboat.

The street life of Granville flowed, bumpily, along wood. The first streets were planked and, where necessary, as with the old Water Street, supported on pilings. Photos of the time fail to convey the rumble and roar that quickened the pulse as carriages sped over the timbers. Vancouver had little cobblestone to represent its early paving, and thus the original surface has long since been composted. The sidewalks too were of plank, spaced to the detriment of women's shoe heels. The recollections of all old-timers, of children who grew up in Vancouver's childhood, include these boardwalks—the ballet step required to avoid the crack that would break your mother's back, the despair when a coin vanished down the gap, and the highly-charged drama of The Night Father Fell Off Into The Ditch. Ambulant, prairie people were of the mud extraction, but early Vancouverites had the forest at their feet.

Beyond the boardwalk, from Granville Townsite a wagon road led diagonally southward across Columbia Street, skirting the waters of False Creek which at fuller tides linked with the inlet, and following the neck of land across which the Indians and early settlers portaged their canoes. The wagon trail proceeded to the Westminster Avenue bridge across False Creek and became the New Road to New Westminster—later Kingsway. Another well-used trail ran from the "residential area" on Cordova Street up Abbott to Pender, and after some directional uncertainty emerged at False Creek, at the foot of today's Granville Street. As one of Vancouver's original aldermen, W. H. Gallagher, recalled it:

> It was used by hunters and loggers from the logging camps out on English Bay, near Jericho. It had been an old Indian trail. When you reached the salt water on False Creek you waved a stick with a rag for a flag, and an Indian would come over in a canoe from the Reserve, and take you across and bring you back again, for four bits. . . . There was lots of excitement down at Greer's Beach in 1886, and the fellows used to go over there to see what the place was like.

Greer's Beach was the Lido for the area, with a touch of Rue Pigalle. For Granville it was an amenity enhanced by the fact that by the time a celebrant had negotiated the trail back to town he was almost certainly sobered up.

Those who failed to make it, and became part of the primordial humus, had their passing publicly recorded as of January 15, 1886, when the first edition of the Vancouver *Herald* appeared. The first edition of the paper also contained notice of application of the town to the legislature for incorporation as the city of Vancouver. A weekly, the *Herald* was Granville's first—and the inlet's first successful—newspaper, a single sheet, folded, and published each Friday. Editor and owner George Brown brought his hand press from Toronto and installed it in an office on Carrall Street. Enthusiastic reception of the paper quickly induced twice-weekly publication and the expansion of the plant to two rooms.

The newspaper was read and its tidings discussed at the cultural center of Granville: Maple Tree Square. Only a bottle's throw from Deighton House, the maple tree shaded a clearing near the beach, on Water Street at Carrall, a congenial spot known to the Indians as Lucklucky. The great maple, which leaned sufficiently to allow dogs to chase cats into its lower branches, was without question the focal point of the townspeople, blending pleasant shelter with the kind of elbowroom essential to intellectual discussion. Fittingly, it was to the maple tree that was nailed the notice of Vancouver's first civic election.

This seismic event had its first tremors at the meeting, in January, 1886, of 125 citizens of Granville to form an incorporation committee. Spurred by the certainty of becoming the railway terminus, and encouraged by the C.P.R. itself, the meeting named a young lawyer, Jack Boultbee, to go to Victoria and nurse the bill through the provincial house. The 125 petitioners were all men and nearly all bore sturdy English names. There was a Brown and a Green. There was a Callow and a Wize. There were one Johns, one Johnson, one Johnston, and one Johnstone, than which nothing could be fairer. There was, God bless him, a Quackenbush.

The founding fathers passed the hat in the saloons to raise Boultbee's boat fare to Victoria. In the legislature on February 18, 1886, member J. Orr introduced a private bill titled "An Act to Incorporate the City of Vancouver." After some token opposition by members objecting to appropriation of the name "Vancouver," the bill received third reading at 7:30 P.M., April 2, and on April 6 the lieutenant governor gave the royal assent. Vancouver was now a city.

The date marks the beginning of the most tumultuous summer in Vancouver's history, a season of comedy both high and low, of terror-filled melodrama, and an epic of pioneer pluck in the finest tradition of other parts of the West.

The curtain-raiser of comedy began when the citizens of the new city gathered under the old maple tree to nominate candidates for the first city council. The mayoralty race was the highlight of the campaign, and as races go the winner would have failed a saliva test.

Of the two candidates the initial advantage lay with Richard

H. Alexander, manager of the Hastings Mill and owner of the special charisma of being the boss of most of those voting. Alexander was a man of parts, all moving with considerable energy. Born in Edinburgh, he had come to Canada at the age of eleven, with his family, which sent him to school at Toronto's Upper Canada College, from which he graduated. At eighteen he led an expedition across the continent in search of gold and adventure, with British Columbia as the best prospect. The goal was partly fulfilled when the canoe upset in the turbulent Fraser River and one of the party drowned. Alexander then worked for a time in New Westminster, cutting cordwood, before moving on to the Cariboo as helper on a pack train. He returned to Victoria where he found employment as a Hudson's Bay Company longshoreman. In December, 1870, he came to Moodyville, subsequently moving across the inlet to work as accountant in the Hastings Mill. After twelve years with the company he became manager, his wife being the first white woman to live in what was to become Vancouver, and his son the first white child born on the site.

Alexander's opponent for mayor, Malcolm Alexander MacLean, was a recent immigrant from Winnipeg, a dark horse that grew darker as his method of campaigning developed. Alexander jeopardized his chances when a strike at the mill, a few days before the election, drew from him the statement to a conciliation committee that he would replace the striking white men with Indians and Chinese and that "Canadians are only North American Chinamen anyway." As electoral tactics go, not the most adroit ever.

Brown of the *Herald* threw his editorial support behind MacLean, urging his readers to "vote early and vote often." In the view of Alexander's supporters, and of the few neutral observers, no public-spirited call received more conscientious response. The qualifications for voting were that the voter had to own freehold property, or have been a pre-emptor or tenant for six months prior to the election. The actual voters' list did not quite reflect the specifications, however, proving to be Vancouver's first creative work of fiction, well worthy of a place in the Literary Institute. The list was open to any male, except an Oriental or Indian, who was over twenty-one and who had paid five dollars a month rental fee. A number of voters rented a corner of a room for the day of the election and for the coincidental fee of five dollars.

The election took place on May 3, 1886, the polling place being the provincial government cottage called "the Court House" that stood on Water Street and more usually served as the home of the lone constable, Jonathan Miller. Both factions, personally led by Alexander and MacLean, showed talent for that branch of taxidermy known as ballot stuffing. The MacLeanites seized on a citizen who was en route to the poll holding, as proof of residence, a lease to a portion of a building on Cordova Street. By persuasive means lost in the mists of time, they obtained from him the lease form, on which there was a space for the name of the lessee. As Gallagher recalled the procedure: "I think fifty men must have voted on that lease. After one man had voted the next voter's name was written on a slip of paper, and pasted in the space on the lease where the name appeared, and so continued until there was a tier of slips, and they were removed and a fresh start made."

The Alexander forces were not to be outdone, however, when it came to ringing in the voters. Again according to Gallagher:

> About eleven thirty a.m. the old paddlewheeler *Yosemite* drew in from Victoria with about one hundred and twenty-five voters on board, and after she passed Brockton Point the band on her deck began to play "Hail the Chief," but the chief they hailed was Mr. R. H. Alexander of the Hastings Mill.

The campaign of the Alexanderites called for not only the water-borne reserves but also a flanking movement overland:

> The Hastings Sawmill, of which Mr. Alexander was manager, was owned by Victoria and San Francisco people, and about midday the mill people sent up fifty or sixty Chinamen to vote. Charlie Queen, who drove the Westminster-Gastown tallyho . . . got up on a stage coach in front of Mr. Cyr's hotel on Water Street, and made a speech blaming the Hastings Mill people for sending the Chinamen up. The crowd grew hostile, started to drive the Chinamen back to the mill, the Orientals took to their heels, and the crowd took after them down the Hastings Road.

If Gallagher is to be believed, both racial tolerance and electoral process were struck cross-eyed by a single clout for municipal government.

Four hundred and ninety-nine votes were cast by an undisclosed number of voters. For Alexander: 225. For MacLean: 242. Spoiled ballots: thirty-two. MacLean having been declared elected, the loser displayed the graciousness to be expected, entering a protest before Mr. Justice McCreight at New Westminster on the grounds of fraudulent registration, among other things. The case was never heard because of the sudden and very decisive cremation of the records.

Of the thirty-two candidates for aldermen, the names of eight of the ten elected succeeded one another, alphabetically, from the top of the ballot. This phenomenon has characterized Vancouver's civic elections in subsequent years, voter apathy riding heavily on the shoulders of the candidate named Zilch. The repeated return to office of Alderman Earle C. Adams demonstrated the principle, whereas the record aldermanic run of Halford Wilson has been a stirring example of overcoming a natural handicap.

One of the MacLean backers was Leaping Louis Gold, who loaned his buggy as the mayor's conveyance for the victory celebrations that included chairing the new mayor and parading him around the block. On May 10, 1886, Mayor MacLean and the ten aldermen of his council met in the tiny courtroom. When it was discovered that Alderman Gallagher was the only member with previous experience in civic administration, he stood out in an assembly notably lacking in *savoir-faire:*

> There were insufficient chairs. Charlie Johnson [the deputy returning officer] found some in the prisoners' cells and passed them out into the Court room, there was some agitation, some shuffling about; Mayor MacLean was standing at the head of the table. Then he sat down, and was the only man sitting when he called the meeting to order. Tom McGuigan, afterwards, for so many years, city clerk, took a seat on the corner of the table at the left of the mayor. Charlie Johnson, who up to that time had been master of ceremonies all day, whispered to me "What do we do next?" I was a young man, it is true, but I had once been through a similar experience in Wolseley, Manitoba, and had a general idea of the procedure. I replied "If you'll wait a moment I'll show you," and I went out into the street and around to Tilley's stationery store, bought a pen, a bottle of ink, a pad of paper, and, returning, wrote down on the head of the first sheet "City of Vancouver."

The procedure was a model of efficiency such as later councils would have done well to emulate, possibly after checking again with the mother of parliaments in Wolseley, Manitoba.

Having appointed a full establishment of civic officials, with salaries, the first meeting of city council had it brought to its attention that it was bereft of funds. Indeed the city didn't even have a bank account. Instant, though marginal, solvency was attained by fining the drunks and rowdies picked up during the election victory celebration. Since many of these worthies had helped to fiddle the MacLean triumph, the scales of justice teetered giddily when, says Gallagher, MacLean, as chief magistrate, took to the bench to thunder a warning against lawlessness. Civic financing has never been as readily expedited as in that time when the council chamber was under the same roof as the jail.

Diminutive though the newly elected council's realm appeared, an enclave of little more than a square block in the wilderness, the city was already the largest in Canada—on paper. In his plans Hamilton provided for a city four miles wide, extending from the present Nanaimo Street to Jericho Beach, and south from Burrard Inlet a full two miles to the Sixteenth Avenue of today. Most of this area was still totally covered by forest, the giant that struck back with one last devastating blow at the magnificent dream.

CHAPTER 6 1886

The Fire

Origin of the holocaust • The city explodes in flames • Recovery from shock, and City Hall a tent-out

IF THERE IS one day of the year that deserves to be named "Vancouver Day"—as indeed it was, officially, in 1925—it is June 13. It was on a June 13 that Vancouver, the site, was first seen by Captain George Vancouver. On a June 13 the survey ship *Plumper* discovered the coal seam that attracted attention to the inlet. And on June 13, 1886, Vancouver was lost, in the Fire.

Other cities—Rome, London, Chicago, San Francisco—have had their histories glamorized by a great fire, but none has been as precocious in the accomplishment as Vancouver, which only two months after its incorporation lay a smoking waste. If it is the first intimation of a city's greatness that it burns itself down, Vancouver lost no time in qualifying for fame.

The student of Vancouver's first civic election may be excused for assuming that the Fire was the direct result of the city's becoming emotionally overheated, spontaneous combustion sparked by politics whose alcoholic content made it highly flammable. The causes of the Fire were otherwise, and more awesome than the isolated accident of Mrs. O'Leary's cow kicking over the lantern. No Nero fiddled while Vancouver burned. The holocaust drew inspiration not from a sly emperor but a shifty wind. And its strength had been years in the making, a colossal bonfire, built around a stake of spar tree, by the men who were to be martyrs to their own transcendent stupidity.

By 1886 the immediate environs of Vancouver had been logged. Some of the finest timber on the entire coast had stood at the crest of what is now the heart of downtown Vancouver, the Pacific Centre-Bay store area. One Douglas fir that stood on Georgia Street between Seymour and Granville was reported to be thirteen feet in diameter at the stump. The fallen giant was measured as four feet thick at a distance of two hundred feet from the butt, sections of which were shipped home to a British garden show as a colonial phenomenon.

The method of logging the area that is today's business section and West End was, to put it as charitably as possible, rude. The loggers chopped only one side of the trunks of the smaller trees, Gallagher recounts, "and then let a big tree fall down upon them; the whole thing would go down with a crash, like a lot of ninepins." This domino method of forest husbandry was soon improved upon: "As the felling progressed southwards towards Davie Street—they started from Burrard Inlet and worked south—a whole section of ten or more, perhaps twenty, acres would go down with one great sweeping crash. The axemen cut down firs and cedars only; the smaller trees were knocked down, crushed, smashed."

Such was the scene of silvi-slaughter come upon by the crews hired by the C.P.R. to clear the area for the new terminus and attendant land development. "People of today may gather some conception of the general appearance of all that tract mentioned," says Gallagher, "if they will imagine brush, limbs and timber to a depth of ten feet or more lying strewn over the ground in an almost solid mass in every direction. . . ."

The stage was set for the melodrama of revenge. On June 13, 1886, the curtain—among other things—went up. In the best tradition of dramatic irony, those who actually initiated the disaster were relatively innocent, except to those convinced that the C.P.R. could do no right. That the railway gaveth, and the railway tooketh away, was true of this event insofar as the Fire started where the C.P.R. men were clearing the site of the roundhouse. The land-clearing operations, the burning of stumps and debris, had been under way for some time west of the settlement. The citizenry had become accustomed to the pall of smoke that dimmed the June sun into a deceptively pale disk. The feckless population was increasing daily with the influx of drifters and get-rich-quick artists attracted by the prospects of a boom town, transients in whose nostrils the smell of loot was too strong for them to notice the atmosphere redolent of Gomorrah chastised.

The spring had been dry. The humidity level was at that low point where men who work in the woods, who know the woods, do not burn, do not so much as touch off an oath, but keep their snoose moist and spit where it is driest. The C.P.R. crew burned slash, at a distance from the main tangle of forest wreckage, taking the calculated risk that there would be no sudden change in direction or force of the breeze. The blazes they played were tigers, unpredictable, making sudden rushes, waiting for the split second of situation in which the trained servant becomes the master fury, striking swift, deadly and implacable.

It was a Sunday. Shopkeepers, some of them, had taken temporary leave of their livelihood, and of the stock and records for which the small businessman would risk his life in the effort of rescue. This dislocation assured the running in opposite directions essential to full-blown panic. Many of the absentees were fortunately as far removed as New Westminster, attending a funeral, a rare instance of the dead saving the quick and a harsh moral lesson to those who failed to pay their respects. For generations afterward a Vancouver Sunday reflected this debt to the deceased.

About 2 P.M. of that Sunday afternoon in June the forces of violated nature swung into attack. The wind veered and gained in velocity. The crews tending the fires made a frantic effort to smother the blazes whose sparks were showering into the tinder-dry wasteland of wood, then fled for their lives.

Accounts of what happened in the next frenzied forty-five minutes, during which the town was reduced to a few acres of red-hot embers several feet deep, are as various as the individuals that survived it. But none comes closer to the epic style of Virgil describing the immolation of Troy than that of the *Daily News* of June 17. Burned out, the newspaper required only four days to find its voice, on borrowed New Westminster presses, and chronicle as stirring a story of disaster as ever moved the bowels of journalism. Even the typography catches the faltering flight of the fire's victims, each subhead a dramatic shout among the smoke-streaked columns of type. If the comparison to Pompeii strikes the reader as extravagant, it must be remembered that in 1886 the Roman antecedent was still very incompletely excavated.

> THE FIRE
>
> Probably never since the days of Pompeii and Herculaneum was a town
>
> WIPED OUT OF EXISTENCE
>
> so completely and suddenly as was Vancouver on Sunday. . . . It was about two o'clock in the afternoon that the breeze which had been blowing from the west
>
> BECAME A GALE,
>
> and flames surrounded a cabin near a large dwelling to the west of the part of the city solidly built up. A few score men had been on guard with water and buckets, between this dwelling and the cabin, but when the wind became a gale they were forced to
>
> FLEE FOR THEIR LIVES,
>
> and in a few minutes the dwelling was a mass of flames and the whole city was filled with flying cinders and dense clouds of smoke. . . .

The ubiquitous Gallagher, who was a railway contractor by trade, returned to his office, leaving three of his men to fight the fire, which according to his recollection broke out earlier, "before 10 A.M."

> I secured our books and money; pay day was nearing, but there was not much time; I had been in our little office but a few moments when I saw, through the window, a rabble of people running by. They were coming down Hastings Road, from the direction of the Deighton House, Gassy Jack's place. I went out on the road, walked up towards Gassy Jack's, but by the time I got there the Sunnyside Hotel across the street was a mass of flames, and before I could get back to the office I had just left, that was on fire too; I had not even time to save clothing.

Gallagher saved himself by wading into the harbor and sucking air close to the surface of the water.

> The city did not burn; it was consumed by flame; the buildings simply melted before the fiery blast. As an illustration of the heat, there was a man driving horse and wagon, caught on Carrall Street, between Water Street and Cordova Street; the man and horse perished in the centre

> of the street. The fire went down the sidewalk on old Hastings Road, past our office, so rapidly that people flying before it had to leave the burning sidewalk and take to the road; and the fire travelled down that wooden sidewalk faster than a man could run.

"The only time I remember being scared was when the roof blew off the soda water factory," recalled Mrs. W. E. Draney later. Then a little girl living with her family on Pender near the rail crossing, she was nearly incinerated when her father made the near-fatal misjudgment of going to the stable to fetch a wagon for their belongings. "The first thing we knew we were surrounded by fire. Father took us to the back of the lot and we crouched down in a hollow. He kept wetting blankets in a pond or stream and putting them over us. He had to keep it up for three quarters of an hour." Mrs. Draney, at the time two years old, had her hair badly burned when a flying ember pierced the blanket.

Those who had a choice other than staying put fled to the nearest large body of water: either the inlet, if they happened to be on the north side of town, or False Creek, if they were caught to the south. One of those who retreated north was volunteer firefighter George Cary, who very quickly gave up the unequal struggle: "Chunks of flaming wood as big as my leg were flying clear over us and dropping in the town. I gathered up a mother and two children from a shack behind the hotel and started east, but all Water Street was ablaze. So we turned back and scurried down to an old float at the foot of Cambie and waded into the inlet. The tide took a raft near me and I grabbed it. The mother said something about throwing the children into the sea because she would rather see them drown than burn. Then a boat came in and pulled the raft out."

Black Joe Fortes was also in the thick of the fight to save the distraught. Yet another of the firefighters later described the scene with a metaphorical *feu de joie:* "The fire apparatus had not arrived. The country west of Cambie Street was a mass of trees, and on that day becoming a screaming tub of fire, from which flame tentacles reached out and licked up the village like bits of paper."

Such a conflagration was of course the cynosure of all eyes on the North Shore, where many of the Indians rushed to their canoes with the intent of aiding in the rescue of their neighbors across the inlet. According to the curious tale of a witness, they were deterred by the mission priest, who stood on the beach, face ruddied by the glow across the water, and said: "No, my children. The white man will lose many things in this fire. If you go you may be blamed by some bad man for stealing. Who knows?"

More verifiable is the fact that the hundreds of people who fled before the Fire straight into the waters of the inlet had no choice other than swim or burn. Captain Soule's ship, the old *Robert Kerr*, lay at anchor off the beach. No wharf led to the ship, but the small boat-landing held a number of oared craft such as canoes that were quickly commandeered for the short haul to the ship. A watchman aboard the sailing ship tried to object to the boarders with what the *News* described as "insect authority," but was in short order persuaded to be hospitable to the 150 to 200 persons who scrambled over the rail. Those who could not find a boat, or were poor swimmers, rolled logs down from the beach into the water and frantically paddled out of range of the searing heat.

People whom the Fire caught on the False Creek side of the peninsula had some of the more harrowing escapes. As the *News* reported:

> . . . John Boultbee and C. A. Johnson saved their lives by lying down and
>
> BURROWING THEIR FACES
>
> in the earth. Both are still suffering from their injuries. . . . Many men were completely crazed, and did not recover their senses for hours. . . .

Indeed, some of the behavior in the moment of crisis was singularly odd. For example, a storekeeper who was running to the rescue of his stock passed a shop window in which a baby was sitting, apparently deserted. The storekeeper then saw the mother sitting nearby, paralyzed with fear. Breaking open the door, he snatched up the baby to carry it outside. The mother at once struggled with him, screaming that the child could not go outside without its shoes on. He broke away from the hysterical woman and saved the baby. Luckily, a week later he was able to return the child to its mother, given up for dead but in fact taken across the inlet to Moodyville.

The same storekeeper (A. M. Herring, who had come from New Westminster by horse and buggy to visit his branch drugstore, and who had left his family at the Bridge Hotel at the end of False Creek bridge) on the same street passed two men carrying a wire bedspring and mattress. One was moaning, "Oh, my poor wife, my poor wife!" When Herring asked the man what had happened, the man replied that he had had to leave the good woman behind, to certain death. Asked why he did not return to save her, the man cried: "I can't let go of this mattress, can I?"

In the moment of truth a man's values become incandescent. Another witness saw a man race back into the flames to save a dead goose. Yet another helped to drag a man from the roof of his house, which he was dousing with water from two small tins. A pioneer who had a piano box in his back yard hurriedly filled it with books, silverware and clothing, nailed up the piano box with a hatchet and lit out down the trail to New Westminster carrying the hatchet, which survived.

With equal presence of mind a citizen threw a bundle of books down a well. They drowned.

Most poignant sight of all, if it is to be believed, was that of the Vancouver homeowner who at the height of the inferno went out of his mind and died trying to save his stock of firewood.

As the *News* reported with accuracy, "the total number of victims and their identity will probably

NEVER BE KNOWN

> With the exception of Mrs. Nash and Mr. Craswell, the bodies recovered were all burned to crisp and barely recognizable as human remains. Mr. Craswell's body was found in a well wherein he took refuge and died of suffocation. A young man named Johnson, and his mother, were found in the same well. Johnson was dead and Mrs. Johnson has since died. The body of Mr. Fawcett, the soda water manufacturer, was identified by his wife by means of his watch-chain.

Druggist Herring, having rescued as many reluctant survivors as he could persuade to abandon the prospect of certain death, returned to the Bridge Hotel, whose location at the end of the False Creek bridge spared it from destruction. He assisted in comforting the burned and homeless as they straggled in during the long afternoon. As there was no first-aid equipment available, those who manned the makeshift receiving station tore up skirts and shirts for bandages. "I did manage to find some flour, linseed oil and some big skunk cabbage leaves," Herring reported, and the poultice was effective enough to support the claim that what the laurel was to Rome, such to Vancouver is the skunk cabbage.

Soon help began to arrive from New Westminster. From Port Moody, the antagonist town, four sailors, as soon as news of the fire reached them, loaded medical supplies into a rowboat and rowed, part of the way against the tide, the full distance to the stricken Vancouver waterfront. They were rewarded with fried egg sandwiches packed by a New Westminster woman.

Mayor MacLean sent messengers to groups of survivors asking these to assemble at the south end of Westminster Avenue, just over the bridge. Says Gallagher:

> Mayor MacLean's call to assemble was followed by what was probably the sorriest looking procession Vancouver ever had, and I hope ever will see, and long to be remembered by those who witnessed it. Hungry and temporarily despondent women, children and men, who had lost all they possessed, some even their clothes, straggled in in twos, threes or larger groups, along that rough old trail, through the woods in the blackness of that dark dreary night, and gathered together to await the arrival of food.

The coming of darkness and its chill added to misery and confusion. "A man with a blanket that night was wealthy," says Darrel Gomery (*A History of Early Vancouver*). Many survivors simply wandered all night, too dazed to respond to weariness. More than a hundred slept on the ground in a clearing at the south end of the Westminster Avenue bridge. In the morning, their demands on the water pump of the Bridge Hotel caused the owner to chain it for fear the well would go dry—a precaution that nearly got him tarred and feathered.

The hotel became an improvised morgue as bodies began to be removed from the smoldering ruin of Vancouver. Gallagher:

> We gathered together some bits of board and built a table about three feet high, five feet wide, and thirty feet long, and as each body, or part of body, was brought in, it was reverently laid upon that table. Some bodies had not an arm, nor foot, nor head left; some of the poor remains would not hold together; some weighed a few pounds, perhaps twenty or thereabouts; all had so suffered

> by fire that they were not recognizable. The Bridge Hotel gave us their blankets, and on these were wrapped such remains as were found, with a little note attached to each parcel saying where the contents were picked up. Altogether there were twenty-one parcels, and I know of others, those which were not discovered until the work of clearing away the debris of the burned buildings began. . . .

The grisly business of collecting the remains of the fire's victims had its touch of macabre humor. On that Sunday Dr. H. E. Langis of the C.P.R. construction medical service was out of town, and the human skeleton that was one of the appointments of his office had been temporarily placed in McCartney's store. "After the fire they picked it up in the ashes," Langis later told archivist Major Matthews, "and took it to the morgue. And do you know what I am told they said when they picked it up? 'Poor fellow, he must have been sick before he died—his back is all wired together.' "

Alderman Gardiner Johnson witnessed one of the more agreeable aspects of the relief work: the distribution of underwear to the women. "I remember when a carload of whitewear of this description arrived. The women used to come to the relief tent for a pair of corsets or something else white, and securing the things, they would run off into the bush to try them on. If they fitted they came back smiling, but if they did not fit, another trial had to be made in the bushy boudoir."

The dawn light of the morning after revealed the full devastation of the fire. Every structure, every living thing above ground and for a foot below it, had been effaced, except for the Hastings Mill buildings, the Regina Hotel on Abbott and Water streets—a freak survival thanks to a change of wind direction—and the Bridge Hotel with its eight or ten smaller buildings on False Creek. Another odd exception to the rule of rubble: a survivor climbed a mound of smoldering sawdust to scan the horizon for a brother who was missing. His feet slipping on the sawdust, he fell and was astonished when his hands encountered ice beneath the charred chips. The Sunnyside Hotel's supply of ice had been preserved when the icehouse collapsed and dropped its insulation of sawdust atop the ice blocks. Thus some of the first water Vancouver drank after the fire was ice water.

West of the fire zone, the Spratt's fish warehouse and the C.P.R.

offices were untouched—further irony, in view of what started the fire. Of the buildings destroyed—numbered upwards of six hundred to perhaps a thousand—few were insured, and those only for a fraction of their value. The fire tempered the crude steel of frontier spirit into pioneers more provident.

By three A.M. on Monday, however, the first tent had been pitched on the still-warm cinders of Vancouver. From dawn onward wagons loaded with lumber rumbled down the baked streets. R. H. Alexander, the defeated candidate for mayor, rose to the occasion splendidly, inviting all who needed lumber for rebuilding to help themselves to sawn lumber stacked in the mill yards. Within three days a dozen firms, including a clothing store, a three-story hotel, a public hall and a hardware shop, were doing business in jaunty if jerry-built quarters; and four hundred houses would be erected during the next three months.

Typical of the poise with which Vancouver's people recovered from the disaster is a morning-after photo of survivors in which, according to the caption, "Walter E. Gravely, later well known in financial circles, lies reading on the ground." Reading what? The casual reclining does not suggest Scripture. The mind has difficulty conceiving the kind of aplomb that enjoys a little light reading, alfresco, a few hours after Herculaneum.

Another sign of how coolly the phoenix would arise flapping from its own ashes was the resurrection of Vancouver's City Hall. In a letter, L. A. Hamilton describes the deed: "In all history, no City Hall has been built more rapidly than the one I erected in five minutes the morning after 'The Fire.' We got a tent. I was senior Alderman. I got a can of paint, a brush and a piece of board, and labelled it 'CITY HALL.' We held Council meetings in it; a magistrate's court sat there; at the foot of Carrall Street at Water Street."

The panoply of spreading canvas, and its occupying dignitaries, were captured in one of the aftermath photos. Unfortunately no pictorial record exists of the prisoners, released from jail during the fire, who were chained to stakes beside the tent that was City Hall. The felons had taken advantage of their sudden parole by breaking open whisky kegs and enjoying the civic house-warming too well. A witness described the flimsy bastille: "Its white canvas sides stood out against the blackened embers to whisper to the people that, though the city was in chaos, yet were the steel muscles of the law tensed in readiness to enforce the Queen's commands."

Except for the drunks, the sinewy servants of law and order were not called upon to cope with much in the way of mischief. Everybody was too busy rebuilding to have time for disturbing Her Majesty's peace. That most of the population had escaped the fate of their homes and chattels lent to the work a gratitude to Providence which had formerly been negligible in Vancouver's devotions. One minister appraised the Fire as a blessing in that it occurred "on the day that the Church was celebrating the coming down of the Holy Spirit under the outward symbol of tongues of fire."

The first church service on the Sunday following the Fire was an impromptu but, according to Gallagher, memorable ceremony:

> Rev. Mr. Thompson, the Presbyterian clergyman, came along, and suggested to the workmen who were grading Cordova Street and covering it with planks—three by twelve planks—that perhaps they ought to cease work for a moment, and give thanks to the Almighty for the escape the previous Sunday. Everyone in sight laid down their tools; the teamsters left their horses standing. Then they picked up the empty spike kegs, and some planks, and carried them into an empty store in process of erection for Geo. L. Allen, the boot and shoe merchant, and made rows of seats out of the kegs and planks. About one hundred and fifty went in to the service.
>
> Just at that moment His Worship Mayor MacLean came along, and he joined in the simple yet deeply impressive service. The men were, of course, in their working clothes; the service was not long, and was soon over. At its conclusion those big, rough, hardy bushmen paid as gentle a compliment as ever I have witnessed. The service over, none moved; they all stood motionless while His Worship moved down the rude aisle. His Worship halted at the entrance, and stood to one side; Rev. Thompson on the other, and both shook hands with each member of the impromptu congregation as they slowly departed from the half-finished building. Then the men went back to work to make Cordova Street passable.

As sustenance for the body, the Hastings Mill Store experienced a dramatic run on stock and was soon down to its large reserves of soda crackers. Some veterans of the Fire suffered no permanent injury except a lifelong aversion to soda crackers.

Nearby, another lucky survivor was the home of the Jones family, whose telephone kept Vancouver in touch with New Westminster, the house becoming the city's temporary telephone office.

More permanent structures were soon under way. The same June 17 edition of the *Daily News* that reported the Fire also published a list of new buildings already begun four days after it—including a photographic gallery. Along with the abundance of photos of the period, this haste in providing a photographic gallery points up the narcissism that is part of Vancouver's personality. Few places have been more in love with their own image, or more willing to believe, like Dorian Gray, that excesses and self-indulgence would be reflected only in the portrait.

One week after the Fire the city council passed a building bylaw requiring more solid construction than heretofore. Soon buildings of brick and stone were rising as replacements of the wooden Topsies that just grew. For the next decade Vancouver was to build with an emphasis on durability unknown before or since. Some of the sturdiest structures of brick and stone in North America remain as evidence of the architectural concepts inspired by flames licking at the heels. They may lack the grace of the Acropolis, but they are fully competitive in endurance.

George Brown's *Herald* was among the irrepressible enterprises that soon found new premises, as Cordova, Water and Carrall streets filled with fourteen office blocks, twenty-three hotels, fifty-one stores, nine saloons, one church, two stables, one wharf, one mill, and one skating rink, all completed by the end of 1886. Also by the end of that momentous year the population of Vancouver had soared to five thousand persons, inhabiting completed construction valued at $521,000, and waiting impatiently for uncompleted buildings worth another $524,000. Tinderbox though the great fire had proven the city's physical presence to be, Vancouver's confidence in itself was firmly packed in asbestos.

CHAPTER 7 1886–1888

The Phoenix Arisen

First, a fire department • Then hospital, schools, police • L. A. Hamilton and the inspired notion of Stanley Park

So EAGER was Vancouver to become a great city that it was born with smog—the haze of brush fires, the pall of smoke that drifted over the place for days after the fire. Chary of overdoing air pollution as an index of progress, however, one of the city's first projects after the Fire was to improve the fire department. The first civic loan, for $6,900, to purchase a fire engine, hose, reels and other equipment, was followed by a second, for $14,000, for construction of a fire hall, well supplied with water tanks, and hopefully for a city hall.

The hope was underfinanced. The city council was unable to raise the $1,280 to complete payment for its first permanent home, on Powell Street just west of Main. Contractor F. W. Sentell, who built the two-story frame building, designed as a police station, four-cell jail, council chamber and civic offices, was not mollified by the $50 deposit. He locked the door till he got the rest of his money. In the meantime the council continued to meet in a Powell Street warehouse owned by David Oppenheimer, who was to be elected mayor in 1888. When they did gain entrance to the new premises, and held their first meeting there on November 8, 1886, the aldermen stood for the proceedings—as they had at their first meeting anywhere—because funds had not been enough for both the building *and* chairs.

During these embarrassments men were digging pits about the city as reservoirs for water for the engine, in case of fire, until the waterworks were completed. The volunteer force obtained its first engine with an audible sigh of relief in May, 1887. Arrival of "Vancouver's Leviathan" provided the occasion for a benefit ball held by the firemen in aid of the department, a great social success at which some of the guests extinguished themselves. These dances attest to the vigor with which Vancouver rebounded from its disaster. Less than five months after the fire, on October 30, 1886, the Vancouver *News* reported the Hastings Bachelors' Ball:

> A ball was given on Thursday night at Hastings by the staff of the C.P.R. and other residents of that place. The steamer *Senator* brought a number of people from Moodyville, Port Moody and this city. Carriages conveyed others from New Westminster and elsewhere. The guests were cordially welcomed by Messrs. D. Oppenheimer, Walkem, Marmette and others. From the popular Brighton Hotel to the ball room—the skating rink—plank walk was laid and lighted with lanterns. The ball room was rendered fittingly festive by numerous flags and other gay decorations. Its illumination was brilliant. Its floor was well waxed and helped to speed the flying feet right merrily. The dressing rooms were very comfortable. In the gentlemen's waiting room there cheerily burned a large fire in an open fireplace, while the card tables served to divide the attractions of the ball room with those who were unable to secure partners for every dance, or with those from whose heads all lightness had fled. In the ball room was one of the happiest gatherings that ever chased the flying hours in pleasure. Matron and maid, paterfamilias and son, all banded together to revel in the delight of mirth, music and dancing. The costumes of many of the ladies were very rich and that, added to the beautiful faces which peered coquettishly above their fans when engagements were being made, or glanced coyly upward when a sudden burst of inspiration in the music made hearts beat more speedily, completed the bewitchment which draws susceptible mankind to scenes such as these.
>
> The programme of the dance was 1. Quadrille; 2. Waltz; 3. Polka; 4. Lancers; 5. Waltz; 6. Schottische; 7. Quadrille; 8. Waltz; 9. Varsouviana; 10. Cotillon; 11. Waltz;

12. Galop. The above numbers were repeated after supper, the grand finale being the old-time "Sir Roger de Coverley." The dancing ended at 5 A.M., the majority of the guests returning at once to their homes.

With human shanks as sturdy as these to bear the engine and reels to a blaze, the purchase of horses for the fire department in 1888 seems almost a luxury.

Stamina and a merry heart would not alone have sufficed, however, to convert the sooty Cinderella of '86 into the princess city of the West. This required the magic of the fairy godmother, the Canadian Pacific Railway Company, which was as anxious as ever to transform the pumpkin into the coaches of transcontinental rail travel. In 1886 the C.P.R. spent $200,000 clearing lots and grading streets, selling $290,000 worth of property. Some of these lots, in the West End, were bought by company executives who built large, rambling mansions which as housing were very distant relatives indeed of John Morton's shack.

This activity was a prelude to that long-awaited event, the keenly anticipated arrival of the first passenger train to complete the journey from Montreal to Vancouver.

On July 4, 1886, the first through train from eastern Canada arrived at Port Moody with 150 passengers. For Port Moody, the original terminus for the line, the event marked the end of the beginning. The train was met by the steamer *Yosemite* from Victoria, with that city's mayor and the Victoria brass band aboard, as well as a few additional passengers that the steamer picked up at Vancouver. The bouquet that Mayor Fell of Victoria presented to the first woman passenger, a Mrs. Hurchburg, was also a floral wreath laid on the hopes of both the erstwhile termini.

For Vancouver the date on which everything was coming up roses was May 23, 1887. The city was *en fête*. So was the train from Montreal comprising a baggage car, a colonist sleeper, a first-class coach, a Pullman coach and a drawing-room car. The locomotive's number plate bore the talismanic words "Arcadia" and "Eldorado," and this being the golden anniversary of Queen Victoria's reign, and the next day (May 24) her birthday, the engine headlight bore her portrait. On the flower-bedecked smokestack of No. 374, engineer Peter Righter at the throttle, hung the bannered message MONTREAL GREETS THE TERMINAL CITY. Montreal has not greeted Vancouver much since, but on that day regional indifference succumbed to sentiment intensified by the railway tie that binds. No better account of the arrival can be given than that appearing in the Victoria *Colonist*, whose reporter documented Vancouver's yeasty faculty of rising to the occasion:

> As the train reached Vancouver carrying the officers of the road it was greeted with cheers in every direction. Streamers floated to the breeze across the track at different points, while the ships and boats in the harbor were resplendent in their variegated colors. At the railway wharf, which was reached sharp on time, it seemed as if all Vancouver had congregated, and a mighty shout went up as the train thundered into the station under a handsome double arch of fir. As the engine rolled on, it was greeted with the following mottoes, "The Occident Greets the Orient," and "Confederation Accomplished," while facing the city, "Labor Omnia Vincit" and "Vancouver" surrounded the arch.

Something of Vancouver's feeling of obligation to the railway company, gratitude bordering on the fulsome, was expressed by Mayor MacLean addressing the multitude and C.P.R. Western Division superintendent, Henry Abbott. Shunting platitudes to make up his train of thought as only a politician can, he said: "We have assembled here today to welcome the arrival of the first through train, which is the greatest asset in the history of our city, and which is of the utmost importance to the city at large. To the Canadian Pacific Railway is due the prosperity of our country and the progress our city has made since the fire of the 13th of June last, and the occasion should be memorable in honour of the Canadian Pacific Railway Company, its directors and the Government of Sir John A. Macdonald, who have placed Vancouver among the important cities of Her Majesty's possessions."

Thus between Vancouver and the C.P.R. began a love-hate relationship perhaps unique in the histories of a city and a rich, powerful company. With time the fairy godmother came to look less and less like the matronly goodbody, and more and more like the Wicked Witch of the East.

The fond glow grew only warmer in 1887, however, as the visible evidence of Vancouver's global status swung around Brockton

Point. Exactly one year and a day after the Fire, the S.S. *Abyssinia*—the name alone was enough to convince the skeptical that the Seven Seas were tributaries of Burrard Inlet—dropped her hook in the harbor and unloaded a cargo of silk for waiting C.P.R. freight trains. She was the harbinger, as was in fact nearly everything in that time of forerunning, of the rich trade with the East that was the first vital factor in the evolution of the mill town to major port.

Among the amenities contributed to Vancouver by the C.P.R. was the first hospital, on Powell Street, completed in 1886. This was later supplemented by the City Hospital on Beatty. The facilities and staff of the first hospital fell well short of the optimum. The original staff consisted of Dr. J. M. Lefevre and his assistant, who also performed as cook. Operations were done on the dining-room table. The patient who had a good appetite could safely be declared cured.

There was in fact nothing effete about the young city's vitality. One of the ex-pupils of the pioneer school recalled that the boys were full of devilment and gave their male teacher a hard time. "One Saturday two of the boys overtook the teacher at a lonely spot and pitched into him. There was a fine fight, but the boys got the best of it. The teacher was a good sort. It was suspected that there would be trouble over the incident, that he would report the rebellion to the trustees, but he did not say a word about it, and consequently won the respect and regard of the very lads who had attacked him." Student revolt is no novelty in education. Only the merits of silence have been devalued.

One of the school trustees spared the need to act was R. H. Alexander, the mill manager who also served as alderman, secretary of the first school board, justice of the peace, consul for Peru in Vancouver and Lloyd's agent for the mainland of B.C. In that halcyon era of administration a man could wear several hats without taxing his head.

Indeed, no man wore fewer than one hat, outdoors, regardless of weather. A man's hat was the status symbol that distinguished the white man from the aborigine, the God-fearing from the heathen, the clad from the unclothed. The hat was something to raise to a lady, to remove in church, and to hang in the home. It had the magic properties of the amulet, warding off evil, shielding the wearer at the most vulnerable part of his anatomy: the crown of his skull. A half-century was to pass before the bareheaded man was accepted as a respectable member of outdoor male society, and before the *décor* of a restaurant was built around something other than placing the hatracks where each customer could keep an eye on the protector of his manhood.

Another of those who wore more than one hat was George Brew, the inlet's first policeman, who peddled milk as a second career. George lived at Brew's Point, later Brockton Point, and his former homesite became part of the most extraordinary feat of spare-time endeavor ever to bestow upon a city the heritage of beauty: the creation of Stanley Park.

This magnificent natural park, the finest municipal park in Canada if not North America, is familiar to every visitor to Vancouver. It is part of the Vancouver experience. Unlike London's royal parks, or the sporty ambiance of the Bois de Boulogne, Stanley Park means, to the Vancouverite, a permanent preserve of wilderness and the virtues of *le sauvage heureux et bon*. Older cities have long since forgotten the natural state of innocence that man's habitation expunged. Vancouver holds it in trust, zealously, within the nine-mile perimeter of "the Park." Vancouver citizens half expect their daughters to be violated, but he who lays a rapacious hand on the Park is begging for violence avenging.

This sense of mission in the preservation of Stanley Park was born with the city itself. To later generations accustomed to seeing the conservation of parkland placed very low on government agendas, it is little short of incredible that the first resolution of the first city council, meeting for only the second time, on May 12, 1886, was for the acquisition of the military reserve as a city park. Between the minuscule courthouse and the proposed park lay the West End forest, heavily timbered and swampy—for this event antedated the Fire. To the east, a matter of a few hundred yards, lay the East End forest. To the south: forest, and more forest. Yet these city fathers, in a moment of fantastic vision, had the foresight to preserve for all time a tidal island of natural forest as a park for the future generations of Vancouver—*as their first official action.* The document is so phenomenal as to merit reproduction in full:

> A meeting of the Mayor and Aldermen was held in residence adjoining Court House, Vancouver at 7.30 P.M. on Wednesday, 12th May 1886. His Worship the Mayor presiding. Present Aldermen Balfour, Gardiner, Coldwell, Griffith, Hemlow, Humphries, E. P. Hamilton, L. A. Hamil-

1. Captain George Vancouver

2. A somewhat romanticized view of Stanley Park's Siwash Rock.
(Illustration from Roper's By Track and Trail Through Canada)

3. Hastings Mill wharf. The Princess Louise Tree is just visible at left. Toward Stanley Park burn slash fires of the kind that caused the burning of Vancouver

4. Oxen logging in the Vancouver area. Log (right) has been barked and sniped (end beveled) to ride over the greased skid road

5. The Maple Tree, Granville. Guests sit on the porch of Gassy Jack's Deighton House

6. A somewhat later view of Carrall Street and the Forum, to which is nailed notice of Vancouver's first civic election

7. Strictly a gag shot, the tree the butt of the joke

8. Looking toward Stanley Park, Vancouver before the Fire, 1886

9. Temporary quarters for the first council, 1886. Mayor MacLean is seated behind second table leg from the left

10. The arrival of the first train, May 23, 1887

11. William Van Horne, general manager of the Canadian Pacific Railway

12. All dressed up for the queen's birthday and the arrival of the first train, May, 1887, this Sunnyside was the successor to the more fabled Sunnyside destroyed by the Fire. The saloon was on the corner nearest the crowd.

13. Stanley Park entrance and causeway, 1888

> ton and Northcott. Communication from A. W. Ross was read requesting the Council to petition the Dominion Government to grant Reserve on First Narrows for a City Park. Moved by Alderman L. A. Hamilton, seconded by Alderman Coldwell, that the Mayor be authorized to forward a petition to the Dominion Government through the Member for New Westminster District praying that the whole of that part of the Coal Harbour Peninsula known as the Government Reserve, or such part as in the wisdom of the Government they might see fit to grant, be conveyed to the city of Vancouver for a Public Park.
> Carried.

The idea of retaining the old military reserve as city parkland grew out of the receipt by L. A. Hamilton, then the C.P.R. land commissioner, of a letter dated January 12, 1885, from C.P.R. general manager Sir William Van Horne informing him that the company had asked the Dominion government for the portion of the military reserve south of a line drawn from Second Beach to Lumberman's Arch on today's map. The company's plan was to open all this section to streets, docks, warehouses and other buildings. In the mind of Lauchlan Alexander Hamilton, however, grew the notion of retaining the rest of the reserve as park. In the ensuing year the idea developed to embrace the whole peninsula. Thus it was for the promontory intact that the Vancouver City Council (including Alderman L. A. Hamilton) on June 23, 1886—ten days after the Fire, when council members might have been expected to be absorbed in such immediate matters as putting roofs over their heads—petitioned the secretary of state for transfer of the reserve to the city.

The Dominion government responded with the ponderousness of men who have never stood in the cathedral of vaulting Douglas fir, or heard the wind-tossed boughs in choir, or smelled the pitchy incense of bark and needles that purges the soul of perfumed East. In short, Ottawa replied a year later. The report of the committee of the honourable the Privy Council, approved by His Excellency the Governor General in Council, on the Eighth Day of June, 1887, bore traces of the military's reluctance to yield ground without firing a shot:

> On a report dated 10th May, 1887, from the Minister of Militia and Defence, stating that he had had under consideration a petition of the mayor and aldermen of the

> City of Vancouver, B.C., praying that the Dominion Government Military Reserve near First Narrows, bounded on the west by English Bay, and on the east by Burrard Inlet, may be handed over to the said corporation for use as a park. The minister reports that he sees no objection to this proposal, provided this corporation keep the park in proper order, and the Dominion government retain the right to resume the property when required at any time. The minister further states that he does not deem it advisable to recommend that this property be transferred to class 2 as not available for military use, as he is of the opinion that it will be required for military purposes, but until this he recommends that the corporation have the use of the same as a park, subject to the provisions mentioned. The committee advise that the Minister of Militia and Defence be authorized to take the necessary steps for carrying the same into effect.

If the Minister of Militia and Defence hoped to gain some good military roads at no expense to the federal government, he miscalculated. Without waiting for the reply from Ottawa, L. A. Hamilton had surveyed, personally, the first path around the park, a route better suited to lovers than to light infantry.

This was the man who was later to be known as "the godfather of Vancouver." Hamilton, whose photographic portrait suggests the face of a bright, beneficent bird, planned Vancouver's first streets and named them, served as senior alderman on the first council, was chairman of the relief committee after the Fire, and erected the first post-fire city hall. His water-color paintings of the Park reveal a pretty fair artist. There is a tale which explains the affection in which Hamilton was held by his fellow citizens: when the C.P.R. offered West End lots drawn by ballot, it was Hamilton who marked all the ballots with an "X" so that Sam Brighouse, who coveted a certain lot in particular, on drawing the first ballot found to his elation that he had his lot. Hamilton then threw the rest of the ballots into the fire.

It was in character that this hero of early Vancouver used a telescope to sight not the masts of enemy ships but the surveyor's stick. Hamilton sighted well. The path he blazed, with the help of a couple of C.P.R. axmen, circumambulated the Park so agreeably, with such leisurely regard for alternating vistas of bay and meadow, of the turbulence of the Narrows and green, tranquil arcades, that the motor driveway of later years followed its course almost to the last engaging curve.

The path ambled past the grave of one of the Park's better-known Indian residents, Khay-tulk, or Supple Jack, who owned a cow and whose friendliness to the Royal Engineers earned him the gift of a bull. With the resultant dairy herd Supple Jack supplied the Hastings Sawmill Company with milk for some years. On his death, the stock ran wild and became known as "the wild cattle of Stanley Park"; the bulls were so dangerous they had to be hunted and shot. The renegades were only part of the volatile peninsula that in 1887 still sheltered bear, cougar and wildcat, as well as deer, raccoon and the logging operations of the beaver in Ahka-chua, or Beaver Lake, centered in the Park.

For many years Hamilton's path passed close by, at the Narrows, the sheltered canoe in which the Indians laid the body of old Supple Jack shrouded with red blankets. The resting place remained undisturbed, as a kind of symbol of the bond of respect the Park itself represented.

Hamilton's personal involvement with the Park was almost matched by that of A. G. Ferguson, an American civil engineer who for ten years not only served as a park commissioner but spent a good deal of his own money—according to Gallagher as much as five hundred dollars in one year—acting as works foreman and establishing grades for the Park roads. Ferguson's name was later given to the point and pleasant tearoom overlooking English Bay, small enough memorial to the man who, after the annual appropriation for park upkeep had been exhausted, dug into his own pocket to pay the bills to the end of the year. This outlay of personal funds for the privilege of administering the physical attractions of Vancouver has to some extent persisted, and the mayor of the city who does not sacrifice a little of his private fortune in the exercise of his functions is considered to be unworthy of the office.

When it came time to choose a name for the Park, however, officialdom looked beyond the hearts of gold on site, toward the glory that is brass. The new mayor of Vancouver, David Oppenheimer, a pioneer of the Cariboo gold mines who with his brother Isaac had formed a syndicate to buy some of the holdings of the Hastings Sawmill Company, in July of 1888 applied to the C.P.R.'s Sir Donald

Smith the request "that you will grant the City of Vancouver the favor of selecting a name for this highly appreciated resort of public recreation."

Sir Donald (later immortalized by Stephen Leacock with the words "Then came the final day when Donald Smith drove a gold spike into the heart of the Rockies, and ended them") did the diplomatic thing, inviting the governor general, Lord Stanley of Preston, to allow his name to be affixed to the distant park. Lord Stanley graciously accepted: ". . . and need hardly say what pleasure it gives me to accede to your proposal—that the new public park at Vancouver should be named 'Stanley Park' after me. I hope ere long I may have an opportunity of paying a visit to that city, which promises to become one of the most important in the Dominion."

The family name of the sixteenth Earl of Derby and Stanley, whose own estate in England had a circumference of ten miles and was somewhat larger than Stanley Park, also graces another symbol of Canada's savage splendor: the National Hockey League's cup awarded to the winner of the annual play-offs. The governor general did not have to wait long to receive his invitation to dedicate the more peaceable scene of recreation. The formal opening and naming of the Park provided occasion for not one but two public ceremonies and celebrations. The arrival of the first train had imbued Vancouver with an appetite for fiesta and as much dancing in the streets as was compatible with puddles.

The first opening of the Park, September 27, 1888, lacked high dignitaries and was the better for it. The *Daily News-Advertiser* of that morning sounded the note of euphoria:

> . . . The procession will leave Carrall and Powell Streets at 11 o'clock sharp, with Mr. R. C. Ferguson as marshal, and headed by the City Band of twenty pieces, will proceed along Cordova Street to Granville Street, and thence to Georgia Street, crossing the Coal Harbour bridge and following the Park road round Brockton Point until the open grassy space, near where Supple Jack's grave used to be, is reached. . . .

The name chosen for the Park had been kept secret, to spur on those whom physical frailty caused to flag or fail during the route march. Few fell by the wayside, according to the *News-Advertiser*'s account the following day:

> First came the City Band in a large wagon drawn by four magnificent horses followed by the members of the Fire Brigade in uniform in another four horse wagon. A carriage containing Mayor Oppenheimer, Mayor Grant of Victoria, and Aldermen Humphries and Couth came next; another one containing Hon. John Robson, Rev. E. Robson, and ladies followed, and then a long string of vehicles of every description containing the aldermen, city officials, visitors and citizens brought up the rear. A number of equestrians accompanied the procession, while crowds thronged the sidewalk and overflowed on the roadway, the small boy, of course, being in his glory and enlivening the proceedings with his antics. A sensation was caused by the appearance of a big black mule ridden by a youth whose dignity was only exceeded by that of the animal he bestrode. . . .

It is interesting to speculate at what point in a city's history and progress it loses the togetherness expressed in both such an event and the newspaper's report of it. Certainly on that balmy September afternoon community spirit was cohesive enough to survive the many speeches, including that of Victoria's Mayor Grant, whose address hit a high point of good sportsmanship when he conceded that Stanley Park had an advantage over Beacon Hill Park, Victoria's pride, in that while the magnificent mountains seen from the latter across the strait belonged to the United States, those seen from Stanley Park were Canadian. Vancouver has never ceased since to take credit for the loyalty of the mountains to be viewed from the Park.

The ball at the Opera House that followed the opening was crowded with celebrants unwilling to bring to an end their rejoicing in paradise regained.

A year later, the dedication of the Park by Lord Stanley in person produced an even more extravagant carnival: nine hundred school children greeting the governor general with song, rockets exploding a flutter of toy balloons, a four-horse butcher's wagon glorious with bunting, and Lord Stanley himself throwing open his arms to the sky and declaring: "To the use and enjoyment of peoples of all colours, creeds and customs for all time, I name thee Stanley Park."

Lord Stanley was sufficiently impressed by the young city exulting in its fine park to exclaim how glad he was to know there was "a place without a grievance." This situation was soon rectified when the Park gained a zoo, consisting of a bear chained to a stump. One day a minister's wife poked the bear with her umbrella. The bear took exception to the familiarity, responding with a swipe of the paw that caught the good lady's ample dress and reduced modesty to a minimum. The gentlemen present averted their glances, but the incident caused the park commissioners to debate whether the bear should be given a deeper pit or a longer chain. The pit advocates won out.

Over the years Stanley Park was to be the focal point for countless social and sports events, as well as the egalitarian playground for all races and religions as envisaged by Lord Stanley. The only unkind stroke of fate manifested at the Park was the wrecking in 1888 of the *Beaver*, the first steamship on the North Pacific, when she ran up on rocks below Prospect Point just a couple of months before the official opening of the Park. The hulk rotting on the beach was mercifully out of sight and no hindrance to contemplation of the living ships bringing more people to the city without a grievance.

CHAPTER 8 1888–1890

The Romance of Real Estate

The Opera House as a pride • Oriental riots for shame • The building boom, and the C.P.R. Hotel • The holy water • The Beastly Electric

Proud feather though it was in the city's cap, Stanley Park was not at first Vancouver's popular playground. One pioneer recalled the rackety single-track car line to Stanley Park "with its little single truck cars, on whose platform no Scotchman wearing a hard hat would ever ride." The Park was the place for an occasional outing, on a day that promised to stay fair long enough for completion of the excursion, but for dependable, on-the-spot recreational violence Vancouver's sporting life favored the Powell Street Grounds and, subsequently, after Joe Fortes had helped to clear the stumps, the Cambie Street Grounds, only a couple of blocks from the heart of town. The city's first cricket team played at the Cambie Grounds, but the hard-packed pitch was better known for the soccer and lacrosse matches—the latter against the ferocious New Westminster Salmonbellies—that for many years fulfilled the citizens' need for internecine strife. The Cambie Grounds also played host to the annual visit of the circus, the block-square rectangle of dirt supporting the promise of unspeakable excitement for generations of small boys.

Vancouver also provided accommodation, early on, for more genteel cultural events: the Opera House. The name evokes the image of La Scala or *L'Opéra de Paris*. Hart's Opera House, however, was a plain, plank-sided building, a former skating rink in Port

Moody, where it was patronized by C.P.R. construction workers, before being transported to Vancouver by former coffinmaker Frank Hart and re-erected on Carrall Street, in Chinatown. By way of seating the level floor had chairs and benches, bleachers lining both the longer walls of the building, which was lit by oil lamps. The small stage was poised over the mud flat of False Creek, a circumstance which, combined with the heat of the wood stoves, made for a very high type of artistic endeavor. The interior of the Opera House was lined with white cheesecloth, but what the patrons lacked in Gobelin tapestries they more than made up for with enthusiasm for the wide variety of presentations.

One of the early productions at the Opera House was a minstrel show to raise money for uniforms for the fire brigade. In October, 1888, the Marquess of Queensberry, visiting Vancouver, was invited to referee a prize fight at the Opera House, but arrived too late to administer his celebrated rules for the manly art—one of the pugs had been knocked cold. Another cultural triumph was a performance of the play *The Texas Steer,* which called for the entrance of a live horse. The production was only momentarily marred when the stage planking succumbed and the horse fell through to his belly.

Within this same Opera House the Salvation Army held its first indoor meeting, in December, 1887, testament to the management's wide taste in music. For many years the Sally Ann band was the only Sunday entertainment audible in the skid road area around Chinatown, undoubtedly a factor in hastening the return of loggers and fishermen to a healthier environment. For its own change of air, the Army held its picnics in Stanley Park, on the little jut of land near Brockton Point that became known as Hallelujah Point, and that later jogged the conscience of the city with the vocal offering by the Nine O'Clock Gun.

Considerably less sanctified than the Army's ministrations were the Chinese riots of January, 1887. Vancouver lost no time in blotting her history notebook with racial bigotry. Among the flux of newcomers to the city, the disenchanted prospectors from the Interior and the States, the adventure-seekers from eastern Canada and the Old World, the C.P.R. men and their ballast of profitable respectability, were the Chinese immigrants—boatloads of coolies from Hong Kong, lured by relatives whose strong backs had laid track from Craigellachie to Coal Harbour.

Hostility toward the growing number of Chinese employed in

and around the city had been swelling for some time. The animus had less to do with the hue of skin than the color of the money for which the Chinese—or "Chinamen," as they were almost invariably called long after the riots—did more work, at ungodly hours, than suited the white laborer. That the largest sticks cut by the Hastings Mill had been for the Emperor of China's palace at Peking had not diminished the community's chafing about "the Oriental Menace." The Knights of Labor were organized to combat "renewal or increase of Mongolian competition to citizen labor," and pledged "as men bound together by knightly principles and obligations, to do our utmost to prevent the increase and to lessen the grievance by an active and persistent action against all persons who continue to encourage or employ Chinese."

It is doubtful that knights ever assaulted the dragon with less credit to chivalry. Those employers who defied the "knightly principles" by hiring "Mongolians" were labeled "white Chinese." It was also widely held that the "Asiatic plague" had been imported from Victoria, the spiteful source of contagion. Gallagher describes events of the day on which resentment boiled over:

> . . . After a few speakers had addressed the crowd, a procession was formed to go up to where the Chinamen had been landed, up at McDougall's camp, and drive them out; that would be well on towards midnight; there was snow on the ground; it was quite clear, and we could see what we were doing. There were many tough characters among the crowd, navvys who had been working for Onderdonk, hotheaded, thoughtless, strong and tough, and many went along with the procession to try to prevent anyone from being hurt. I was not in the procession, but I was within fifty feet of the front of it when they started. The column was singing as they marched along in the semi-darkness.
>
> When the Chinamen saw all these men coming they were terrified. The crowd came up to the camp singing "John Brown's Body," and such songs. The Chinamen poked their noses out from beneath their tents; the rioters grabbed the tents by the bottom, and upset them. . . . The Chinamen did not stop to see; they just ran. Some went dressed, some not, some with shoes, some with bare

> feet. The snow was on the ground and it was cold. Perhaps, in the darkness, they did not know that the cliff, and a drop of twenty feet, lay in front of them; perhaps they had forgotten. Some may have lost their direction. The tide was in. They had no choice, and you could hear them going plump, plump, plump, as they jumped into the salt water. Scores of them went over the cliff. McDougall was supposed to have two hundred of them up there. . . .

The "Victoria Chinamen" having been seen off, the rioters passed a quiet night getting some rest before reassembling at 8 A.M. before the Sunnyside Hotel and marching upon Chinatown, with wagons hired for the forcible eviction of the Chinese merchants.

> . . . The Chinamen in each building were permitted to select their own custodian to be left behind; no goods were damaged; there was no pilfering. One Chinaman was left in each store. The remainder, probably one hundred, assembled quietly, were loaded onto old-fashioned horse-drawn drays. They all stood crowded together on the drays, and one by one the drays and wagons moved off to New Westminster—a pretty rough ride in a springless dray over a rough road—and put on a steamer for Victoria.
>
> I have heard it said that four Chinamen were tied together by their pigtails, and thrown into the creek at McDougall's camp. If so, I know nothing of it. I do know that some of them were tied together by their pigtails, to prevent them escaping, in Chinatown the following morning. . . .

The provincial government stepped in to forestall any further taking of the law into Occidental hands, and to check the abiding urge to "run 'em out of town." It was a mark of shame bitterly resented by the young city that the Victoria government virtually suspended Vancouver's charter and sent in a special force of constables to keep the peace. Although less than a year old, the incorporated Vancouver had developed a civic pride that took precedence over concern for either civil rights or the brotherhood of man. Righteous indignation at Victoria's intrusion fulminated in the newspapers. After months of fanning the sparks of anti-Chinese feeling, the Vancouver

News-Advertiser of March 2, 1887, responded editorially to the criticism across the gulf: "We have long felt the Victoria *Times* to be one of the most degraded and vile sheets that the Province has had the misfortune to be burdened with. A miserable failure in itself with no moral tone to back it up, it attempts to draw other journals into the slough of blackguardism in which it apparently delights to wallow. . . ." Whatever the other faults of Vancouver's journalism of the time, an excess of moderation in defending the city's conduct was not one of them.

This was not to be the last extension of Vancouver's courtesy to its Chinese citizens. For years the sign in a shop or restaurant window "All White Help" was a mark of distinction. When the Dominion Bank Building developed the infirmity of shedding chunks of its ochre terra cotta to the street below, it was called "The Yellow Peril." It is little short of miraculous that the Chinese community survived the obloquy without an enduring rancor, and that the younger generations of Chinese have maintained the quiet pride that makes the difference between a ghetto and the charm of Chinatown.

Despite the pretensions to silk purse, therefore, Vancouver 1887 remained very much sow's ear. The elegant revels of the Coal Harbour Bachelors' Quadrille Club were more than offset by the marathon poker games patronized by the Hastings Mill workers. Out of respect for these communions the mill sometimes closed down till the game ended, usually violently. In fact gambling was so popular that if cards and players were not available a sporting man would improvise, like the saloon patrons—one of them the Keefer whose name adorns a Vancouver street—who stared at two flies on the bar mirror till Keefer said: "I'll bet one hundred dollars that fly on the left flies off before the other."

Another gambling story of Vancouver's early days involves the Oppenheimer brothers, David and Ike. One of the players in an all-night poker game woke from a doze to find that he held four queens.

"Who dealt?" he asked.

"David."

"Who cut?"

"Ike."

"I pass," said the player, resuming his nap.

The number of Vancouver streets named after gambling men was, however, relatively few. More commonly the proper streets of Vancouver bore the names of C.P.R. officials: Abbott, Cambie,

Hamilton. Hamilton himself described how the streets were planned: "I took numbers for avenues running east and west, while for the streets running north and south I chose the names of trees." The species of trees were soon exhausted, but the streets continued to be named rather than numbered, a gallimaufry of English, Spanish and Indian nomenclature.

To align the streets east of Burrard with those of the West End, Hamilton did his surveying from a point marked by a nail driven into a wooden post. He received some obstructive opposition from Spratt, the fish-oil man, who owned four waterfront lots, with the result of a few unexpected jogs and dead ends that lend variety to the grid in that part of town near the Marine Building.

A visitor to the Vancouver of the period noted that the streets had been laid out on "the American plan," i.e. intersecting at right angles, and that the houses in the resultant rectangles were spotted in rather irregular fashion, a sociable cluster here, a lone abode there, with enormous stumps in between as doleful reminders of whence the lumber was liberated.

One reason for the scattered pattern of building, which often found a substantial building of brick or stone cohabiting a block with a wooden shack, was that land speculators, obliged by law to erect solid structures to a specified value, built these in different localities to encourage development of the intervening property. The value of a lot was enhanced by the neighboring presence of a permanent building. However, to the eye untrained in the occult ways of real estate, the dispersion of lone edifices suggested a community with a remarkably low threshold of claustrophobia.

Another good reason for the checkered pattern of development was the cost of clearing lots. One of the first of many visitors to record their impressions of Vancouver during the eighties and nineties, Mrs. Algernon St. Maur (Duchess of Somerset) reported in her *Impressions of a Tenderfoot:*

> Without having seen the forest in its wild state, one cannot understand the amount of labour necessary to bring a "building lot" into condition. Each of the large stumps left in the ground when a tree is felled costs $30 to remove. They have partly to be burnt, partly blown out with giant powder and the rest dug out with picks. Speculators in such lots are asking very large prices, which

> we are told are still going up. We saw a lot which had just been sold for $5000, with only room for one small house between two already built on adjacent ground. . . .

It should be noted in passing that Mrs. St. Maur was one of many who disapproved of the choice of name for Vancouver: "It seems rather stupid to have called the new town, which is the terminus of the railway, by the same name as the island, as it must sometimes lead to confusion." Confusion came easily to Mrs. St. Maur, who describes the start of her canoe trip to Howe Sound: "Fine weather smiled on us, and in the distance Vancouver Island was visible; thus we crossed to the lighthouse, which is on the other side of the entrance to Buzzard's Inlet."

The slip of the pen was perhaps excusable. The buzzards were indeed hovering over every ship or train that brought in another quantity of quail for plucking. Real-estate agents were on hand to welcome the passengers disembarking from every mode of transportation except a wheelbarrow. One dazed traveler reported: "The bare fact of a man's coming to Vancouver by train was almost sufficient introduction. Inside of an hour every real-estate man in the place would know him and his business in Vancouver and probably whether he had any family or a hereditary disease."

For sheer profusion of premises, the only competition for the saloons—reckoned to number one to every hundred of population, including women and children—was the real-estate offices. A widely distributed photo of the time showed a realty office housed in a huge hollow stump, upstaging the spruce budworm. Real-estate agents were said to be so numerous in Vancouver during this period that they were obliged to sell to each other. Their siren song reached to every corner of the globe: in 1889 a group of American soldiers raiding a village of hostile Indians in Arizona discovered in one of the tepees a cache of pamphlets beating the drum for purchase of lots in the Brighouse estate in Vancouver's West End.

The real-estate furor did, however, have its effect. Vancouver literally exploded with vitality. Mrs. St. Maur vibrated: "Blasting goes on daily at Vancouver, and few precautions are taken to warn passers-by. A man was killed last week in this way. The workmen get so accustomed to the use of these dangerous explosives that they leave them lying about. Two days ago enough giant powder was found close to the hotel to have blown up the whole town, but it did not excite much attention. . . ." One of the deans of demolition, stump-blaster Ernest Gortley, later known as "the Powder Wizard," summarized his career as "one blasted thing after another."

Vancouver, 1887, was a scene made for the panavision motion-picture camera that unfortunately had not yet been invented. The English traveler Roper (*By Track and Trail Through Canada*) described it: "There were many people about, some well-dressed ladies, sundry Chinamen in Celestial clothing, but generally with English hats upon their shining polls, some Indians dressed like whites, many business men, and crowds of working men. Above all rose the increasing noise of sawing and nail-driving, the ring of the bricklayer's trowel, and the stroke of the lumberer's axe; for everyone was busy, in one way or another, building up the city."

Not only real-estate agents but newspaper reporters and hotel criers met all the arrivals by land or sea. One English visitor was badly shaken, as he detrained, to be greeted by the wild supplications of hotel touts yelling from beyond the platform that was out of bounds to them. "There were but half a dozen hotels worth calling so at that time in Vancouver City, and all the racket made was quite uncalled for." This experience was not assuaged by the detonations that rocked this traveler's room at The Leland at regular intervals, nor by his finding that the boots he had left outside his door overnight to be cleaned—the English traveler's birthright—were untouched in the morning and possibly a shade dirtier from blast dust.

A year after the Fire, Vancouver boasted twenty-four large frame hotels, with equally uncertain service. According to one account, perhaps fanciful, guests of one of these hotels were hurried out of bed in the morning because the sheets were needed for the dining-room tables. Such contingencies were partly offset at hotels like Tom Cyr's Granville Hotel, where every guest was entitled to a free eye-opener before breakfast. The guest was encouraged to think in terms of the essential comforts, such as buying a round before going up to his room. He also could expect to receive no nickels in his change, the "short bit" (ten cents) and the "long bit" (a quarter) being the basic coinage of the bar.

Such caravansaries were soon outshone by the splendid inn erected by the C.P.R. to protect its investment in the welfare of the globe-trotters the company was enticing to use its route. The chain of itinerary being no stronger than its weakest link, and Vancouver having been forged in a fire indiscriminate as to quality, the railway company began in the fall of 1886 the building of a brick hotel of one hundred rooms. The hotel stood on the southwest corner of Georgia and Granville streets—"away out on the hill" and utterly foolish in the opinion of most citizens. But the company proved to be accurate in assessing the location of Vancouver's Mayfair. Georgia at Granville is the natural crest of inclines from the four points of the compass. At first the Hotel Vancouver was surrounded by forest, and for a time only a handful of guests rattled around in its splendor. Van Horne himself had some doubts about the design, if not the site. On being introduced to the original architect, T. C. Sorly, he remarked: "So you're the damn fool who spoilt the building with all those little windows."

The guests had something better than large windows: a veranda that was the talk of the Empire. Other Vancouver hotels had spacious verandas, on which the guests after dinner took their teetering ease, passing the time of day with other visitors or guffawing when a wagon rumbling along a planked road spurted a geyser under the unwary pedestrian. But only the C.P.R. hotel offered the superlative view of the inlet afforded by its choice vantage point. Even the redoubtable Mrs. St. Maur was mollified: "In the evening we sat in the wide verandah of the hotel, and had a glorious view of the Sound and the mountains beyond, by pale moonlight."

For the predictable wages of the sin of veranda-sitting, the Duchess of Somerset is good enough to prescribe the nostrum: "My face was very much swollen from mosquito bites, but carbonate of soda with a little water, dabbed on gently with the end of a bit of cotton wool, at once removed all irritation."

An American report on the luxury of Hotel Vancouver veranda-sitting was published by the San Francisco *Journal of Commerce*, whose correspondent wrote:

> You've just dined! Well, come out with us then on the veranda and smoke a cigar. Stretch yourself at full length on that bamboo chair, throw your leg over that elongated arm; that's right; now what have you to say about it? Isn't that a magnificent view over the bay? It is two miles across. You would scarcely think so, would you? Those foothills are ten miles off, whilst the distant peaks, you see due north, we are told are over forty miles away as the crow flies. Those white specks you see over the water

> are the houses of the Indian mission. You may just distinguish the spire of the church; some distance to the right you see the Moodyville settlement; here is the largest sawmill in the province. On this side of the bay, there to the right of where you see those fine ships lying at anchor, is the Hastings Sawmill. . . .

With such endorsement the Hotel Vancouver flourished, spread its wings of brick along both Georgia Street and Howe, and became a celebrity, so homely she was endearing, a hotel such as survives today only in those parts of former Empire that are too poor to reduce hotels to parking lots.

Travelers from Europe who arrived in Vancouver tensed for confrontation with wild beasts found the most formidable fauna right in the C.P.R. hotel, in the form of the huge frontier breakfast. One visitor who survived an encounter with this monster wrote: "They do not use an English egg-cup, but a glass double-ender, one cup of which is like a tumbler, into which is broken a half dozen eggs, stirred up with butter, pepper and salt, and eaten as a sauce accompaniment to the main course." He was also bemused by being served salt "in a small castor, in which is a branched iron affair, that rattles as you shake it, and thus keeps the contents from caking."

The same traveler noted that "the ladies did not leave the table with the dessert; and I doubt if there was any other room for them to go to." In the beginning, Vancouver was a city in which women and cigars were to be enjoyed together. The assimilation of womanhood into a male society was exemplified by the event reported by the *News-Advertiser* of February 3, 1888: "At a general meeting of the members of the Vancouver Reading Room, held last evening, the Rev. H. F. Clinton in the chair, it was decided to repeal the by-law restricting the privileges of the reading-room to persons of the male sex only, and in future to allow ladies to become members on payment of the usual fees."

Segregation of the sexes came later, when hotels were required to have separate beer parlors for "Ladies" and "Gentlemen" to frustrate the floozies who found the tavern door the shortest route to a logger's wallet. Visitors from the Old World for many years found it curious and slightly inhumane that a man was spared a woman's presence in the one place where his condition made it bearable.

Such circumspection was not the name of the game in the

Vancouver of the late eighties. "It just makes a 'Friscan's mouth water," wrote the *Journal of Commerce* correspondent, "when he compares the business men of this infant Vancouver with the poor, dollar-limit fossils of San Francisco. . . ." He voiced the prophecy that was almost a catechism among the citizens: ". . . in a very few years to come, groans will be heard in the streets of Vancouver, and many a slap upon the thigh, as people bewail the chance they missed by not investing in the early days."

The Tragedy of Hindsight has been the most popular piece played outside the old Opera House, the blind Oedipus being almost blithe compared to the remorse of the investor so myopic as to miss the chance to make a fortune speculating in real estate.

The C.P.R. on the other hand was almost too long-sighted. The company put through Granville Street all the way to False Creek, the plan being to make it the prestige street for new businesses. Besides the hotel it established foci of social activity: the new Vancouver Opera House flanking the hotel, and the railway depot at the foot of Granville. The Hudson's Bay Company store moved from its old site to the intersection of Georgia and Granville, kitty-corner from the Hotel Vancouver. And British investors were wooed with the promise that Granville would be the main artery of commerce.

However, the artery remained capillary till after the turn of the century. For the first decade and more, the main business thoroughfare of Vancouver was Cordova Street. For years empty stores lined Granville, while Cordova boomed—a situation reversed fifty years later. Old Granville Townsite was the first business section to prosper. Water Street, planked immediately after the Fire, was joined by Cordova, Carrall, Hastings, Cambie, Powell, Oppenheimer and Westminster Avenue. The aspiration, represented by the C.P.R., was to the heights, but the dollar preferred the waterfront.

On the waterfront streets was always a saloon within easy weaving distance. The Opera House presented no concert music as mesmeric as the honky-tonk pianos of The Fountain, The Bodega, The Woodbine, and The Hole in the Wall. J. M. Clute, who helped to organize the first Vancouver YMCA in an effort to counteract the powerful suction of so many swinging doors, ruefully admitted later that the founding fathers were obliged to hold their first meeting in a room over a saloon, no other space being available.

These men who played hard, worked hard. Between June, 1886, and December, 1888, they graded thirty-six miles of streets, not including the nine miles of Park road. They planked twenty-four miles of sidewalks and 5,280 feet of bridge. They embarked on a comprehensive system of sewers. They built the new section of workingmen's homes south of the mill, on Cordova and Dunlevy, with a straggle along Westminster Avenue (Main Street) and East Pender, formerly Dupont Street.

Main Street developed from a narrow logging road running south from the city, flanking the famous trout stream that cascaded from a lake to a beaver dam, thence to the waterwheel of a brewery and finally to the flume that served the Hastings Mill. Few other trout streams have afforded the convenience of buying a bottle of beer within sight of the lure. The trail winding farther southward through the Fairview forest passed the cedar stump of which a pioneer hermit had fashioned a three-room residence straight out of "Burgess Bedtime Stories": kitchen, living room and bedroom, plus front steps in the form of a ladder nailed to the outside of the stump. With the municipal clerk sitting perched on this stump, was held the first meeting (1892) of the council for the Municipality of South Vancouver.

The Vancouver district north of Pender and east of Granville not only rapidly became commercial but did it so gainfully that in 1888 the officials at City Hall grumbled because citizens were paying their taxes ahead of the due date and demanding the discount for prepayment. The Vancouver council was also regretting already the twenty-year tax exemption granted to Yaletown, Vancouver's first real suburb. Centered by the Yale Hotel, at what was to be the intersection of Granville and Drake streets, close by False Creek, Yaletown grew in the 1886–87 period as C.P.R. work gangs set up camp near the company's engine shops. The company had originally planned its yards for Point Grey, complementing the proposed terminus in Kitsilano, because the Granville Townsite had no fresh water other than that from wells, whereas on the south side of False Creek ran the streams full of trout vital to any roundhouse crew.

The C.P.R. ran into more fight than that offered by the fish, however, in the person of Sam Greer, a fiery Irishman who manipulated property rights to the Kitsilano area known as Greer's Beach, and who refused to be evicted when the C.P.R. disputed his claim. When railway agents came to exercise their rights, Greer promised to welcome the sheriff by shooting him. Sam ripped up the railway ties at night as fast as men could lay them by day, and was equally industrious about filling in the holes they dug for telegraph poles. When at last the sheriff from New Westminster, accompanied at a safe distance by various railway officials, marched to the railhead that was Sam's property line, and shouted the suggestion that Greer, barricaded behind his door, come forth to parley, Sam replied by squeezing off a shotgun blast that caught the sheriff in the face and chest and felled several other aides. If the volley had not been fired through the door the damage might have been serious.

The date of Sam's thus simplifying the dispute without resolving it was September 26, 1891. Sent to prison, he obtained his release through the intervention of the local Orangemen, of whom he was one of the deeper shades.

Meantime, the railway company needed its shops. A special bylaw passed by the Vancouver council granted the C.P.R. the section of land on the north shore of False Ceek that became Yaletown, a generosity spurred by the anxiety of Vancouver merchants at the prospect of a rival center on the opposite side of the creek. Named after the town up the Fraser where the company had other engine shops, Yaletown consisted of shacks for married men, "Bachelor Hall," a barge moored in the creek for the single men, and huge piles of cordwood to fuel the locomotives, most of the wood being lost to the Fire. At first separated by wilderness, off the C.P.R. right-of-way, Yaletown later blended with the southward-expanding Vancouver.

As for Greer's Beach, it became a popular resort for summer campers during the nineties, people pitching their tents beyond the swamp of rushes and muskrat. The swamp was not replaced by beach sand till the dredging of False Creek.

By this time the young city had a voice in its newspapers, which from the beginning were strong of lung. William Brown's *Herald*, which survived the Fire only to die almost at once of natural causes, yielded place to Vancouver's first daily, the *Advertiser*, born May 8, 1886, also burned out, revived and finally amalgamated with the *News* to become the *News-Advertiser*, a morning daily whose hyphenation reflected the conservative, English background of its publisher, F. L. Carter-Cotton. Carter-Cotton was an able businessman and competent writer not too familiar with the western scene. His matinal diffidence was balanced by the *World*, founded in 1888, an evening paper of liberal tendency. This journalistic pattern of two dailies, one starting off the day with English understatement, the other concluding it with the unbridled gusto of the frontier, has been repeated from time to time, notably with the *Province*, after it became a morning paper, and *The Sun*. The Vancouver *World* was Vancouver's senior newspaper till it was sold, in 1924, to the *Morning Sun*. The *Province*, which began publishing in Vancouver as a daily March 26, 1898, proved the most durable of the several newspapers that discovered that in a city of ten or fifteen thousand news travels faster than the presses can print it. Taking over the site of the *News* at Cambie and Hastings, the *Province* building was for seventy-five years a landmark—"the Old Lady of Victory Square."

The principal source of stories during Vancouver's first decade as a city was the waterfront: the ocean liners and their passengers who brought exotic whiffs of the Orient as well as globe-girdling Britons with news from "home." When the *Abyssinia*, the first of the China ships, inward bound from Yokohama, berthed in Vancouver harbor the local press had prepared the populace so thoroughly for the event that the city was in an ecstasy of excitement. For years thereafter one of Vancouver's favorite sources of a small thrill was to "go down and watch the boat come in."

Visitors who failed to praise the city were summarily dealt with by the press. For example the *News* of July 23, 1886, editorialized under the heading "Skipped to the States":

> The Victoria *Times* says: "Sherman Heck and family have returned to Seattle from Vancouver. Mr. Heck gives a gloomy account of the outlook for the Canadian terminus. He says few people are coming in and all who can get away are leaving. He lost everything he had by the fire, and is thankful to get back to Seattle with his health." Heck is a swindle who skipped this city very quietly and very suddenly, leaving several mourning creditors in debt to the tune of $1000. The dupes, if asked, would doubtless give a "gloomy account of his doings at the terminal city."

Vancouver never entirely lost this predisposition to assume that those that left the city, especially if they did so quietly and without a ritual flagellation, were compelled by circumstances that did them no honor. On the other hand the visitor who gave the city a good name was assured of the heartiest of notices.

An initial bad impression of Vancouver was responsible for

the Bank of British Columbia's being the first chartered bank to open for business in the city. L. A. Hamilton had invited the general manager of the Bank of Montreal to come out and assess the value of opening a branch. The gentleman arrived on a wet day, had a misadventure with a mudhole, found the gray and sullen skies depressing, and returned to Montreal unconvinced that the place would sustain life long enough for a bank to recoup its loans.

In August, 1888, that part of Vancouver's water supply that was potable became marvelously more so with completion of the pipeline to the North Shore and the mountain watershed of the Capilano River. The city that had been plagued by typhoid fever from time to time gained at one swoop a water supply without peer, for purity, coolness and sudsing in the tub, among all the cities of America. The kind of veneration inspired by the vestal virgins has been lavished on their water by Vancouverites. P. J. McDougall, writing in the *British Columbia Magazine* of June, 1911, was hardly more lyrical than average: ". . . the tinctured draught he gulps down in the heat of midsummer inspires him with the utmost of respect. It is out of the heart of these towering piles that the welcome water comes, fresh to his lips from glacial ice beds ages old."

Vancouver's is, in effect, sacramental water. Blessed by pure luck, her water far more than her wines Vancouver has jealously guarded from adulteration. For Vancouver the Fifth Commandment is "Honor thy father and thy mother and thy water"—not necessarily in that order.

The Capilano and Seymour water systems, gravity-feeding hundreds of millions of gallons of ice water the short distance across the inlet, made Vancouver prodigal with its water. Relatively few public fountains were built to take advantage of the abundance, but this austerity was more than offset by private sprinklers whose display on a summer evening was a magnificence of volume such as Versailles could never conceive.

The new houses being built a mere two years after the Fire enjoyed not only the luxury of water mains but also the somewhat more contaminated pipeline of the telephone. The telephone antedated the Fire in Vancouver, the first switchboard being installed in 1885, with thirty-five subscribers. After the Fire the icon of civilization was taken for granted in the new homes. By the turn of the century, the amenities for the "hello girls," as the operators were affectionately dubbed, included, according to a contemporary account, "light, airy and well-furnished retiring rooms . . . where the operators off shift may rest and amuse themselves. Appreciated features of such rooms are the pianos." For the largely male population of Vancouver of those years, the telephone office had much of the magic of the seraglio, nonetheless engrossing for being built of red brick.

The safety of the young ladies who emerged from the building was improved, if not guaranteed, by the installation of street lighting, by the Vancouver Illuminating Company, whose first bulb glowed in August, 1887. The company built an incandescent plant, on Abbott Street between Pender and Hastings, capable of operating seven hundred lights. Because of lack of a transformer, however, the street lights became progressively dimmer with distance from the plant, those on Granville Street shedding a gentle glow that attracted only the most susceptible of moths.

John Clough, the city lamplighter, who had a rather short career because of Vancouver's passion for modernity, became the city jailer. It was rumored that Clough had been jailed so often for drunkenness—a lamplighter to whom the call to light up was something of a mission—that the police commission decided that it was cheaper to take him on staff.

In 1889 the city council granted the charter for construction of a street railway. Initially the cars were to be drawn by horses but, as with Clough's coal oil lamps, progress was so impetuous that the plans for a carbarn and stable for the street railway were scrapped to make way for electrified public transit. The Vancouver Electric Railway and Light Company was born of union of the street railway and illuminating companies. Official inauguration of the electric trams —accelerated by the report that New York City had yet to get them—was scheduled as part of the Dominion Day, 1890, celebration. But it was on June 26 that the first electric streetcar (No. 14), built in Baton Rouge, Louisiana, trundled out of the Westminster Avenue carbarn, escorted by many excited small boys. The ride cost five cents, collected by the conductor who moved along the running board beside the open-end seats.

The nickel was not enough. Expansively, the company accepted liability in 1893 for a cow killed on the Granville Street line. The urge to lay track becoming a delirium, it built the Fairview line, running up Granville Street and across the wooden Granville Street Bridge (completed in 1888), crossing seven gullies and streams with bridges up to 150 feet long, east on Broadway to join the Westminster

Avenue line. The Fairview line served an ungrateful stretch of dense bush whose raccoon and deer declined to give up private transportation. The company went broke.

It was bought out, in 1895, by the Consolidated Railway and Light Company, which amalgamated with the New Westminster Street Railway Company to become the New Westminster and Vancouver Tramway Company. In the natural business process of big fish swallowing smaller fish only to be swallowed in turn by yet larger, the new company in 1897 was absorbed into the British Columbia Electric Railway Company, which ruled as grand poobah of electric plants and street railways for Vancouver, New Westminster and Victoria.

The B.C. Electric Company, or "the Beastly Electric" as it came to be known to generations of Vancouver commuters waiting damply at car stops, owed its health to an energetic Scot, R. M. Horne-Payne. So much muscle was quickly developed by the company that much of Vancouver's animus against the C.P.R., the absentee landlord, could be diverted against the more omnipresent rails of the B.C.E.R. While the citizens of cities elsewhere vented their spleen against czars and petty potentates, the people of Vancouver cursed an oligarchy whose palace was a carbarn, whose temple was an aromatic silo of gas produced from coal, and whose benevolence was limited to providing, on foggy nights, the red light on the rear of the streetcar that served as bellwether for a flock of private vehicles feeling their way home.

In the same year, 1890, that the first electric tram rolled on steel in Vancouver, the city saw its first automobile—a Stanley Steamer. The rival means of transit had an even start. For the time being, however, the only commercial competition for the street railway was the several teams of cart horses owned by the "merchant princes," as Vancouver's grocers were called. This class of cabbagey Bourbons flourished because of the fact that city builders have healthy appetites. Vancouver's second mayor, David Oppenheimer, owned one of the wholesale grocery stores that began to fill up the flats between the C.P.R. tracks and Hastings Street, with what was to become a three-block-wide repository of victuals. One of the more rural customers, attempting to take a short cut from Fairview to False Creek, arrived upset because he had been chased by wolves. Sensing a deterrent to trade, the merchants built an auxiliary wholesale center near Granville Street Bridge, where wolf-chased clientele would at least have a shorter run.

Another commercial enterprise doing well was sale of hardware: ship's chandlery, mill chains, wire ropes for the logging camps. The loggers who previously went to New Westminster to buy their "best clothes" now had retail stores closer at hand. The stock of Vancouver's first department store, the Hudson's Bay Company, was at first limited to groceries, provisions, wines and spirits, with a nice regard for the priorities of civilized living. The sale of alcoholic beverages in private retail stores was to become one of the victims of Prohibition, but in these years of innocence the government liquor store had yet to lay a clammy hand over the mouth that spoke directly to the cork.

Of more immediate interest to city council, restless in its quarters in the Sentell Building, was the opening in 1889 of the Market Hall on the northwest corner of what is now Main and Pender. The ground floor of the new building was a public market for poultry and farm produce, the lane outside accommodating horses, cattle and swine. The second floor, known as City Hall Theatre, housed itinerant entertainments such as concerts and political rallies. The combined ambiance of politics and pig fights was irresistible to the aldermen, who moved into the second floor and gradually evicted the other livestock, till by 1898 they were in complete possession of this city hall.

Able to afford something in better taste, the Hudson's Bay Company moved from its first store on Cordova Street to the corner of Granville and Georgia to partake of the tourist trade centered by the C.P.R. hotel. This second store was replaced in 1916 by the classic columns of the emporium known to the next half-century of Vancouver shoppers as "the Bay." On Hastings Street David Spencer would build his department store (later Eaton's), while Charles Woodward provided major competition for both with his store, first on Westminster Avenue, later moving to Hastings Street. From the start Woodward's was the workingman's store, the aisles barely wide enough to take the broad Scottish accent of the customers.

Thriving though it was, however, this domestic trade would have buttered few parsnips for the growing city without the global commerce for which Vancouver was fast becoming an entrepôt.

14. The Big Tree, Stanley Park, and guests

15. Hastings Mill store, approximately 1888

16. Loading at Hastings Mill, around the turn of the century. Note ramps by which lumber entered the hold

17. Early wedding of industry and art

18. Klootchmen, sometimes called squaws by those who had not studied the pride and dignity in the faces of these coast Indians. (1901)

19. English Bay Beach and pier, and the West End. Three horse-drawn rigs are discernible at left

20. Joe Fortes shows the youngsters how it is done, at English Bay

21. Canadian Pacific Railway station festive on the occasion of the visit of the Duke of Cornwall, 1901

22. 1914. Off to war? No. Militia called out to defend Vancouver against the *Komagata Maru*

23. Returning aboard the *Komagata Maru* after a parley, the Sikh on the ladder is the ill-fated expedition's organizer, Gurdit Singh

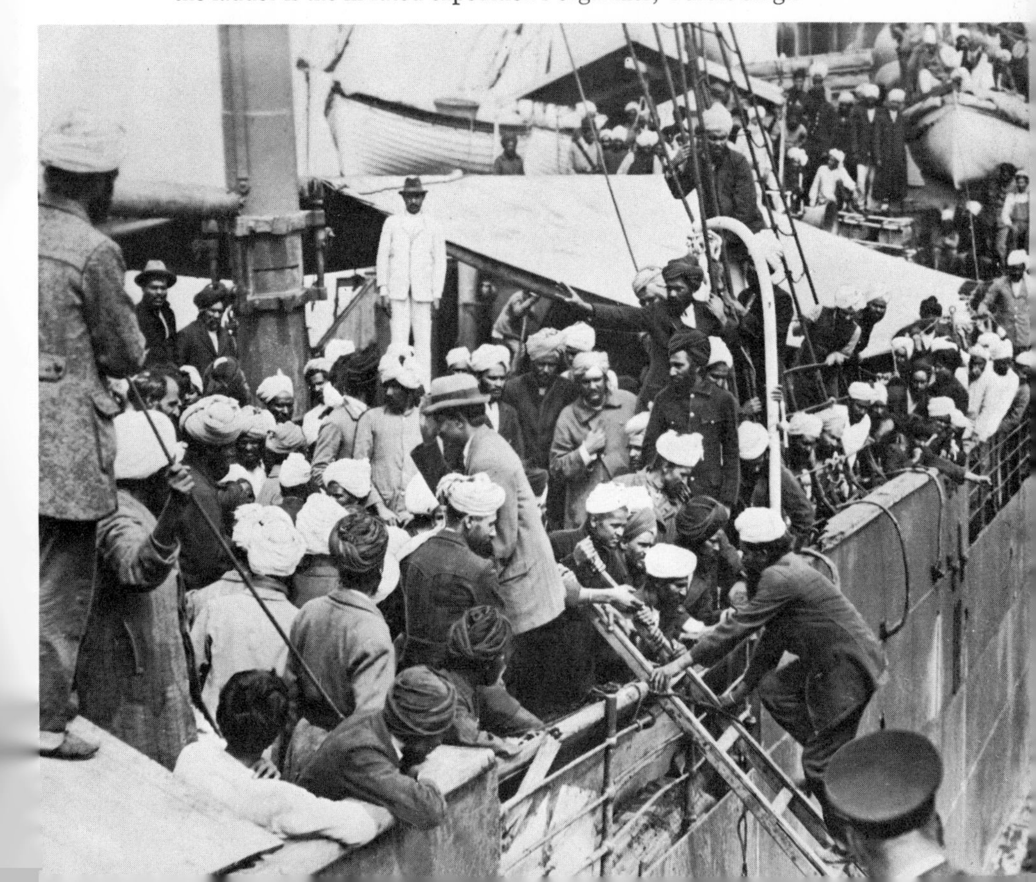

24. The *Empress of Japan* slips gracefully outward-bound from the First Narrows. West Vancouver is populated by one farm at the mouth of Capilano River

CHAPTER 9 1890–1913

Port of the Wider World

The Empresses grace the All-Red Route • The new commerce, and the old racial prejudice • The Klondikers prime the pump • Beginning of a university • Edwardian airs, travelers' impressions, and the cloud no bigger than a lady's glove

FROM the beginning, the most important business street in Vancouver has been that paved with water: the harbor. Also from the beginning the C.P.R. knew that the revenue produced by freight and passengers bound only to and from the terminal city would not even pay for axle grease. Van Horne saw the railway as a link in the All-Red Route, and the company lost no time in convincing the British government that C.P.R. vessels could carry mail and tranship Japanese tea from the Orient to the eastern seaboard with more dispatch via Burrard Inlet than was possible by way of Portland, Oregon, with its problems of river navigation.

As the Canadian Pacific Steamship Company, a fleet of ex-Cunard liners—the *Abyssinia, Parthia* and *Batavia*—kept the new wharf in Vancouver piled high with cargoes of tea, silk, mail and general merchandise. That most of these delicacies were consigned to the fleshpots of the East, principally Montreal and New York, detracted not at all from the heady aromas drifting over Vancouver's waterfront.

On their return journeys westward across the Pacific the ships were at times embarrassingly empty, as almost the only product Vancouver could load for the teeming but indigent Orient was flour from mills in Portland. The C.P.R. blandished the world's supply of globe-trotters in an effort to fill up the vacant space with people as well as produce, and during the period from 1887 to 1890 actually carried more than ten thousand passengers. Ninety per cent of these travelers were steerage class, however. The company had its sights trained on the seagoing carriage trade, and it was partly to satisfy the particular passenger that in 1889 it ordered three steamships destined to become famous as a fleeting part of the Vancouver scene: the *Empresses*.

The *Empress* ships—the *Empress of India*, the *Empress of China*, the *Empress of Japan*—began to enter service from 1891, creating the key link in the new fast route from Britain to the Far East. The sleek liners, which embodied the grace of a schooner with the speed and efficiency of steam, for a time outpaced anything on the Atlantic, and for nearly half a century were the pride and effulgent joy of the Vancouver citizens who watched them cleave the eddies off Brockton Point. The white ships brought dependability as well as acceleration to scheduled sailings, between Vancouver and Hong Kong, Yokohama, Shanghai. Within a few years the liners, which connected with a transcontinental rail service that now boasted a dining car, in addition to the C.P.R. resort hotels opening in the Rockies, brought a new bustle to the foyer of the company's hotel in Vancouver. Thousands of travelers who stopped at Vancouver en route to someplace else suddenly found that they had found their destination.

One of the first of the secondary industries born of the exotic trade with the South Pacific was the British Columbia Sugar Refining Company, established in 1890 with the initiative of an American, B. T. Rogers, capital provided by Canadian businessmen, and a $30,000 grant from the city. The B.C. Sugar Refinery profited from the favorable cost of importing raw sugar from the Pacific islands and Australia, finding an expanding market wherever steel rail was opening up the Canadian Northwest. The same improvement in shipping fostered wholesale businesses such as Oriental Traders, not only importing tea, silks and spices but also processing products such as coffee and coconut. The smell of raw lumber, along the docks and Water Street, vied with and at last yielded to that of copra and roasting coffee beans. Henceforth a man could stand where the old maple tree had stood, and breathe deep, and fancy himself to be on a tropical isle—if he kept his eyes tightly closed—where the natives worshiped a god other than Real Estate.

Of more immediate relevance was the fact that each sailing

of an *Empress* called for $6,000 worth of provender and $2,000 worth of oil and general supplies. The tendrils of commerce grew from the harbor area through the city and began to find their way into the hinterland of British Columbia, that vast and rugged region that had yet to respond to the vibrations from the potential metropolis. Vancouver sat in the lower left-hand corner of the province like a Venus's-flytrap, thriving on the swiftness with which it seized the unwary and paralyzed him in the sticky mortgage.

For the time being the center of trade on the Lower Mainland remained New Westminster. The farmers' market in that city, and its Royal Agricultural Exhibition, overshadowed the neighboring city's claim to principality. The value of valley spuds, as compared to pineapples from Fiji, became sharply apparent during the world-wide depression that hit Vancouver in 1890 and affected its growth for most of what was left of the nineteenth century. For a time land values fell off, and the speculators moved on to fields if not greener at least less burdened with stumps. Among the victims was the fledgling Bank of British Columbia, which found the winds of finance no easier to navigate than the muddy Vancouver streets that it had chosen to brave. Vancouver was to become known as "the graveyard of bankers" when the Bank of Vancouver, founded later (1910), succumbed after four years of attracting mostly small deposits by children. Vancouver has never quite managed to develop an equivalent to Wall Street, Bay Street or Rue St. Jacques, something in the air impairing the moral cohesion of bankers. Possibly it is the Potlatch People whose ghosts discommode concretions of wealth in buildings with facades of Roman columns and vaults of Pittsburgh steel. The Bank of British Columbia, at any rate, was absorbed by the Canadian Bank of Commerce, and with it went the chance for Canada's financial tail to wag the dog.

By 1890, however, Vancouver had grown past the danger of succumbing from pup diseases such as economic worms. The 2,700 buildings in the city included five schools with 1,200 pupils, a City Hall, seven lumber mills, fifty-five hotels competing with two iron foundries, the sugar refinery, the provincial government building and courthouse, and three chartered banks, as well as the telephone, light and tramway services. And on November 21, 1894, St. Paul's Hospital opened as a wooden structure with twenty beds, under the auspices of the Sisters of Charity of Providence.

The Vancouver fire department had two stations and thirty-three men, stalwarts ready to minister to the combustible Achilles' heel of a city that for the next century was to have in abundance the lumber mills stacked for spectacular three-alarm fires. Whenever possible these fires have occurred, in keeping with precedent, on a Sunday, when viewing a good, uncontrollable blaze was the only diversion that Vancouver afforded.

The fire department was also a comfort to the C.P.R. officials whose fine homes in the West End provided the nuclei of bon ton for the socially ambitious. The railway executives built their expensive homes on the bluff at the foot of Howe Street, to overlook the magnificent view of the inlet without observing the shacks of the Kanakas still resident on the beach of Coal Harbour. Of this fine prospect visitor A. G. Bradley (*Canada in the Twentieth Century*) wrote:

> There is here no maze of projecting wharves and docks to keep all these great steamers . . . at arm's length. They float right up to the back gardens of the houses. As you sit at the club window, and look across its tennis lawn of English hue and texture, the masts and hull of an Australian liner seem almost to touch the garden fence, while through their yards and rigging the snowy peaks of the Cascade [sic] range look down upon the blue waters of the inlet.

By the turn of the century a fairly solid section of residences reached five blocks west of Granville Street as far south as Nelson Street. Georgia Street, between Granville and Jervis, was known as "Blue Blood Alley" because it served the homes of the most prominent citizens. It may be noted here that Georgia has never lost its association with status, developing from the showplace of homes into the prestige street for office buildings, hotels and restaurants. Vancouver's aspiration to a Champs Elysées has been directed along Georgia, Stanley Park substituting for Place de l'Etoile, and a wistful single row of tree plantings emulating the great boulevard's leafy splendor.

Until as late as 1905, however, and after the streetcar line had been extended to Stanley Park and down Denman Street to English Bay, the few houses west of Denman were cut off from the city by wilderness. It was during the building boom of 1907–10 that cheaper houses and apartment blocks rapidly filled the gaps. Previously, the West Enders took their pleasure in other parks besides the rather remote Stanley Park, and Douglas Sladen, an Australian author who visited the city in 1889, remarked on "a superb athletic ground where, by the influx of English and Australians, cricket is restored to its legitimate place of pride." It did not take long for Britons to draw stumps of the more gentlemanly sort.

These new arrivals were facilitated by the first rail connection between Vancouver and Seattle, by 1892, but to permanent residents there was greater consequence in the incorporation, in 1889, of the Union Steamship Company, a union of the Burrard Inlet Towing Company and the Moodyville Ferry Company. This inglorious fleet, under the direction of Henry Darling, son of John Darling of the Union Steamships Company of New Zealand, consisted at first of three tugs augmented by three small passenger ships brought across the Pacific in sections, by tramp steamer, and reassembled in the inlet. The three welded wonders were renamed the *Capilano,* the *Comox* and the *Coquitlam,* a rather left-handed compliment to Indian tribes whose canoes were sightly as well as speedy. If the departure of a C.P.R. *Empress* was a spectacle to catch the breath, that of a Union paddleduck waddling through the First Narrows was less ennobling.

Yet the vulgar black-and-orange funnels of the Union boats were in a way dearer to the people of Vancouver during the decades when the ships pottered up and down the coast and its inlets. The "C" scapes, later supplemented by the *Lady Rose, Lady Alexandra* and other *Ladys* fated to mingle with the masses rather than the classes, brought supplies to coastal settlements, and company picnics to playgrounds. For the city bounded by mountains that discouraged the building of highways for the first fifty years of its existence, the day-boat excursion was the standard outing. The determination to have a good time called forth resources of energy and stamina that strike awe into those today who take their relaxation lightly. Spilling off the streetcars at the foot of Main in the early morning, families were herded by fathers across the railway tracks and down the wharf. There the Union boats leaned wearily into the pilings, their stacks wisping, as each vessel summoned the strength to endure the indignities of yet another holiday horde.

Bruising battles, none the less fierce for being wordless, were fought in the crush of bodies striving to be the first ashore, with the consequent advantage in the footrace to stake out the choice picnic table. The halt and the elderly, and those unschooled in the contest, spread their tablecloths and blankets on peripheral rocks, and took what vengeance they could when a child of the victors came within range of a volley of wet tea leaves.

The weekend sailings were called "the Daddy boats" because they brought fathers to the summer cottage at Sechelt, Half Moon Bay and other coastal resorts. For the young unmarried, the height of bacchanalia was the Saturday night "booze cruise" to Bowen Island, aboard what should have been called the *Lady Chatterley.* The enthusiasm with which several generations of Vancouver youth dedicated itself to proving the truth of Donne's words—"no man is an island, entire of itself"—stunted vegetation on that part of Bowen within a half-mile of the dock.

Not so entertaining as the Union boats was another arrival from the Orient, in 1895: smallpox. As usual, Vancouver accused Victoria of being the immediate source of the scourge. The "Battle of the Hoses" resulted from Vancouver's quarantine against arrivals from Victoria. When the Canadian Pacific Navigation Company boat *Premier* attempted to land passengers on the C.P.R. dock at the foot of Howe Street, a policeman deterred a passenger, who persisted in trying to disembark, by authority of a solid punch on the nose. In the melee that ensued, the Vancouver fire brigade arrived and turned a hose on the unwelcome visitors, who responded with a jet from the ship's steam hose. It was not to be the last time that Vancouver gave a visiting ship a reception of water display less cordial than that accorded by New York to liners on their maiden voyage. Fortunately, the smallpox proved less obstinate. For a time the bell of the wagoner was heard daily in the streets, as he carted the stricken to the isolation hospital on Deadman's Island. Then the disease abated.

In spite of plague and poor times, the Mount Pleasant and Fairview districts of Vancouver expanded settlement, moving out toward the Tea Swamp, east of Little Mountain, where Jim McGeer, milkman, poet and father of Vancouver's first political McGeer, pastured his cows in the muskeg. The trestle bridge across False Creek helped to open up this area. Still farther south, in Kerrisdale, roughly where the Point Grey High School would be built, the fertile soil grew flowers for the tables of C.P.R. dining cars and hotels. Kerrisdale began as a country village (named by a resident related to County Kerry) on the Vancouver–Lulu Island tramline. Strung along Wilson Road (later 41st Avenue), the homes drew their water from wells and had to wait till 1912 for the east-west tramline. South Vancouver and Point Grey thus grew as separate municipalities, incorporated in 1892 and 1908 respectively. South Vancouver evolved from rugged individualists like Jim McGeer, farmers who preferred solvency to comfort and practiced a do-it-yourself type of local improvement that broke a few axles. Point Grey, logged off, opened up as streetcar lines arterialized blood to new residential areas.

West of Kitsilano, and where Vancouver's first golf course, the Jericho Golf and Country Club, would be built, lay a ranch owned by the Dalgleish family. Because English Bay was safer anchorage for the sailing ships of the British Navy than that gained through the swirling tides of the First Narrows, it was not unusual during the early days for crews engaging in gunnery practice to arch the occasional cannon shot over the Indian village on shore into the higher levels of Kerrisdale and Dunbar heights. The Dalgleishes chose the lower levels, filling in the swampy elk pasture of their Jericho ranch. During the nineties their place was popular with church picnics for which the parishioners loaded onto a scow in False Creek, to be towed by paddle-wheel tugboat to Jericho Beach, where they were welcomed by the Dalgleish family.

On the opposite side of the Point Grey peninsula, the farm of Fitzgerald McCleery was less isolated than when it was the first cabin on the shore of the Fraser and called "St. Patrick's Cathedral" because it was used as the first place of divine worship in Vancouver. The cabin subsequently served as a school, and after the building (1909–11) by the government of Southwest Marine Drive (dubbed "Dick McBride's baby" after the premier), was destined to hear the Lord's name invoked by the faithful occupying the sand traps of the several golf courses, public and private, that spread their special version of the gospel along the sunny southern slope.

In the early nineties the biggest boy in Mount Pleasant school, field captain of the lacrosse team and the only student of either sex who wore long pants, was milkman McGeer's son, Gerry. In his speech on becoming mayor-elect of the city in 1936, Gerald Grattan McGeer recalled a youthful appreciation of a city made doubly wondrous by his first visit to the circus in town:

> The mountains seemed very much higher than they now appear and apparently lay closer to the city. No doubt the circus tents looked very much bigger than they were. The morning breeze was exciting the waters of the

> Bay and the white caps were dancing in an ecstasy of enthusiasm akin to my own. It made me think that all the fairy nymphs of Neptune were just as excited and thrilled as I was at the prospect that lay before me. The mountains formed a vast amphitheatre, a perfect caravanserai, to welcome the mighty legion of wonders that posters, generously placarded on stumps, barns and wood sheds, had for weeks been promising.

Between visits of the circus, Vancouver improved itself with patronage of the new Vancouver Opera House, built by the C.P.R. at a cost of $100,000 on Granville just south of the company's hotel. The Opera House opened on February 9, 1891, with a performance of *Lohengrin,* for which the better ladies' shops pushed the sale of "opera colors in cashmere, in silks; opera silk gloves; wool shawls, fans, opera hose, opera corsets (pink, blue, black) and opera kid gloves." The éclat of the season was made even more resonant by the eminent diva Emma Juch, who was so impressed with the young city that she bought several lots on a speculative basis and was said to have made a killing even more dramatic than the Wagnerian.

Miss Juch was not the first luminary to celebrate introduction to Vancouver by purchasing a speculative lot. Two years earlier the youthful Rudyard Kipling had been similarly taken with his new acquaintance—"The place is full of Englishmen who speak the English tongue correctly"—and became a landowner of "400 well-developed pines, a few thousand tons of granite scattered in blocks, and a sprinkling of earth. That's a town lot in Vancouver. You order your agent to hold it until property rises, then sell out and buy more land out of town. . . ."

Another gifted writer came to Vancouver, to stay, when Ethel Wilson, later the *doyenne* of belles-lettres for the west coast, arrived in 1895 with her grandmother who was joining three sons in the city: J. F., W. H. (later a mayor of Vancouver) and Philip Malkin, who had established themselves in the grocery wholesale business. As a proper young lady Ethel went to Crofton House private school:

> As I walked to and from school (thirty-five blocks a day), I passed the chain gang clearing land for building-lots on Davie and Jervis Streets. The men of the chain gang were shackled. They were driven to work in a wagon with

> a team of horses and were guarded by keepers who cradled guns in their arms in traditional style. I was always a little afraid and did not turn to look at the chain gang although I wanted to explore their faces, and understand why this had come about.

When she went shopping with her aunt on Cordova Street she saw "beautiful ladies in black, usually travelling in pairs." Recalling the impressions of a seven-year-old:

> Their skirts were long and would have trailed (given a chance) but were held up by an elegantly crooked elbow, their cheeks were very pink, their eyes were large, and lingered as they looked, soft and hard with experience.
>
> "Oh, Aunty Belle!" I used to say, "do look at that lovely lady! Who is she?" I was rather ashamed that my aunt did not know any of these lovely ladies nor did she seem to wish to know them. . . .

Ethel Wilson was one of those whom Joe Fortes was teaching to swim at English Bay. "He taught nearly all the boys and girls to swim. I can still hear Joe Fortes saying in his rotund rich voice, 'Jump! I tell you, jump! If you don't jump off that raft, I'll throw you in!' So we jumped. Joe was a heroic figure." Ethel's great-aunt joined in the vogue of the late nineties of appearing in the company of a bicycle, as did all the family except her grandmother. "My great-aunt did not ride her bicycle; she preferred to walk it about and talk to people—her favourite occupation."

It was considered very stylish to have the whole family on two wheels, tooling around the packed-shell drive of Stanley Park or racing down the plank sidewalks to the continuing outrage of retired army officers who wrote letters to the editor abominating this peril to pedestrians. The bicycle rack was a mark of rank of every building with any pretensions at all. At Pender and Granville a school for bicycle riding covered several lots, the cinder practice track screened from the gaze of the irreverent. The Vancouver Bicycle Club, representing the velocipedic Establishment, spurned the new pneumatic tires being adopted by the younger Terminal City Bicycle Club. In *fin de siècle* Vancouver the generation gap was expanded with a bicycle pump.

Vancouver's outdoor pastimes of this period were not, however, a totally unmixed pleasure. A sportsman touring the country, Joseph Adams, reported in his *Ten Thousand Miles Through Canada:*

> The difficulty in Vancouver is to find a boatman to whom the destiny of the angler and the fishing can be safely entrusted. It speaks well for the prosperity of the city that there is practically none of the sporting leisure classes, such as one finds in dumping quantity in Ireland and Scotland. There the shoemaker's last and the crofter's hoe are willingly set aside for a day with rod or gun. In Vancouver it is otherwise. One might spend a week in quest of an efficient attendant, and fail to discover him.

In Vancouver Adams picked up a makeshift gillie who undertook to row him to a fishing ground and who, once in the lively current of the inlet, admitted that it was his first experience with oars. Suddenly less interested in salmon than in survival, Adams returned to shore under his own power, and left town saddened by the flaw in its menials.

At that time the commercial fisherman was better catered to by Vancouver, which had become the headquarters of the fish-packing companies. As early as 1867 James Symes was experimenting with preserving salmon in hermetically sealed cans. Although the canneries developed in neighboring parts of the Fraser and the coast, the companies like B.C. Packers were to have their business offices in Vancouver, and the city was becoming home to hundreds of commercial fishermen, either full- or part-time.

Similarly mining development in the interior of the province stimulated economic recovery in Vancouver. Machine shops and mercantile houses grew in numbers in the late nineties. To this orderly development a brief but dramatic boost was the Klondike gold rush of 1897–98. Victoria was quicker to seize on the commercial significance of the news that gold had been struck in the Yukon, the capital city laying in supplies with the experienced hand of the veteran of the Cariboo campaign. But Vancouver was a close second in stockpiling the canned salmon, the miners' gear, the tents and sleds. Indeed the city became infected with a gold fever more virulent than the pox Victoria had visited upon the mainland. Real-estate hucksters whose trade had been languishing suddenly became experts in properties north of the Panhandle. The church picnics were scattered out of False Creek to make way for the laying of keels of stern-wheelers and river craft. Instant authorities on canine obedience opened classes to train the novice prospector in the management of a dog sled. Skid Road was never more slippery, with adventurers of every stripe, from the four cut corners of the earth, overspilling from hotels and lodginghouses. The red-light district glowed more roseate than the glasses through which the tenderfoot viewed his gold-finding chances, the streets gaining a fillip of Stetson-hatted lasses, sturdy girls determined to bring the comforts of home to the nugget seekers. The plainer of these camp followers profited from the wisdom of the East, as represented by Vancouver's Chinatown, by learning to double on laundry.

By the time the last boatload of Klondikers had shipped northward, Vancouver had a brand new carriage trade, numerous mansions, new business blocks—all derived from the good fortune of having been on the itinerary of rampant lust. The passage had been so spirited that the Granville Street Bridge suffered degeneration of the planking, the *Province* complaining editorially (June, 1900) that two wagons passing on the bridge shook it as if it were afloat. The building boom was on again. Vancouver's second-stage booster had fired, fueled by various volatile kinds of folly, rocketing the city safely out of the depression and into the twentieth century.

Vancouver's enthusiasm for the Boer War bespoke its fresh reserves of energy. Although only seventeen city men were chosen for duty with the Royal Canadian Regiment in South Africa, they formed the nucleus of the Duke of Connaught's Own Rifles and bore the standard of west coast valor into thirty-seven battles. The contingent suffered three dead, a captain and two privates, with four privates invalided home. When the first wave of seven veterans returned home, December 30, 1900, they received the welcome of a tumultuous crowd at the C.P.R. station, were paraded to the Royal Theatre for the accolade delivered by the lieutenant governor of the province, and later partook of a procession, scanned by searchlights atop the B.C. Electric Building, to the Opera House, where each hero was presented with a gold watch and a new suit of civvies.

Even more thrilling to Vancouver was the visit, September 30, 1901, of the Duke and Duchess of Cornwall and York: the future King George V and his Mary. The head of the committee in charge of decorating the city for the event was a young man named Louis Denison Taylor. Exactly five years earlier, as a penniless young man from Ann Arbor, Michigan, Taylor arrived in Vancouver, found a job at the C.P.R. dock, worked overtime and was taken to dinner at the Oyster Bar by the man who had signed him on and who was not too surprised to learn that it was the first meal Taylor had had in thirty-six hours. Working overtime became an occupational disease with the young man, who soon had substance enough in the community to help raise the funds to bring the *Province* newspaper, originally published in Victoria, to Vancouver as competition for the *World.* With Walter C. Nichol (later a lieutenant governor) as publisher, Taylor, as circulation manager, had begun his career of personal appeal to the public.

The royal visit of 1901 was just one of the occasions that gave Taylor an opportunity to inch up in the public's esteem. It was a moment of truth for a community short on both silk toppers and proper curtsies, but everyone agreed that the bunting draped on the C.P.R. railway station, a turreted castle redolent of fairy tales, was thoroughly regal without being gaudy. The American boy had made good as a loyal subject.

Vancouver was well and truly launched into the decade generally agreed to have been her *âge d'or.* As one of her biographers commented, in the mélange of metaphor that is a collector's item of commercial history: ". . . in 1903 came another panic in New York and the ripples of it affected every city on the coast. But this time Vancouver was better buttressed, she had begun to hear the music of the deep sea chanties and the smell of the ocean was in the nostrils of her traders." Another aroma that helped to fortify the buttresses was that of trade opened up to the south by the linkage, in 1904, with the Great Northern Railroad.

The only disharmonious note was that struck by the Ludgate Affair. This was the first, and classic, instance of how Vancouver's love of nature triumphed over commerce, with the help of xenophobia. The Ludgate Affair began, by popular account, in 1898 with the arrival in town of one Theodore Ludgate. Identified with a Chicago bank (indictment enough), Ludgate had selected Deadman's Island as the site for a sawmill. Worse, he had obtained a lease from the Dominion government, which in the grossness of its nature had apparently forgotten that the island's trees were the living tombstones of Indian warriors, as well as part of the view from the Park. When Ludgate showed up with his crew he was met by an outraged Mayor James F. Garden and police constables chosen for their indignation. The mayor read the Riot Act, Ludgate listened politely, and at the end of it he and his men set to chopping down a fine stand of cedar and fir. Singling out his adversary, the mayor shouted: "Mr. Ludgate, you must not destroy that tree." Far from sparing the tree, and having gone to considerable trouble and expense to ensure that he had every legal right to destroy the tree, the woodsman doubled his stroke. The police arrested him. Ten years of litigation ensued, the bewildered but stubborn Ludgate having his lease upheld in every court till at last a federal order-in-council ceded the islet to the city. Meantime most of the trees had been felled to clear the field of battle, and the squatters driven off by occupying forces of either Ludgate men or Vancouver police. But at least one Chicago bank had learned that the territorial authority of Canada's federal government ended at a line drawn by the tree-worshiping natives of Vancouver.

As early as 1892 the nature-oriented city council was approving the purchase of sea lions, for the city museum, "at a cost not to exceed $115," reported the *News-Advertiser*, "but the minutes do not state whether the animals are to be first stuffed and mounted or not."

More prosaic methods of education also occupied the city, though less emotionally. The opening of the first high school in Vancouver, in 1890, had attracted small registration, indicative of the lack of interest in higher education among the largely mature hustlers moving into the city. The first city college, a private institution called Whetham College, turned belly up after three years in the Smith Block, at Granville and Georgia, the corner later occupied by the Birks Building. In 1890 the provincial legislature passed an act establishing "The University of British Columbia," but did not choose a site for the institution because of the familiar rivalry between Vancouver and Victoria. The act did, however, specify that the university was to enable "all denominations and classes to obtain academical degrees." Aside from considering sacred all virgin stands of timber within view of the city, neither Vancouver nor Victoria had a sectarian basis for their universities such as that in eastern Canada. From the beginning it has been possible for a student to rise to the doctorate level at the University of British Columbia in such a religiously neutral atmosphere as to preserve him as a heathen, except for those sylvan mysteries he shares with the Druid.

"The Capital will not forsooth support the University because it is not to be located there," the Vancouver *World* said editorially in 1891; "why should the Parliament buildings be placed across James Bay, when the more central and more convenient place for them would be the Mainland where the bulk of the population is, and where it would suit the convenience of the majority of the members to meet?" To which the Victoria *Colonist* riposted three days later: "The action of the Mainland senators is capable of but one construction, and that is that their sectionalism got the better of their common sense. . . . The question of a University for this Province is dead."

As indeed it was, for a quarter of a century. A clear case of abortion it was; the fetus of the university shriveled in the womb by the same septic instruments of politics that continued to infect schooling at all levels. Higher education for Vancouver had to grow from its own high school. In December, 1897, formal application made by the Vancouver School Board for affiliation with McGill University was approved. Renamed the Vancouver College of McGill University, the school was authorized to teach first-year Arts only, graduates then being eligible for admission to the parent university. In 1902 the curriculum was extended to include second-year Arts.

University graduates adopting Vancouver as their home became increasingly vocal in their promotion of a separate university for British Columbia. The University Graduates' Society was formed to press, initially, for a land endowment. This program received enthusiastic support from the *World*, which "approved the immediate reservation of a million acres of the wild lands of the Province for the purpose of advanced education." Not to be outdone, the University Club of Nelson, B.C., thought that "such endowment, to be ample for the needs of a Provincial University, should consist of the revenues from not less than ten million acres of land."

Unfortunately the willingness to be generous with wild lands was not matched by money forthcoming to construct buildings in any given location. Instead the existing colleges were combined to create McGill University College of British Columbia in Vancouver and Victoria (1906), variously known as "University College of British Columbia" (to the legislature that approved the measure) and "McGill B.C." to everyone else. Classes for the first session, 1906–7, were held in unused rooms of the Vancouver High School, later known as King Edward High School and later still as Vancouver City College, at 12th Avenue and Oak Street. Soon crowded out of these quarters, McGill College moved into the vacant brick buildings formerly occupied by the City Hospital, at Cambie and Pender streets. These premises were cozy, with the requisite growth of ivy, but the building was condemned by the city health officer. Meantime (1910) the University Sites Commission had chosen Point Grey as the home of the future University of British Columbia. Denied the prospect of growth, McGill College sifted into shingle-covered frame buildings on the same site as the Vancouver General Hospital, then starting to rise. Intended to be temporary quarters only, these two flimsy structures at Laurel Street and 10th Avenue became known to a generation of U.B.C. students as "the Fairview shacks." The dreaming spires of Oxford slumbered in absentia.

Vancouver accommodated itself much better in the matter of private homes. From 1904, when good times returned as though they meant to stay, to 1909, when the college was playing gypsy caravan about the city, housing kept pace with a population that doubled from 38,414 to 78,900. "The dweller in flats is an uncertain and unsettled quantity," wrote the author of "Vancouver, City of Beautiful Homes" in the *B.C. Magazine* of June, 1911. "The man in an office may be a foot-loose adventurer. Homes alone indicate the extent and quality of citizenship. It is in them that patriotism is developed and cherished." The period's kaiser of real estate was Alvo von Alvensleben, owner of the grandest porch in Kerrisdale. A get-shelter-quick scheme of the time, titled "Free Homes," described in its prospectus what the buyer might look forward to: "The best models of every land have been studied, and something taken from Oriental pagoda, Swiss chalet, California bungalow, Mexican patio and even from the Maori whare and Indian wigwam." The architectural bloodline obviously was not of classic purity, but the styles did have something of the traditional vigor of an illegitimate son.

The Kitsilano area was filling up with homes built in the style later known as Kitsilano Gothic. Large, wooden-frame houses skirted with capacious verandas, these residences were shortly outclassed by the district known at Shaughnessy Heights, situated on the crest of the rise south of False Creek and opened to development by the C.P.R. In Shaughnessy, Vancouver had found its true Nob Hill. For decades the first families mounted their mansions on the Heights' crescents and other arcane drives suited to persons who didn't need to hurry to arrive.

The main problem of the mansion was that of finding servants. The moneyed class drew heavily on Chinatown, but the demand exceeded the supply. A 1907 visitor from Britain, Harry Brittain, in his book *Canada There and Back* remarked on "one lady we met who had paid the passage of a girl from Scotland and her railway fare from Quebec. She had arrived on a Monday, was moved in Tuesday, and was looking for a servant herself on Wednesday." The same amiably bigoted commentator said of the "Chinaman," who was the low man on the menial totem pole: "He seems quite content to remain a faithful servant, and unlike the Jap has no desire to be constantly improving his position or poking his nose into his adopted country's politics."

For Vancouver housewives the Chinese was freely described as "a labor-saving contrivance" having the work capacity of three English servants including the cook. Since this bifurcated appliance sent most of its earnings home to family in China, it was not subject to failings of operation found in European types that required frequent lubrication. Because the Chinese was content with minimal use of the English language, his complaints were equally rare. A student of the mores of the time tells of a young Vancouver society matron who became curious about the cryptic Chinese symbols that constituted her address on her returned laundry. She at last found an interpreter who rendered the address as: "Big long woman, top hill."

A more perceptive visitor from France, Jean Lionnet, in his *Chez les Français du Canada* (1908) views the city's Chinese community as not altogether as submissive as it appeared to Colonel Blimp: "Ici l'on constate le groupement, on perçait la menace. Bien entendu, ils n'arrivent pas arrogants, supérieurs, comme les Anglais chez des nègres. Silencieux, lents, sournois, obstinés, ils se glissent à pas de chats."

The relative placidity of the Chinese may or may not have derived from the circumstance that these pioneers remained largely without womenfolk, because of immigration laws, and made life bearable with fraternal societies bound together by fondness for gambling, particularly fantan. Whenever it was expedient for the city police force to demonstrate its vigilance, without disturbing Anglo-Saxon violations of the law, it raided a "Chinese gambling den." Because the Chinese previewed all visitors through an aperture in the front door, and because their alarm system was almost occult in its efficiency, the police adopted elaborate means of infiltrating the den. As one chronicler of the constabulary, G. Weston, put it:

"The Chinaman has eyes which can penetrate an ordinary disguise. The policemen are such fine, clean fellows that they find difficulty to pass as the inmates of a Chinese 'joint.'" Fake pigtails fashioned by braiding the silk covers of umbrellas scarcely camouflaged the wholesome aspect of the gambling squad. For one of the more successful raids the policemen disguised themselves as Sikhs. "Each wore a long beard, old clothes and a dirty turban." Having got past the guards, "they entered the room where the gambling was in full swing, and stood gazing about with the gently curious manner of the Indian." Police outside then crashed the doors, while the Trojan "Hindus" prevented the inmates from closing the series of doors leading to the den.

Public hostility to the growing number of Asians arriving in Vancouver was, however, undisguised. In one year more than eight thousand Japanese had come to British Columbia, some from Hawaii, where they had been stranded by a sudden cutoff by U.S. immigration and where they chartered ships to B.C., others arriving from the States to populate communities like Steveston and create in Vancouver the concentration of residents around Powell Street known as "Little Tokyo." In the same year two thousand Sikhs arrived from India, and hundreds of Chinese filtered into the city despite the head tax of five hundred dollars. The result, among Vancouver working people sensitive to labor available for coolie wages, was formation of the Asiatic Exclusion League.

The League's membership of five hundred whites on August 12, 1907, passed a strong resolution against admission of the Japanese, and received endorsement by the leaders of all political parties. Meetings of this highly flammable organization climaxed with the September 8, 1907, assembly, which was scheduled to prelude a protest march to City Hall. Instead, after a number of incendiary speeches, including one by the secretary of the Seattle Exclusion League, the meeting turned into a mob that marched on City Hall, where it burned an effigy of Lieutenant Governor Dunsmuir, whose coal mines employed Orientals, then charged through Chinatown and beyond, into the district of Japanese. Here the rioters met a passive resistance that rapidly turned active as the Japanese armed themselves with knives and bottles to throw back the invaders. Cries of "Banzai!" filled the air the following Sunday morning when the mob made a second sortie and was routed by the aroused Orientals. In his report of the affair to the shocked governor general,

Wilfrid Laurier said of the inglorious retreat: "This is at once a cause for rejoicing and for anxiety: rejoicing, because the rowdies got a well deserved licking; anxiety, because this may make the Japs very saucy, and render an adjustment of the trouble more difficult."

To take some of the spice out of *la sauce japonaise,* Laurier dispatched to the coast his deputy minister of labor, W. L. Mackenzie King. King's assignment was to assess the causes of increased Japanese immigration and the claims for losses by the rousted Orientals. His mission was charged with concern at the highest level of the Colonial Office. The Great Powers were engaged in the delicate maneuvering of prewar diplomacy, accommodations in which East Asia figured both militarily and economically. Here in the outpost of Empire a hoodlum city was rocking the Imperial boat.

Displaying the tireless tact that was to characterize his career, claims commissioner King smoothed the ruffled Oriental feathers by approving payment of losses to a total of more than $25,000. But even sensitivity to diplomatic considerations could not prevent his boggling, with all the easterner's sense of propriety, at claims of $600 each for damage suffered by two opium manufacturers. Reported King:

> I also personally inspected the premises and saw the process by which the manufacture of opium is carried on. In the case of one of these establishments it was stated by the proprietor that he had been engaged in the business for a period of ten years, and was employing, at the time of the riot, ten persons; that his gross receipts from this source alone for the year 1907, totalled $180,000; that his wage bill for the month amounted to $485; and that his estimated net profit, for the year 1907, was $20,000. . . .
>
> Both manufacturers stated that they sold to white people as well as to Chinese and other Orientals, that the opium was consumed in different parts of the Dominion; and that, in addition to their own factories, there were three or four other opium factories in the city of Victoria and one in New Westminster, all of which were doing an extensive business.

King not only rejected the claims for losses to this flourishing local industry, he urged the federal and provincial governments to enact such measures as would "assist in the eradication of an evil which is not only a source of human degradation but a destructive factor in national life."

The racial prejudice that was considerably more destructive to national life was temporarily assuaged by Japan's voluntarily accepting restriction of emigration to Canada to four hundred persons of selected categories each year. But Vancouver was still many years away from the racial harmony of the Hawaii that was spared having Victoria for a noxious neighbor.

The white population of Vancouver did, however, value the Chinese as a tourist attraction. The Vancouver Tourist Association booklet *Vancouver, The Sunset Doorway of the Dominion*, published shortly before the 1907 riots, draws attention to a picturesqueness: "One is but a short time in Vancouver when the Celestial in his Oriental dress is observed." (The Celestials wore the pigtails that were the symbol of submission under the Tartars.) "The Chinese baby is an object of curiosity. The jet black slanting eyes of these atoms of humanity are just as shiningly inquisitive as those of white babies, and the voice when plaintively raised is the same. . . ." Having stared closely at a Chinese baby, thereby testing the plaintive raising of its voice, the tourist is urged to visit a Chinese rice mill, operated by human treadmill. "The peculiarities of another people are always interesting, and the study of them at close range, which may be obtained without difficulty, is an attraction to visitors."

As a change from being closely peered at for their peculiarities, the Vancouver Chinese had their own theater, which kept alive their remembrance of their homeland's history and customs. "The presentation is made by a company of no mean histrionic ability, the members of which command large remuneration," says the tourist booklet. "The costumes owned by the company are handsome and richly embroidered with gold."

Theater was a deceptive index of prosperity, however, during the first decade of the twentieth century, as Vancouver had already become what it was to remain: a good show town. The Vancouver Opera House on Granville seated two thousand and mounted spectacles on a stage fifty by seventy-five feet. Although literally the end of the line for touring theater companies, Vancouver took for granted appearances by the great stars: Melba, Schumann-Heink, Paderewski, Mrs. Patrick Campbell. At Pender and Hamilton streets the Lyric Theatre did not want for novitiates to the "Temple of Amusement." In 1906 the Empress Theatre was built by a syndicate of real-estate agents because property around the site on Hastings near Main was booming. A fine house in the red-plush-and-gilt style, the Empress developed a company of repertory players worthy of any stage, several of its alumni going forth to stardom in Hollywood and London.

Whether or not the readily available lumber encouraged Vancouver actors to tread the boards, it did expedite home building. Larger edifices of the downtown area were of an architecture that blended various European styles into a sturdy mongrel: massive gray-stone block (Scottish baronial) embellished with Roman columns and sometimes topped, as with the Vancouver High School, by a dome suggestive of St. Paul's without the apostolate. Also styled in constipated classic was the Public Library, built in 1902 at the corner of Main and Hastings, succeeding the one-room library in a building on Cordova Street which in 1887 had succeeded the reading room in the Hastings Mill boardinghouse. Pillared and properly intimidating to anyone contemplating borrowing a book, the library later became the city museum as well, and for years stood at the headpoint of Vancouver's Skid Road, a beacon of culture beckoning the bums and drunks who collapsed gratefully over its reading tables to sleep it off. Only the Vancouver Hospital, with its twin sentry towers, was more convincing in its impression of no escape.

"A magnificent metropolis," extolled *Greater Vancouver–Illustrated*, a local publication paid for by its various advertisers and providing a rhapsodic view of the city of 1908. "High moral tone pervades every form of life" (a reference to the multiplying churches). "It is hither that nearly every denomination flocks to found its propaganda throughout the district." Among other saintly manifestations, the schools adopted a savings bank system. "At a time when many pupils are earning money, and the temptations to spend it carelessly are so numerous, the value of such a system cannot be over-estimated."

The children were doubtless tempted by the sight of their elders splurging on the luxuries of prosperity so inflated that an alley corner on Hastings Street East, near Main, sold for $100,000 where only half a century earlier it would have had no takers at a dollar an acre. The Hotel Vancouver now had 205 rooms, 75 with bath connections—a ratio bordering on hedonism. In the spacious lounge the wicker chairs accommodated even the most discriminating derrière in comfort, and the management by Captain Pym was a credit to the service. His bar bucketed champagne to be conveyed next door, down the alley, to the Opera House to slake the thirst worked up by visiting prima donnas. For the less exigent gullet, the Cabin Tea and Lunch Rooms ("Down the Marble Stairs") at 615 West Hastings took quiet pride in its "well-ventilated smoking room for gentlemen," a wistful reminder of the time when good food was savored unpolluted by a miasma of tobacco smoke. Having lunched with his lady, the Vancouver playboy of 1908 who required further transport could call upon the Stanley Park Livery, at Seymour and Dunsmuir, with its stable of eighty-six horses, forty rigs, seven hacks and two tallyhos. A phone call for a hack received prompt attention, and a spin around the Park timed to coincide with the firing of the Nine O'Clock Gun was good strategy in projecting the lady into her beau's arms. Placed near Hallelujah Point, the cast-iron muzzle-loader has been fired daily—except for short periods of absence at the hands of pranksters—since arriving from Woolwich, England, in 1894.

A Park drive naturally culminated at English Bay, with perhaps a stroll along the pier. If the gentleman's campaign was proceeding to her satisfaction, the lady would eventually bring him to the display windows of the new (1907) store of Henry Birks and Sons, jewelers. The store was distinguished by its noble clock, erected about 1902 at the corner of Granville and Hastings by the jewelry store's former owner, George E. Trorey. When Birks moved to its pre-eminent location on the southeast corner of Georgia and Granville, in 1913, the clock went with it. The clock became the prime rendezvous of the townspeople ("I'll meet you under Birks' clock"), the four-faced horologe carefully timing the ardor of a lover by the minutes he was early, witnessing the tears of those whose date showed up not at all, and providing a useful alibi for the lingering of less sentimental sirens to whom neither the hour nor the escort were especially premeditated.

If a lady was a lady, however, she might be picked up for a ride in John Hendry's automobile, the first in the city powered by an internal combustion engine and delivered in 1904 with no gasoline in the tank. As the first gas station in Vancouver did not appear till 1908 (at the corner of Cambie and Smithe), mill owner Hendry had to apply to Major Matthews, then the agent for the Imperial Oil Company, for means of combustion. Imperial Oil stocked only two kinds of gasoline—one for cleaning ladies' shoulder-length gloves, the other used by plumbers in their blowtorches—so Hendry chose the cleaning fluid. (Some say he used stove paraffin.) In any event the fuel was sufficiently eruptive to frighten horses and test the skill of Hendry's chauffeur, Henry Hooper, who later cranked to life Vancouver's first taxi business. The Hendry automobile was for some years a familiar itinerant explosion on Davie Street, where in 1901 Hendry had built a mansion that only in 1968 was torn down to make way for a high-rise.

By 1908, the car and other vehicles had available to them 228 miles of city streets, of which 12 miles were paved with wood block and 104 miles macadamized, with 58 miles of cement sidewalks to encourage the window shopper. For those using public transport there was the interurban electric train of the B.C. Electric, whose lines were extending to other Lower Mainland centers such as New Westminster. The interurban to New Westminster was the lifeline for groceries bought by Vancouver housewives at the Valley market center. Running through forest punctuated by clearings of settlers, around the stations, and past the odd poultry farm, the trip cost ten cents and took three-quarters of an hour. The tramline to Chilliwack brought in produce and took out picnickers, with a daily "Milk Special," while the Cemetery line had its terminus at the Mountain View Cemetery—the B.C.E.R. served its customers from the cradle to the grave.

Probably the fastest and most exhilarating interurban ride was the "Sockeye Special" to Steveston, the flats of Lulu Island permitting quick acceleration with few curves. In its heyday the interurban was a cathartic experience; the cars, which often ran two in tandem, had cane seats so slippery that a sharp curve slid a small boy's buttocks sideways in sweet surrender to centrifugal force. The windows—barred to discourage defenestration on one side and decapitation on the other—were surmounted by panels of stained glass, a basilican touch only slightly profaned by ads for Heinz Apple Butter and Fit Rite Clothes, and entirely redundant to the youngster aware that he was careening at speeds beyond the power of mortals. The drivers of the interurbans were a breed apart, and knew it. To a man, they were filled with a kind of divine rage at the restraints of track and stops. Halted by the despicable requirement of picking up a passenger, both train and driver throbbed in a paroxysm of frustration, and the boarding party not uncommonly stumbled in its haste to scale the high steps before the brakes yielded to the massive surge to go sixty.

To go from the sublime to the bibulous, young Vancouver hitched a ride on the slowest transport in town: one of the two delivery wagons of the Three Star Wine Company, "Canadian whiskies of the best brands, famous Scotch, Irish and American whiskies, miscellaneous liquors of recognized excellence, cigars of foreign and domestic make . . ." (advertisement). Despite the easy access to alcohol and the burgeoning brewery that dated from the city's incorporation, Vancouver of 1905–10 was not a "wide-open town like Seattle and Tacoma," as visitor Bradley saw it. A wide-open town was defined as one whose amusement places ran the gamut of iniquity, seven days a week. There was some argument during this period as to whether the greater attraction of the two U. S. Northwest towns, for the Yukon miner and the lumberjack on leave from the woods, was jeopardizing Vancouver's material progress. Events proved that Vancouver had nothing to worry about, as she later caught up with and passed both Seattle and Tacoma in casting fleshpots. Seattle was to become the staidest city in western America thanks to the soberly bourgeois presence of Boeing Aircraft, while the high-rolling miner, fisherman or logger whose ambition was to relieve his hip pocket of its embarrassing cud found Vancouver liberally supplied with spittoons.

In the Vancouver of the early 1900's, however, revelry was a subsidiary of commerce. The first street fair, held August 5, 1901, was modeled after the European, with booths set up at Granville and Hastings and an inaugural parade. The fair was an immense success, attracting the entire populace to mill about the intersection and watch Professor Rose, the gymnast, dive into a tank of water from a ladder one hundred feet high. It established the tradition of the Vancouver carnival as a festive occasion for selling something. The spirit of Mardi Gras, derived of religion and exhibiting release from inhibitions (kissing strangers on the streets, playing tag with young bulls, etc.) has never functioned in Vancouver. There has been no intermediate stage between commercialized kermess, damped down by Professor Rose, and full-scale riot.

Some notion of the affluence and expensive tastes developed

by Vancouver in this period is conveyed by the banquet arrangements for the visit of Earl Grey, the governor general, in 1906. The banquet was sponsored by the B.C. Lumbermen's Association, John Hendry, president, and the Canadian Manufacturers' Association. T. M. McAuliffe, writing in the *Province* sometime later, gave an eyewitness account of the fare:

> To emphasize the Russian mode of dinner service, golden-colored croutons adorned the table centres, their various shapes and symmetry symbolical of the occasion. Indented or protruding from the taller croutons were receptacles for the rose-hued roasted curlews, whose hovering wings found support in gum arabic, plump outlines of the willow and blue grouse, clothed in scintillating robes of aspic, with their erstwhile means of locomotion and stays of momentum silver-skewered to an amber background; pheasants, truffle-stuffed and galantined, spread their beautiful plumage; the swift-winged jack-snipe, glazed-basted, rested on a nest of asparagus tips, their wings supported by Quesnelles Jolie.
>
> In the centre a spring salmon, boiled whole, peered with whiteish eyes through a sea-like aspic, pistachio-colored, capped with angelica and blown cream, which added a foamy crest to a Neptunistic environment.
>
> From the hors d'oeuvres to the *café noir* it required no invocation to Gasteria—the tenth muse who presides over the pleasures of taste—for the enjoyment thereof.

This Edwardian Vancouver disappointed a few who arrived from the homeland expecting the West to be Wild. J. A. Hobson, in his *Canada Today,* summed up his impressions of the city of 1906: "It is a purely business town, a thing of stores and banks and meagre wooden houses, with no public buildings of account." Hobson had the misfortune to arrive during a lesser celebration organized by the I.O.D.E. in honor of Trafalgar Day. The newspapers were passionately entwined in the ties of Empire, displaying "ostentatious animosity" toward the United States and reviling the bawdy cities just across the border. Vancouver was entering the phase of being more British than the Britons, a state of mind that would prevail for a good quarter of a century. Obviously not Hobson's choice, the city was to disappoint many another visitor from the Old World whose expectation was to find a city to which he could feel comfortably superior, but who found instead one abominably condescending to everything except Buckingham Palace.

Yet Vancouver had the faculty of being all things to all men. The Frenchman Lionnet admired the city of 1908 because its park forest was a jungle of a harmless sort, with no scorpions, poisonous snakes or fever-ridden swamps: "Dans les fossés, je crois voir mes fougères de Fontainebleau." The cascades of flowers in city gardens also remind him of Nice, while his Japanese traveling companion comments: "On croirait le Japon." An earlier visitor, Douglas Slade (*On the Cars and Off*), saw Vancouver as another Stamboul, "the cypress groves of the Seraglio Point represented by the forest primeval of Stanley Park." Slade also envisaged public buildings to rival the minarets and mosques of the capital of Islam.

To the more permanent resident, however, it would not have occurred that he was inhabiting a Turkish delight. The lyricism was more apt to be heavily Britannica, as in the poem *Sea-Room* (1910) by Aubrey N. St. John Mildmay, whom Vancouver inspired to pen (as refrain):

> Sea-room! Sea-room! for the vessel under way;
> For West is East, and East is West, and the best
> is yet to be—
> Star of the night, fling far your light, Vancouver,
> star of the sea!

To a more prosaic imagist: "Vancouver is one of the buckle-holes in one of the great belts of travel that girdle the earth." Besides ruddy-cheeked Britons, the buckle hole picked up a variety of lint in the way of vagrants. Many of these light-footed arrivals found their way to the labor agencies of Powell Street which every morning hung out blackboards listing jobs open in the woods. The sidewalk was the market place for loggers, laborers, every breed of wilderness cat. The loggers in particular came from any part of the world—craggy Scandinavians, Americans seeking an evergreen alternative to the French Foreign Legion, black Highlanders who scented the spoor of a small fortune. "They have the strong, unfreakish character of the outdoors that wilderness workers everywhere, whether cowpunchers, prospectors or lumbermen, have in common," wrote the author of "Lots of Work in Vancouver" (*B.C. Magazine*, June, 1911), "and they have something else that the great woods give to those who long inhabit her aromatic dominions. The logger is a man of much simplicity and directness, and not difficult to analyze." The simplicity and directness with which he brought his woods earnings into Vancouver, to blow the roll in a glorious booze-up, discouraged analysis. When the actress Mae West said: "I want a strong man with a weak mind," she described one way in which Vancouver prospered from the hinterland.

The city did offer to grubstake new industries within its own boundaries. After the disastrous attempts to establish a quartz mill and an iron works, it had become apparent that cost of transportation of minerals and ore made Vancouver uncompetitive with such centers as Trail and Britannia. It was more practical, from the city's point of view, to handle the basic metal—gold—in agreeable surroundings. In 1910 the government assay office, opened during the Klondike gold rush in an effort to recapture from Seattle some of the miners' trade, found new quarters in the Federal Building at Granville and Pender. The seven rooms of this minor palace of Midas included a melting room, a muffle-furnace room, a balance room, the manager's office, and a special room off the vestibule from which depositors could gaze through steel screens into the melting room and watch their gold being reduced to something fetching in the way of ingot.

As a Christmas present in 1905 the city gave itself the handsome new quarters of the Vancouver General Hospital, in Fairview. The opening of the public market, in 1908, received enthusiastic response from the city's housewives, many of whom participated in the 8 A.M. opening-day race for the prize of a hindquarter of mutton offered to the first person to purchase anything. The *Province* reported the event: ". . . over a hundred women, carrying chickens, produce, meat, etc. in their hands rushed for the stairway all at once. One lady had a good start but stumbled just at the turn. The crowd rushed over the prostrate woman and there was a rough and tumble race to the office door, in which Mrs. Jas. Allen of 2210 Columbia Street came out ahead and secured the coveted mutton."

As for the larger market, on January 11, 1909, the first direct shipment of Canadian flour left Vancouver for Britain. The five thousand sacks of flour were shipped in an experiment to see if it was practicable, from the point of view of spoilage, to ship flour via Cape Horn. It wasn't.

By that same year the city had strung out along the streetcar line to New Westminster in a continuous strand of habitation. In

September, 1909, Mayor C. S. Douglas, accompanied by guest of honor Earl Grey, rode a B.C.E.R. observation car as the first vehicle across the new Granville Street Bridge, a swing span structure engineered to provide exquisite frustration to almost half a century of Vancouver motorists. In October the city proposed a memorial to former mayor David Oppenheimer in the form of a stone arch at the entrance to Stanley Park. The arch was of less lasting consequence than the council's adopting the park commission plan of a causeway to replace the Coal Harbour Bridge across the tidal flat, and the constitution of Lost Lagoon as a fresh-water lake, "the slopes of the lake converted into lawns planted with ornamental trees." The original plan for the lake also included two man-made islands, but the council decided that this was painting the lily pond.

A few months earlier, as a last victorious salvo fired in defense of the Park's exposed flank, the council thwarted Theodore Ludgate's effort to lever the city police off Deadman's Island. Declared Alderman McSpadden: "If fifteen policemen can't hold the island we'll put on a hundred men. I'll volunteer to be one of the guards myself. We are not going to allow Yankees to come over here and hammer our policemen." The Churchillian defiance signaled the end of Vancouver's first and last land engagement against a foreign power until the visit of the New Zealand All Blacks.

Lacrosse and Ludgate were not the only contact sports immediately available in 1909. The popularity of baseball, a new roller rink, and a remarkably capacious ice rink provided a variety of ways of getting a thick ear. On the English Bay side of the Park, things were quieter because of the presence of Joe Fortes, whose voluntary vigilance as lifeguard and keeper of the peace was confirmed by city council, on the paid basis of policeman's wages. Demand for more recreational space spurred the council to purchase the Kitsilano park site in 1909. Across the water to the new park would drift the sound of band concerts held each Sunday evening in the bandstand of English Bay's Alexandra Park. When the setting sun gilded the ripples of the bay, and the young ladies lay on the grass in languorous attendance to Rudolf Friml, it could only be assumed that a new subdivision of Elysium had been opened to the living. Those mortals who insisted on a roof over their heads were being beckoned to new residential areas such as Queen Anne Hill (Dunbar Heights), whose developer advertised lots at $700–$800 each with the message: "The West End is, as everybody knows, even now overcrowded."

Vancouver, 1910, took the advent of Halley's Comet as the symbol of the city's rocketing progress. Docks and warehouses jostled in contention for space on the foreshore that had only recently known no wholesaler but the lone heron. Exasperation bloomed as a hardy perennial because the growing city found itself cut off from its own waterfront by the C.P.R. Owning the whole shore the company built fences and allowed access to company property at company pleasure. Although the city felt cocky enough to hurl lawsuit after lawsuit—all lost—at the barriers blocking the crossings of the rail yards, citizens continued for years to have only three streets that extended to the water line, and only one public access at the foot of Gore Avenue.

Gulliver was merely impatient with such Lilliputian binding. The slogan of the Hundred Thousand Club—"In nineteen hundred and ten, Vancouver will have one hundred thousand men"—was made good with several months to spare. The exuberant impulse to outdo was expressed in the rivalry to build Vancouver's first "skyscraper," the word itself having barely arrived from New York. The Dominion Trust Building, raised and completed from 1908 to 1910, soared fourteen stories at Hastings and Cambie and was said to be not only the tallest building in the British Empire but the finest edifice in Canada. It obliged the fire department to obtain longer ladders. The polished red granite columns were imported from Aberdeen, the Carrara of the North, and every floor was to be carpeted with cork for quietness. The building was the first in Vancouver heated with fuel oil and equipped with a vacuum suction plant with outlets for cleaning each floor of offices.

The magnificence was too much for L. D. Taylor, one of whose business rivals had helped to finance it. Taylor invested his earnings in a new building for the *World* that was to be 272 feet high and have seventeen stories—a *new* tallest building in the Empire. Despite the building's cheating a bit (the top dozen stories were contracted into a tower whose tightly spiralled staircase was to cause several generations of journalists a giddiness sometimes reflected in the news coverage), the backers went broke. The Tower Building went into liquidation, was sold to the Bekins moving and storage firm, and became known first as the Bekins Building, and later as the the Sun (newspaper) Tower.

L.D.'s setback was, however, the exception to the rule of the city of 1910. In that year the building of the Second Narrows Bridge was declared to be a certainty. The bridge was actually completed in 1925, fifteen years being the approximate gestation period for a new bridge around Vancouver. Meanwhile commuters from the North Shore swarmed aboard the *Senator*, a steamer of length 51½ feet, width 12 feet and draft 4½ feet. "She had a 'stateroom' in the after part of the deckhouse for lady passengers," recorded one commuter, "while the male passengers either stood on the narrow deck or crowded into the pilot house where they could smoke or chew at will. A horse was occasionally crowded on the deck in front of the pilot house, but if a wagon had to be taken across it had to be loaded on a scow and towed alongside."

Although the Second Narrows Bridge was deferred temporarily in 1910, other local improvements steamed ahead. In July, the council of the municipality of Point Grey, incorporated two years before and still mostly a wasteland logged-over and be-stumped, submitted to its sparse ratepayers bylaws for not only a streetcar-line franchise but also $500,000 for water connections, $250,000 for a sewerage system, $100,000 for roads and $100,000 for parks. All the bylaws were passed, with substantial majorities. One of the few who abstained from the water proposition was a hotelkeeper who had been unable to obtain a liquor license. "It's whisky we want in Eburne, not water," declared this resident of the district at the end of Granville Street.

With the same optimistic regard for the future the municipality provided wide avenues like King Edward and 16th. Vancouver surfaced additional streets with stone and bitumen, Georgia Street and Eburne Road being favorites with the motorists whose wheezy machines were beginning to overlord the horse. Yet as late as 1911 the remaining horse-drawn wagons of the fire department required the services of seven engineers, two linemen, one machinist, two telephone operators, a blacksmith and a veterinary surgeon. The horses were better accommodated than the city council, which had begun the dispute over a new site that was to become one of the city's best-chewed bones of contention. More positive was the council's decision in 1910 that livery stables having more than four horses had to be built of brick.

By 1911 Vancouver had surpassed Victoria in tramp steamer trade. The main curse on commerce was that phenomenon of railway freight rates known as "the mountain differential." The mountain differential was to be Vancouver's *bête noire* for years, no less abominable for being barely understood. It derived from the extra cost, real or imagined, of goods transported from the East by rail. Vancouver housewives came to visualize their housekeeping money going up in smoke with every chuff of the extra locomotives needed to haul Ontario-manufactured products over the multiple ranges of mountains to the coast. In 1911 this phobia of unfair freight rates was temporarily sublimated in the orgy of speculation created by rumors of new railways opening up the interior. Every week the newspapers laid track for another new line: the Vancouver, Victoria & Eastern Railway, the Vancouver, Westminster, Northern & Yukon Railway, extension of the Chicago, Milwaukee & St. Paul Railway from Seattle. Precursor of a new method of transportation, the first aircraft built and flown locally took off from Minoru Park on April 28, 1911, piloted by owner William Templeton, later Vancouver Airport manager.

With improved transportation Vancouver became the clearing house for European capital that was caught by the apocalyptic vision of the new cities (Kamloops was advertised to investors as "the Los Angeles of Canada") from Vancouver to Fort George. In 1912 the provincial government announced the charter of the Pacific Great Eastern Railway, planned to unite North Vancouver with the Grand Trunk Railway at Fort George and spill the treasures of the Cariboo and the North into the lap of Burrard Inlet. The P.G.E., which was to earn the name "Please Go Easy" among others less printable, at last reached Fort George in November, 1952, forty years after its inception. Four years later, in June, 1956, the connection to North Vancouver was complete—a true epic of retardation.

The prospect of a British Columbia latticed with steel hinging on the Lower Mainland faded as war between Britain and Germany suddenly seemed inevitable. The English financiers, the German princes, who had been pumping cash into the all-too-readily-inflated expectations of the city, reduced the flow. Unemployed workingmen began to crowd into Vancouver. Prosperity turned to ash for the nine cigar factories that had established themselves in Vancouver, in addition to the one in North Vancouver and those in New Westminster. These factories had turned out no five-cent cigar; theirs was nothing less than the dime product of genuine Havana leaf, without band, and comparing favorably with cigars rolled on the thighs of Cuban maidens.

The realty offices that had outnumbered the grocery shops in Vancouver 3 to 1 now found themselves stocked with lemons in about the same ratio. And property owners who had refused fantastically inflated offers for their land were mentally conditioned to become the first volunteers for the front.

The temperamental excesses, the mercurial changes of mood of the adolescent city, were about to be sacrificed to the ancient enmities of Europe. The naïve charm awaited introduction to the facts of death on the battlefield, to mature responsibilities of the Dominion as a whole. Vancouver had seen the sun rise on her fortunes to reach a rapturous midmorning, and as Wordsworth said of another's tender years:

> Bliss was it in that dawn to be alive,
> But to be young was very heaven!

CHAPTER 10 1914–1918

Marching to a Distant Drum

The Komagata Maru *Affair* • *Troops go overseas* • *Opening of the Panama Canal* • *Veterans return, and woe to the conquerors*

WHILE the potlid of hostility boiling among the Great Powers jittered ever more violently, Vancouver of the immediate period before World War I continued to grow heated about only one invasion: that of the Vancouver labor market by Asiatics. Japan had accepted restriction of emigration to Canada by the "Gentlemen's Agreement" subsequent to the 1907 riots, but most of the gentility stemmed from the western side of the Pacific. The white population of Vancouver was in no way mollified by the fact that the number of Chinese residents was increasing less quickly than that of the Japanese, who were permitted to bring in "picture brides" chosen by parents in the homeland. The Japanese were showing a good deal of enterprise commercially, and only the fact that Japan was not an enemy in World War I, and that many Japanese Canadians served in the Canadian forces, prevented the outbreak that characterized Vancouver's conduct in World War II.

"We must keep the country a white man's country at any cost, and a British country if possible," wrote the new editor of the *British Columbia Magazine* in the June, 1911, edition. "Imperial patriotism" was thus linked with "the Oriental problem." The coolie was the Commie of this prewar Vancouver, the object of animus and the motivator of fear. On March 14, 1914, the city council accepted from the Board of Works a report that included a clause demanding that none but British subjects and ratepayers be employed on city work until further notice, preference being given to married men (most non-British immigrants were of necessity single).

On the very eve of the great conflict that was to shake civilization to its shallow roots, Vancouver was therefore primed for the ludicrous mini-war called the *Komagata Maru* Affair. This naval saga had its origins in the campaign of the Asiatic Exclusion League, after the Oriental riots of 1907, to raise barriers against East Indian immigrants who were slipping into the country because they were British subjects. Partly as a result of the League's lobbying, the federal government passed an order-in-council that barred the landing of Asiatic immigrants having less than two hundred dollars and failing to arrive "by continuous journey" from their native land. As there existed at that time no direct steamship connection between India and Canada, a small group of East Indians had no trouble testing the order-in-council in court. Whereupon another order-in-council was passed making it illegal for "artisans or labourers, skilled or unskilled," to land at any port of entry in British Columbia.

This patently discriminatory legislation merely exacerbated the wrath of the East Indians already in the province, most of them Sikhs, a spirited lot whose feelings were scarcely mollified by the derision commonly aimed at the colorful turbans in which they entwined black locks, to the abiding outrage of Vancouver barbers. In the spring of 1914 a former B.C. resident and militant Indian nationalist named Gurdit Singh chartered the asthmatic steamer *Komagata Maru*, a Japanese vessel operating out of Hong Kong, and took aboard 376 East Indian passengers, each of whom had been promised the blessings of the new life in British Columbia. The immigrants, some of them veterans of British wars, embarked at various China coast ports, and the ship drew into Vancouver harbor May 23, 1914.

Gurdit Singh's motives in bringing his countrymen to a shore that he knew specifically excluded them have been variously interpreted. He may have been trying to embarrass the British raj in India. He was indeed accused of being a German agent—the ship itself was an ex-German freighter—helping to make the world climate favorable to the Kaiser's precipitating the war. The true story, however, smacks less of international intrigue than of plain, old-fashioned bungling.

On arrival in Vancouver harbor the ship, whose decks were

crowded with East Indians of all ages from youths to gray-bearded patriarchs, was not allowed to dock. The immigration authorities forced it to anchor in the stream and patrolled it with small nautical watchdogs to make sure that the East Indians on board did not communicate with those on shore. All the would-be immigrants were then given a medical examination which despite its remarkable thoroughness found only ninety unfit to land. Some of the Sikhs claimed Canadian domicile, having landed in Canada previously. These were screened and permitted to go ashore. The restless remainder, on short rations, refused to depart. Instead Gurdit Singh demanded a writ of habeas corpus for each passenger on the grounds that the order-in-council barring the landing of artisans and laborers on the west coast was *ultra vires*. Singh hired a Vancouver solicitor named Bird, who for the next eight weeks aged rapidly from having a Bengal tiger by the tail.

His first move was to wire the prime minister for permission to visit his clients. The prime minister was also receiving the first of many wires from the India Office in London and from Indians all over the world, urging admittance, and telegrams from all over British Columbia sent by labor organizations, boards of trade, Orange lodges, city councils and political groups, not to mention the provincial government itself, all demanding no admittance. The politically partisan Vancouver press blamed the government for not having forestalled the unforestallable. "They were not wanted here, not only on their own account, but because they would, if admitted, be the forerunners of thousands," wrote an editorialist who was one of those thousands who had only recently taken over the inlet from the Squamish.

Meantime lawyer Bird lodged a formal protest against the positioning of the *Komagata Maru* in mid-harbor. He was informed that the position had been chosen by the harbor master, whose judgment in the placing of vessels was not to be questioned. When Bird also objected to the patrol boats circling the ship he was told that these were for the protection of those on board, against the bloody-minded ashore. Neither the positioning nor the patrols could entirely isolate the aroma drifting from the ship as the summer days grew hotter. Not designed to carry passengers, the ship had been provided with rudimentary quarters on deck and even less sophisticated sanitary arrangements. Because harbor regulations forbade dumping of garbage overboard, the otherwise unarmed vessel acquired a large-caliber smell, as well as an arsenal of rotted refuse that was to be decisive in the battles to come.

To complicate matters, particularly for the haggard Bird, the ship's charter was bought from the original owners with $22,000 raised by the shoreside Sikhs. The "Temple Committee" sought to persuade the authorities that they had taken over the charter so that they could unload the ship's "cargo of coal." The authorities scrutinized the request and concluded that, as the ship had no cargo of coal, it was a ruse to bring her to dockside where the unhappy passengers would have a better chance of slipping over the side without fanfare. When their bid failed, the subscribers to the Temple fund wanted their money back, and the Vancouver officials faced groups both by sea and by land irate because they could not get a refund.

The East Indians on board were the more uncomfortable and cross, however, despite rations furnished by the immigration department. On July 4, after six weeks of enforced contemplation of Vancouver's skyline, five of the passengers were permitted to board the government launch to visit with friends from Nanaimo. The visit over, those aboard the *Komagata Maru* refused to lower the gangplank to reclaim the five guests. Only after a great deal of persuasion were the immigration men able to discharge the hot quintet, and the episode ended the social cruises.

The authorities then gave the ship's Japanese captain formal notice to leave the harbor at once. When the captain pointed out that he was a captive aboard his own ship, the authorities explained further that under Canadian law he was liable to a fine of five hundred dollars for each passenger if his ship was not taken immediately beyond the three-mile limit, and that if circumstances were not favorable to his control of the vessel it was his duty to call on the police for help. The Japanese skipper showed some reluctance to call the police, as he and his crew were in relatively close contact with the several hundred angry Sikhs surrounding them.

Eventually Captain Yamamoto was able to smuggle out a formal application for police assistance, and the scene was set for the only naval engagement ever to take place in Vancouver harbor. The forces of law and order and Imperial preference consisted of 120 policemen and 40 special immigration officers, led by Police Chief Malcolm McLennan and a few police inspectors. Their ship of the line was the seagoing tug *Sea Lion*, a sturdy enough battlewagon but unfortunately fifteen feet lower than the deck of the ship her marines were supposed to board. She was also outgunned. The police had orders not to use firearms. The doughty Sikhs on the other hand had had two months in which to whittle driftwood into clubs and stockpile garbage of truly overwhelming repulsiveness.

Aboard the *Sea Lion* that day were several Vancouver citizens who were to distinguish themselves, though not in this particular fray: Leon Ladner, later one of the city's leading attorneys, representing the department of immigration; H. H. Stevens, the member for Parliament for Vancouver; and Fred "Cyclone" Taylor, an immigration man who was to win a place in sports' Hall of Fame. On that hot July 23, however, there was nothing sporting about the shower of debris that greeted the attempt of the boarding party to grapple with the ship. Bricks, coal, scrap iron, clubs and even bamboo spears were the more solid objects rained down on the righteous, damaging several, including Mr. Ladner. Her decks awash with rubble, the *Sea Lion* was forced to beat an ignominious retreat, to the jubilation of the East Indians, some of whom were apparently under the impression that they had defeated Canada's combined armed forces.

Acting on the report that the Sikhs on shore were trying to smuggle arms across the border from the U.S., the defenders of Vancouver, clearly under siege by a one-ship fleet, appealed for help which arrived from Esquimalt in the shape of the elderly navy cruiser *Rainbow*. On July 21 the *Rainbow* stationed herself in the harbor a short distance upwind from the *Komagata Maru* and trained her six-inch guns on the enemy bucket. This dramatic confrontation was witnessed by crowds along the shore front and by customers of the David Spencer department store on Cordova Street. According to one witness there was a near-panic on the store's roof garden when an old lady shouted: "One of them shells might come right on this roof!" The first casualties fell in the minor rout from household furnishings to women's ready-to-wear.

For the officials on shore the frozen scene in the harbor was rocked by waves of rumors and counter-rumors. Ammunition consisted of round after round of conferences, all duds. Luckily, in town that day was the federal minister of agriculture, an eminence from which the East Indians were taken by the promise of consideration of their claims for reimbursement. The passengers agreed to accept $4,000 worth of provisions, and on July 23, nine weeks after she dropped anchor, the *Komagata Maru* sailed out of the First Narrows. Cooler heads had prevailed, though few of them belonged to the citizens of

Vancouver, who had called out the militia, including the Sixth Vancouver Regiment and the Irish Fusiliers, in order to deal with a shipload of half-starved Asiatics.

The aftermath of the Battle of Burrard Inlet was no more edifying than the event. The subscribers never did recoup the cost of their passage. More immediately galling was that most of the Sikhs aboard the jinxed ship were not returned to their original ports of embarkation, such as Hong Kong, but were directed to their native Punjab whether or not home called. As a result, when the *Komagata Maru* docked at the mouth of the Hooghly, September 27, the passengers were in such a distracted state that they refused to board the special train sent down for them, and instigated the Budge-Budge riot which caused loss of life to both the passengers and Indian police. When released from prison many committed acts of terrorism, including sabotage, and became the ringleaders of wartime conspiracies in the Punjab. All thanks to two months of sojourn afloat in beautiful Vancouver harbor.

It was not an upshot heard round the world, least of all in Vancouver. By September, 1914, the first troops were leaving the city for training camps, to prepare for the War to Save Democracy. It was to be Vancouver's proud boast that she sent more fighting men to France, in proportion to population, than any other city of comparable size in Canada or the U.S. The Vancouver regiments, notably the 72nd Canadian Infantry Battalion, Seaforth Highlanders of Canada, fought with distinction, but their history is that of the war and its battlefields many thousands of miles away, rather than that of Vancouver.

The city itself was probably the safest place to be in the Empire, with the exception of prairie towns whose livability might have been enhanced by a moderate amount of shelling. The Vancouver branch of the Red Cross rolled bandages, the local Council of Women arranged to equip a hospital ship, but the pragmatic truth of the matter was that the war added the string of shipbuilding to the city's bow of industry. Some markets were lost because of attacks on shipping, but the development of aerial combat created a demand for Sitka spruce shipped from the port of Vancouver.

For the city the most consequential event of 1914 was the opening in August of the Panama Canal. The effect of the canal on Vancouver's commerce was not at once appreciable, because of the German Navy's harassment of sea lanes, but after the war the canal meant that Vancouver had graduated to a year-round outlet for western wheat and lumber bound not only to Pacific markets but also to those of Britain and the Continent. The journey to Liverpool was 5,600 miles shorter than via Cape Horn. As historian Walter Sage pointed out: "A glance at the map of the wide Pacific shows the strategic importance of Vancouver. It is nearly a hundred miles nearer to Yokohama than is San Francisco, and is almost equidistant from Europe and Asia. From Liverpool to Vancouver is 5704 miles, and from Vancouver to Hong Kong approximately 5600." Because it transformed the city from a Pacific outpost of Empire to a fulcrum of global trade, the opening of the Panama Canal has been judged to be, after the excellence of the harbor and the choice of the city as terminus for the railway, the third key factor in building Vancouver's sinew as a seaport.

Such long-range benefit was, however, of less interest to the average Vancouver person in 1915 than the opening of Athletic Park, just south of False Creek near Granville, to cap two championship seasons of the local team and its hero Bob Brown ("Mr. Baseball"). In the same year the Millionaires, Vancouver's entry in the National Hockey League, won the Stanley Cup with the help of its great star Fred "Cyclone" Taylor, who according to legend once startled the eastern leagues by defiantly scoring a goal while skating backwards.

Recruits from Vancouver continued to board the trains to eastern training camps and to the more deadly game played by the first Canadian divisions overseas, while the city witnessed the introduction of mobile warfare in the Jitney Affair. During 1914–15 the first jitneys appeared on Vancouver streets, the jitneys being open touring cars, mostly Fords, licensed to carry passengers on any thoroughfare. The name "jitney" came from the American slang word for a nickel, which was the fare on one of these vehicles. By 1917 the two hundred licensed jitneys had become so popular that they were taking a mortal bite out of the streetcar business of the B.C.E.R., which was operating under a charter that gave the company considerable rights and privileges but also set certain restrictive conditions for operation, such as speed limits and frequency of service on routes. The speed limit for streetcars was 8 mph on business streets and a torrid 10 mph in residential areas. The jitneys, on the other hand, traveled as fast as horsepower and passenger bulk allowed.

In June, 1917, the B.C. Electric was pleased to see its employees go on strike, as the jitneys had to absorb the full weight of public transit. Licensed to carry six persons, the jitneys were seen barreling about with as many as fifteen on board, some on the hood and running boards. A commission of inquiry authorized by the provincial government looked into the demand by the B.C.E.R. for sole rights to public transport, while the Jitney League submitted a brief seeking to avoid collision with a monopoly. Whether or not the commission was influenced by complaints about the practice of jitney drivers of waiting till streetcar passengers were about to step off the curb, then braking noisily to scare the people back to the curb where they missed the streetcar, the commission's report resulted in the banning of jitneys from the streets of Vancouver. More important, having broadened the investigation to include public utilities of Victoria as well as Vancouver, the commission set the principle of monopoly control of public utilities under a public utilities commission appointed by the government.

For the young people of Vancouver, however, the blow fell on the young couple who had been able, for one dime total fare, to take an evening ride in the privacy and social congeniality of the back seat of an unlighted vehicle. (One jitney driver told the commission that he was working on an evening-hour jitney composed entirely of back seats, a real break-through in public transit.) All these advances, technological and otherwise, were swept aside forever by the cowcatcher of the utterly public, damnably well illuminated B.C. Electric streetcar. The blissful company granted the previously "impossible" demands of its striking employees, who by 1920 became the first workers in the Commonwealth to gain the eight-hour day and forty-hour week.

The company also shouldered into oblivion the Brown Cars, a Brown Car being an elongated omnibus, a kind of queen bee of open touring cars, often photographed with ladies in white, broad-brimmed hats and smocks occupying the sideless benches with remarkably trusting expressions on their faces. Used for jaunts around Stanley Park, Marine Drive and Capilano Canyon, the Brown Cars yielded to the B.C. Electric observation cars, whose celebrated conductor-guide, "Teddy" Lyons, was to become part of the experience of being young for thousands of Vancouver children who ran to street corners to wave at the majestic open streetcar, whose seats were tiered to a giddy height—a galleon whose glib-tongued captain snapped a mean quip over his rubberneckers.

George Kidd, the company's general manager who masterminded

the anti-jitney campaign, was not unmindful of that being fought in France. He persuaded the London office to allow company employees to use company land in Vancouver to grow food, free of rent, to help solve the shortage. In the same summer of 1917 the first steel steamer built in British Columbia was launched by the Wallace shipyards in North Vancouver. The U-boat toll of merchant vessels rang the cash register in Burrard Inlet and False Creek. The old dream of the city as an industrial center wafted out of the smoke from shot and shell, only to be dispelled by the fortunes of peace.

As the war ground on, Vancouver felt something of the frustration of the emotionally involved combatant who cannot get near the fight. Soldiers like Brigadier Victor W. Odlum were winning glory that rubbed off on the city but made it even more impatient for final victory. A curious mix of professional soldier and newspaperman, Odlum joined the *World* in 1902, rose to be editor-in-chief at the age of twenty-five, took command of the 11th Canadian Brigade and shared credit for the technique of hit-and-run trench raids later adopted by all Allied forces and copied by the Germans. Yet the people of Vancouver were whipsawed by news of reversals of battle.

To make patriotic matters worse, the McBride government in Victoria was in bad odor, from charges not of gunpowder but of corruption. In May, 1916, Vancouver launched a personation inquiry resulting from the importation of a number of Americans to vote in a city by-election. The investigation into the "plugging" of votes was not made more flattering by the disclosure that the Yanks were found rooms in a boardinghouse that advertised itself as "British owned and operated."

Vancouver's response to these banderillos jabbed into a wartime conscience was to go after reform—almost any kind of reform. Banners were raised in the streets demanding prohibition, prison reform, the franchise of women, sanitary government. Members of the University Women's Club, stalled by the freeze on new buildings for U.B.C., led the assault on exclusive voting rights for men, while the "drys" marched behind the standard of the Committee of One Hundred, whose formidable leader was Jonathan Rogers, president of the Board of Trade. As individuals, people saved pennies to send "smokes" overseas, while the Vancouver Trade and Labour Council joined other provincial councils in denouncing the depletion of manpower, and the city in 1917 was home to the Anti-Conscription League.

The trainloads of wounded soldiers who began returning to the city found it racked by strikes, the home fires burning in aid of international labor unions and the socialist movement. The casualty most honored locally was a radical leader killed by police near Comox while attempting to avoid the Military Service Act. Labor's protest, in August, 1918, took the form of Canada's first general strike, of twenty-four hours' duration, which in Vancouver culminated in an attack by returned soldiers on the Pender Street headquarters of the Longshoremen's Association. Vancouver was so distracted by the labor pains attending the birth of unionism, and by the mounting death toll of victims of the world-wide flu epidemic that closed Vancouver theaters, that the last great Allied push on the Western Front passed almost unnoticed.

The telegraphed news of the Armistice, reaching Vancouver early on the Monday, November 11, therefore released a tremendous pressure of pent-up feeling. By one o'clock crowds billowed in downtown streets, an estimated 25,000 gathering at Granville and Hastings, the *World* also reporting: ". . . curses that were prayers were heard; jangling klaxons shrieked; self-confident, prim men and women hammered tin cans, blew horns and shouted in glee. . . . Confetti carpeted the sidewalks, the red paper of fireworks fairly filled the gutters." Boat whistles racketed in the harbor, and at the military annex of the Vancouver General Hospital the wounded veterans staged a pajama parade for which no formal salute was taken.

The Vancouver that woke up sober, with a slight head, was not the Vancouver that had blithely sent the boys off to war. The young veterans bulging the already distended Fairview shacks in 1919 were more mature than the university's students pre-1914. The city received a transfusion of blood, not all British, tested in battle and found to be type "C" for Canadian. A woman, Helen Gregory MacGill, had been appointed a judge of juvenile court, representative of the escapement resulting from opening the Pandora's box of women's rights. Henceforth life in Vancouver, at work and at play, would be a more complicated affair. The war had made a man of the city, and a woman of the city, and the simple gender of childhood, with its time for anything and everything in time, lay buried in Flanders' fields.

CHAPTER 11 1919–1929

Janet and the Money Tree

Prairie gold rolls west • New home for U.B.C. • The Janet Smith Case • L.D.'s finest hour, the greater Vancouver • The luxury of repentance comes too late

On March 3, 1919, the pontoons of a single-engine Boeing biplane cleft the waters of Coal Harbour to inaugurate the first Canada–U.S. mail flight, from Seattle to Vancouver. A year later the first Dominion airmail plane landed at Minoru Park, and an aircraft spun the invisible strand linking Vancouver with Victoria. Vancouver's first air crash, in English Bay in 1922, confirmed that the city had entered the air age without having its feet too firmly set on the ground.

It was to be another thirty years before the airplane became a factor in Vancouver's economic fate. In the water, not the air, lay the business end of cornucopia. Despite the launching in 1918 of the first deep-sea steamer (the *Alaska*, 8,800 tons) built in False Creek yards (requiring the jacking up of the Kitsilano trestle bridge to let her out to the bay), and despite the ships that continued to be built in the yards of the creek and Burrard Inlet, the waters of the harbor remained precious to Vancouver not as a Clydeside but as a port, a place to which more and more ships built elsewhere came to drop the hook.

To satisfy a world suddenly hungry after the exertion of the Great War, the ships' holds gaped for grain. In 1916 Vancouver had dispatched to Liverpool via Panama the first wheat cargo, as opposed to sacked grain. The objection that the port had to overcome was that wheat thus shipped in bulk could not survive the heat of the tropics without "sweating." Eastern shippers were clearly audible in their assertions that such perspiration was a problem well beyond the power of any deodorant, for example the Vancouver Board of Trade, to control. "Stevens' Folly" was the name donated to the terminal grain elevator built on Vancouver harbor in 1916, at the protracted behest of H. H. Stevens, M.P. for the city. The huge elevator, with a capacity of 1,125,000 bushels, was classed with the proposed tunnel under Point Grey as instance of Vancouver's aptitude for a reach that exceeded her grasp. For six years the elevator stood almost idle. The derision lavished on it in Ottawa, Montreal and Halifax appeared to be fully merited. Then, after the six lean years, came the golden deluge.

The break-through began in 1918–19, when five ships loaded with a total of 800,000 bushels of wheat boldly sailed from Vancouver to Europe. Each ship carried a chemist who made daily tests of the condition of the grain. By the early twenties, therefore, the shippers had scientific verification that it was feasible to load grain in bulk at Vancouver. At the same time they were educated to the advantages of the ice-free harbor where deep-sea ships could berth hard by rail spurs and conveyors from elevator to ship's hold. The Panama Canal facility came together with other conveniences at the right moment to swing significant numbers of grain shippers to the western port. Vancouver moved into contention with the heavyweights of the East. More and more grain cars rattled down from the Rockies as Vancouver closed the credibility gap between tidewater and Calgary, then the rest of Alberta, and finally parts of Saskatchewan. In 1924 the climactic message came over the wire: "For the first time on record the exports of Canadian wheat, via the port of Vancouver, have exceeded the exports via the port of Montreal. For the ten months ended June 30, 1924, the wheat going out from Vancouver amounted to 50,691,296 bushels, as compared with an export for the same period at Montreal of 47,262,196 bushels." As poetry it didn't really rank with Homer, but the words fell on Vancouver ears as sweetly as the rustle of currency. Even when Montreal promptly cried "Foul!" and pointed out that the period named included five months when the St. Lawrence was closed by ice, the upstart westerner remained cheeky. Vancouver had Canada's No. 1 port on the defensive and it knew it.

With the palm came its thorn: the mountain differential, sharper than ever. The railways' surcharge for transporting wheat over the western mountains was arrived at through calculations that seemed to Vancouver, and its champion in Ottawa, Harry Stevens, to be based on a theory of mathematics taught only at eastern universities. During the decade that followed the expansion of Vancouver's economic hinterland to include the prairies, two hairy monsters lived in the mountains east of the city: the Sasquatch, which bore off Indian maidens and returned them pregnant, and the mountain differential, which raped the grain shipper and put the illegitimate issue on Vancouver's doorstep.

With less mixed emotions Vancouver watched the development of the harbor to include other than grain ships. The lumber trade, rid of the tourniquet applied during the war, multiplied the number of tugs hauling booms of logs from an enlarged radius of points along the coast, into Vancouver harbor and False Creek. Both the north shore of the inlet and the creek offered shallow, sheltered water suitable for the mooring of log booms, and with Granville Island and parts of the creek reclaimed, the beehive burners of the mills emitted prosperity as a fallout of fly ash. The ash, added to the odor of the creek at low tide, made crossing the Granville Street Bridge something of an adventure for eye, nose and throat. The creek shores became the main industrial area in the city, a motley agglomeration of sawmills, processing plants, gravel dumps, warehouses, cooperages, hog fuel burners, wharves and railway yards—a dirty apron at the city's waist.

Farther out, in English Bay, lay the fixed mooring buoys for log booms and scows, as well as anchorage for the deep-sea freighters waiting their turn at the inner harbor. The yacht clubs, particularly the Royal Vancouver Yacht Club, lent a touch of elegance to the heterogeneous clutter of vessels. While the North Vancouver ferries plodded across the inlet, the smaller ferry to West Vancouver ran the daily gauntlet of driftwood through the First Narrows, and at the eastern end of the harbor, near Indian Arm, would soon mushroom the tanks of petroleum refinery storage, whose tankers would have to thread their way through all these maritime oddments, ranging from sculling shells in Coal Harbour to the C.P.R. coastal *Princesses*—the *Kathleen*, the *Patricia*, the *Marguerite*, the *Louise*—and the new, splendid *Empresses*. On June 26, 1922, the *Empress of Canada* made her maiden visit to the port, the largest ship to have entered the harbor. In Stanley Park the elaborately carved prow of the old *Empress of Japan* was preserved to welcome the new version of that fine ship.

As with all great ports, Vancouver's function was that of the heart whose own life depends on pumping goods into both the major arteries of commerce and a delicate network of tiny capillaries in the immediate vicinity.

Besides the strengthened pulse of legal shipping, Vancouver in the young twenties developed a fibrillation less conducive to sound repute: rumrunning. Prohibition in the States made it profitable for the small fleet of highly independent craft to ply the waters between the gulf islands, nocturnal operations as courageous in their own way as those of the minor armada at Dunkirk but winning no acclaim for rescuing thousands of Americans from the ruthless forces of temperance. "Pussyfoot" Johnson, the celebrated U.S. prohibitionist, was quoted as saying that most of Canada was cooperating, but "British Columbia on the other hand is cooperating only with bootleggers." The judgment was unkind, as the only visible monuments to the overproof navy working out of Vancouver were several magnificent homes built on Southwest Marine Drive, by makers of spirits whose international good-neighborliness extended at least one hundred nautical miles south of the border.

The introduction of daylight-saving time, in 1920, disturbed the sailing schedules of the grog boats somewhat. The rest of Vancouver's night people adjusted readily, the social clubs flouting the law by selling booze, bootleggers thriving at all hours, and use of opium and other narcotics spreading beyond the shadowy limits of Chinatown. Movie theaters gorged themselves on patrons, and up at the Shaughnessy mansion of millionaire financier A. D. McRae the swinging parties were the talk of the uninvited and the prelude to Vancouver's most celebrated scandal.

The first recorded disrobing by the Doukhobors, in 1921 in the C.P.R. station, did not qualify as authentic whoopee, but it did give a fillip to the possibilities of rail travel. As for the automobile, what shook the British imperialists was the stripping of gears that accompanied the change, January 1, 1922, of traffic from left to right. The choice of New Year's Eve for the switch-over was never publicly connected with the fact that there would be no measurable transition for people driving to parties on the left side of the street and coming home on the wrong side.

Less contentious was the announcement, in 1921, of the building of a ferry slip for a car ferry to the North Shore. As embellishment for a somewhat larger ship, the destroyer *Vancouver*, the city sent to

Britain the city's coat of arms: a logger and a fisherman holding the provincial shield above the legend "By sea and land we prosper." The curator of the Imperial War Museum in London tartly described the coat of arms as "heraldically . . . hopeless. The most hideous ever seen, and a disgrace to Vancouver." This was a blow to Vancouver boosters, who had looked upon the logger and fisherman as a tasteful variation on the lion and the unicorn. Nothing, however, was done about the emblem till some years later when council deemed it desirable to revise the prospering to "By sea, land and air."

In 1921 the air traffic around Vancouver was still mostly impromptu. Planes were being used to expedite the rumrunning to the States, and in January the police almost caught the truck that had loaded a plane that took off from Minoru Park and headed on its mercy mission toward the southern desert. Thanks to such enterprise local liquor penetrated deep into the disadvantaged area. In September, 1921, one of the details of the murder charge against Fatty Arbuckle, the Hollywood film comedian, was that the liquor drunk at the famous and fatal party had been traced to Vancouver.

The law, too, employed the airplane in the smuggling war. A government seaplane based at Jericho Air Station conducted regular flights over the gulf to intercept the fast launches and fish boats that picked up cargo dropped overboard from liners incoming from the Orient. Opium and cocaine were the contents of the buoyant castaways, one of which was found on the beach of a gulf island. One of Vancouver's aviation pioneers, Major McLaurin, piloted for the anti-smuggling patrol, sharing his aircraft with carrier pigeons trained at Jericho and released from the plane if it was forced down. Upon receipt of a pigeon the Jericho base telephoned to Steveston for a tug to go to the rescue, as one did on December 13, 1921, in just such emergency, to initiate Vancouver's air-sea rescue service. McLaurin was killed, September 11, 1922, when his seaplane crashed near the cable hut at Point Grey.

The drama of outwitting the nefarious agents of the Orient was played as low farce in city council, where Mayor R. H. Gale during 1921 heard deputations arguing the infamy of a garbage disposal system that permitted Chinese scavengers to bring their vegetable produce to the city in the same "unwashed swill buckets" used to cart garbage away. The city considered giving the garbage disposal contract to a firm that also agreed to cultivate the Burnaby cemetery site, a sort of dust-to-dust package deal.

Whereas the city council could see the value of restaurant garbage as salable to the hog-raising industry, there was less enthusiasm for casting pearls before the swine of higher education. Students were as high-spirited as in any other era, but excesses were severely dealt with. When, in May, 1919, as the climax of their annual "Socks Day," high schoolers donned gaudy hose and dark glasses and marched downtown behind a rube band, many drew suspensions or detentions, ending "Socks Day" forever. With equal severity the taxpayers gazed upon the pleading for funds to move the University of British Columbia from the Fairview shacks to the chosen land of Point Grey. Since the university's casting off from the mother ship McGill, in September, 1915, students had literally sweated out the war in primitive accommodations that cribbed everything but the ebullience of the students, who popularized the "yell" that was to be the *chanson de geste* at college games for years:

Kitsilano, Capilano, Siwash, Squaw,
Kla-How-Ya Tillicum, Skookum Wah!
Hyu Mamook! Muck-a-Muck-a, Zip!
B.C. Varsity! Rip! Rip! Rip!
V-A-R-S-I-T-Y—Varsity!

Anthropologically, the cheer left something to be desired, but there was no questioning the spirit. Without it, the university would have simply withered on the vine. The death in 1918 of U.B.C.'s first president, Dr. Frank F. Wesbrook, who chose the motto *Tuum Est* ("It's up to you") and kept enthusiasm alive during the wartime austerity, had been a blow to the drive for a new campus. Point Grey was still well outside the perimeter of Vancouver's interests, yet was close enough to the city to be identified with it by Victoria, where the purse strings were held, by a government headed by Premier "Honest John" Oliver, an ex-dirt farmer who took some pride in his freedom from formal education. Similarly, if not actually anti-intellectual, Vancouver has never been in danger of being confused with Cambridge, Mass.

It was not till October, 1922, that the twelve hundred students bulging the flimsy walls at Fairview mounted a province-wide petition and campaign that culminated in the Pilgrimage, a well-organized parade on foot of all the students through downtown Vancouver, with floats and decorated cars. From Davie and Granville the pilgrims piled into streetcars that took them to the end of the line, at 10th Avenue and Sasamat, from which point the parade re-formed and trekked to the campus. There, the Israelites hailed the wilderness and had their photo taken astride the steel beams that were the eight-year-old skeleton of the unfinished Science Building.

And the Lord heard them. Contracts were let for the construction of buildings which, in September, 1925, accepted the surge of students who were all that was holding up the old shacks. Vancouver had acquired a new polarity, that for young people at the tip of Point Grey. On the Endowment Lands rose the Dutch colonial houses of the first residents of the university district that was to be of Vancouver though not in it. Vancouver was not destined to be a university city, in the sense that McGill and the University of Toronto became part of the vitals of their respective metropolises. The University of British Columbia was the jewel on the hand that the city extended to the western sea, while her other hand pulled down her girdle.

A good appearance was mandatory when Vancouver welcomed the twenty-ninth President of the United States, Warren Harding. Ties of blood and smuggled liquor made the occasion, July 26, 1923, a deeply moving one for host city and eminent guest alike, the citizens relishing the distinction of receiving the first American President to pay a social call on Canada. Harding's response to the experience was to die a week later in San Francisco, his Vancouver speech virtually his last public utterance. To commemorate the visit a memorial was raised in the gardens of Stanley Park between the tea pavilion and the future site of the Malkin Memorial Bowl—two bronze female figures representing Columbia and Canada, flanked by eagles. Forty-six years later, an unidentified critic of foreign policy sawed off a hand from each lady and amputated the birds' beaks. But for the time being, amity reigned.

In the mid-twenties Vancouver welcomed representatives of powers not only foreign but supernatural—evangelists, theosophists and other itinerant wise men from the east or more often from the south. The unveiling, in April, 1924, of the cenotaph in Victory Square, a memorial modeled on that in Whitehall, by Mayor W. R. Owen, attracted a vast throng, but nothing to compete with the audiences hanging on the words of Dr. Clem Davies, the evangelist credited with establishing the first standard broadcasting station in western Canada, and a voice heard over Vancouver's CJOR for years before Davies passed on to the better life in Hollywood.

25. Great Trek students flesh the partly finished Science Building on the new campus of the University of British Columbia, 1922

26. Old Hotel Vancouver, started in 1905 and completed in 1916, was not the first Hotel Vancouver at Georgia and Granville. The original was officially opened May 16, 1888

27. Louis D. Taylor

28. An early (May 23, 1919) aerial photograph of Stanley Park, the causeway of a tidal Lost Lagoon, and Coal Harbour. Big building is the Arena, destroyed by fire in 1936. Upper left, Deadman's Island and the large field that was the Buffalo Park

29. Lions Gate Bridge, on completion, Stanley Park and the city in the background

30. Gerald Grattan McGeer

31. "Gerry" McGeer

32. Chinese community's arch, Vancouver Golden Jubilee, 1936

33. The Post Office Riot, June, 1938; RCMP wear the banded hats

34. The wake of the Post Office Riot. Casualties on the sidewalk are store window dummies

35. Impounded vehicles of Japanese residents, Hastings Park, 1942. In background the Shoot the Chutes and Giant Dipper

36. The celebrated photograph by Claud Dettloff of a daddy leaving for war and (inset) safely returned

Vancouver had entered the new era of mass communication with the first radio news broadcast, March 1, 1922, by the *Province*, from what became station CKCD in the Merchants' Exchange. The four hundred receiving sets in Vancouver at that time rapidly became many times that number as the people responded to the pleasure of hearing immediately of any local disaster.

This was a period of some emotional instability for Vancouver, as it was for other cities whose values and orientations had been rudely shaken by the war. The smoke pall over the city—Mayor C. E. Tisdall decried it with the comment "I lived in the 'Black Country' in England as a boy, but I have never seen the equal of the grimy condition obtaining in Vancouver"—was merely a continuing nuisance. Feelings ran higher on such matters as compulsory smallpox vaccination for all school children. Mothers manned the barricades against the Needle, the length of which ranged in rumor, among the children, up to three feet, and many a first-grader cried himself to sleep because he had been labeled a Conscientious Objector, a name synonymous with cowardice and forced labor in a logging camp hundreds of miles from home.

One of the chronic causes of nervous twitch among Vancouver people, the mountain differential of freight rates, appeared to be cured by the long-awaited report, October 10, 1923, of the railway commissioners ordering a 10 per cent reduction on freight rates of grain to Pacific ports. Ships were already under way from foreign shores to Vancouver, to take advantage of the lower rate, when Ottawa referred the whole matter back to the commission to consider "equalization of rates east and west"—a tactic in a game of political football almost as old as the Grey Cup. Despite the carefully preserved confusion, one hundred deep-sea ships arrived in the port of Vancouver during February, 1924—a new record for any month.

Unlike most other cities, Vancouver experienced an event that brought together all the elements of the city's postwar neurosis in a single sensational mystery melodrama, one that did not want for comedy relief. That event was the Janet Smith Murder Case.

Janet Smith was a young nursemaid employed to look after the twenty-month-old child of Mr. and Mrs. Frank L. Baker, who at the time of the murder were occupying the residence of Baker's brother, R. P. Baker, who was out of town. The 3851 Osler Avenue address distinguished it as one of the mansions of the rich who were making Shaughnessy Heights the Westmount of Vancouver.

Although the district was part of the municipality of Point Grey, the homes gracing the crescents and avenues around the General McRae estate were Vancouver suburbia's *crème de la crème*. Gossip of the envious, along the lower reaches of Granville Street, whispered that the tone of the parties held in some of these homes was not as elevated as the topography.

On Saturday, July 26, 1924, workmen nearby heard a voice singing in the Baker house, a voice they recognized as that of the girl they called "the Scottish Nightingale"—Janet Smith. One hour later, although nobody reported hearing a shot, Janet Smith was found dead on the concrete floor of the basement, a bullet hole in her head. According to his account, the body was found by the Chinese houseboy, Wong Foon Sing. Wong was peeling potatoes in the kitchen, he later testified, when he heard a shot and ran down the stairs to find the girl dead beside her ironing board. Wong's own room was in the basement. The houseboy phoned Frank Baker at work, and Baker called the police.

At the inquest a few days later Frank Baker told the jury that he believed that Janet Smith had, out of curiosity, been examining the gun—a heavy army automatic pistol—which belonged to his brother and had been kept in a haversack in the front hall of the house. This implied that the girl had interrupted her ironing to come upstairs, remove the fully loaded revolver from the haversack, return to the basement and accidentally pull the trigger with the gun aimed at her head. Two doctors testified that the skull fracture additional to the bullet wound could not have been inflicted by a fall on the concrete basement floor, nor did the girl stumble down the stairs. The supposition was that she fell sideways, striking her head against the granite sink. Suicide was ruled out, as Janet was known to be an exceptionally cheerful lassie, engaged to be married to a lumber camp employee at Roberts Creek.

Finally, and decisively, a Point Grey policeman testified that there was nothing in the evidence to indicate foul play. The jury brought in the verdict of accidental death.

Neither the discovery of the body nor the inquest received much attention from the Vancouver newspapers, which were agog at the Loeb-Leopold "thrill killing" of Robert Franks in the U.S., coincidental with the relatively prosaic death in Point Grey. The city was also in the midst of a crime wave that had elicited from Mayor W. R. Owen orders to clean up the police blotter stained by holdups and burglaries. Nothing more would have been heard about the unfortunate Miss Smith had not the united Scottish societies persisted in muttering darkly in their porridge about "Orientals," and the bizarre pastimes of the wealthy. The societies pressed for further investigation, in particular into information they believed to be in Janet's diary, which was in possession of the Point Grey police. Their rumbling produced a second inquest, at which it was proved conclusively that it was a physical impossibility for anyone to shoot himself as Janet Smith had been shot. Also, though her outer garments had been thoroughly soaked by blood, her underclothing below the stains was spotless. Odder still, no brain tissue was to be found on the floor or anywhere in the basement despite the gaping wound blown open by the heavy-caliber bullet. It was also disclosed that burns on the body could not be explained by the victim's falling against the iron she was presumably using before she was shot. As the final blow to public confidence in the Point Grey police department, the same policeman who at the first inquest dismissed the possibility of homicide now testified that he had been misunderstood and that this was now a case of murder.

The back-yard comment that had been a buzz now became a hum clearly audible in Victoria. The provincial police took over the investigation, appointing a Victoria lawyer, M. B. Jackson, K.C., as a special investigator. He replaced the private detective hired by the Point Grey police commission, O. B. V. Robinson, head of the Canadian Detective Agency, who received $1,250 for his services to the utterly tarnished badge of the Point Grey police. Attorney General Manson assured the public, with a special release to the press, that all the rumors "afloat" were being thoroughly "sifted."

The restless natives were appeased somewhat by these developments, which were supplemented by a bill introduced in the legislature to prevent the employment of Orientals in homes where white girls worked. In case anybody missed the sinister implications of this landmark in British legislation, a member for Saanich told the house that Janet Smith's death was at the hands of "higher ups" in the dope racket. On January 6, 1925, speculation was kept bubbling by the news report that the provincial investigators had unearthed valuable information. No details accompanied the announcement, however, with the result that everyone was able to put his own interpretation on the major clue and help to brighten a drab winter month.

The Scottish societies, smelling blood, resumed their demands for something more solid to seize upon. Officialdom surfaced with promise of a third inquest, then sounded the deeps once more. The surface remained suspensefully placid till the night of March 20, when the turgid waters erupted where totally unexpected. During the night Wong Foon Sing was spirited away from the Baker home by a gaggle of rather substantial spirits, men dressed in flowing robes and white hoods. As there were no witnesses to the kidnaping, the description of the abductors' garb added a dimension of mystery to the page-one news stories the following day. From sources in Vancouver's Chinatown came the account of how, while the Baker family was conveniently absent, the robed kidnapers hustled Wong into a waiting car, taking along his belongings as if planning for him a protracted holiday. The *Province* theorized that the abduction was "possibly a method of seeking to converse quietly with the China boy."

To Vancouver people of the mid-twenties the costumes ascribed to the abductors seemed by no means as bizarre as such theatricals would appear today. Part of the Americanization of New Liverpool was the overspill from the south of Ku Klux Klan activities. In November, 1925, during a debate in the provincial legislature on banning the Klan in British Columbia, a member rose to declare that if the Klan was against Catholics, Jews and Negroes there was no place for it in a British community, but "if it freed the province of Orientals" he would be for it. The Klan outriders from the States had picked up a fair amount of support, once they had established the fact that a person did not need to be black to qualify for persecution. Yellow was a perfectly acceptable color.

Vancouver's Chinese community, whose patience has been one of the city's inexhaustible resources, this time ran short of it. It held mass meetings that gave notice to the city police that it expected action due a first-class citizen and it brought the Chinese consul into an affair already surfeited with ethnic groups. The spectacle of the Chinese Benevolent Association ranged against the Scottish societies was one that edified Vancouver's racial relations hardly at all. The Chinese refuted the conclusion to which much of the city had jumped, namely that the abduction story was a smoke screen behind which Wong had skipped town aboard the *Empress of Australia,* which had left for the Far East the same evening that Wong disappeared. The Vancouver police were preparing to send a plane after the ship when the captain of the vessel wired that there was no visible Wong on board. Lending weight to the argument of Wong's friends that he was not the type to pick up and leave so precipitately was the report—mysteriously omitted in earlier accounts—of evidence at the Baker home of a struggle: scuff marks on the door and other indications that Wong had left under duress.

During the next few weeks the news reports were such as to suggest that nobody knew what was going on except everybody. The Chinese consulate was the most reliable news agency, on April 4 revealing that Wong's captors were becoming exasperated in their efforts to interrogate the houseboy, that they badly needed an interpreter for the prisoner, who spoke no English, and that "he may be punished by the mysterious tribunal. . . . He has had one trial, and will have another this evening. Tonight however his captors hope to be able to break him down and have him make a further statement." The bulletin was received, by police and public alike, with a minimum of inquisitiveness about the Chinese consul's source of information. He enjoyed diplomatic immunity from the conspiracy of silence.

The silence was shattered at 3 A.M., May 1, the time given by police as that when they picked up a dazed Wong Foon Sing wandering on Marine Drive. The police promptly charged the Chinese with murder and clapped him into Oakalla prison, in nearby Burnaby, before anyone else could speak to him. The *Province* obtained access to a story, however, that described Wong's long auto ride the night he was abducted, a trip intended to make the terrified houseboy believe that he was being transported to Mexico, even including a stop for checking by spurious U.S. immigration officers. The "underground refuge" in which the kidnapers held him was identified as a place where, early in World War I, machine guns and German weapons were found cached in preparation for a coup on behalf of Kaiser Wilhelm. Again, as with the *Komagata Maru* affair ten years earlier, the inscrutably Asiatic was parlayed into the machinations of the Hun. In Vancouver, East was East and West was West, and if the twain did not meet, an assignation was arranged by the press.

The *Province* story also made the first press mention of a party held at the Baker home the evening before Janet Smith was killed, and hinted at the involvement of prominent persons in the continuing drama. The paper reported that Scotland Yard was "investigating aspects of the case." That the Yard was showing interest raised the mystery to a new plateau of homicide. Vancouver had been placed on the crime map, for the first time in its history, and the populace delighted in the distinction.

The following day, May 2, the newspapers were emboldened to repeat the questions on everyone's lips: "What did the police have on Wong, and how did they get it?" They also suggested that private operatives were involved in the kidnaping. On May 3 the headlines burst into the full blossom of what was to be the longest-blooming story ever to scent the front page. The Chinese community, and the counsel they hired for the houseboy, obtained permission for a doctor to visit the prisoner in Oakalla. To lend a touch of technological modernity to the case, it was reported that a dictograph was used by the kidnapers to record Wong's statements. That the statements themselves left something to be desired was implicit in the revelation that the Chinese interpreter who assisted at the second inquest had also been abducted while Wong was being held. "Third degree methods"—another attractive novelty from the U.S.—were said to have prevailed during the questioning of Wong, who was quoted as saying that his captors threatened to kill him.

The number of local personages being "shadowed" now verged on a major eclipse. A gauge of the amount of rumor rampant in the shadows was the writ for slander issued by F. L. Baker against a Vancouver woman because she was alleged to have told a friend: "Isn't it too bad that the Bakers had the party the night before?" It is doubtful that libelous insinuation could sound more innocuous out of context. Matters had in fact reached the point where the provincial police felt constrained to recall Inspector Forbes Cruickshank, its top detective, from Washington State, where he was investigating the *Beryl G.* case, *Beryl G.* being a boat involved in a rumrunning plot that had higher priority in Victoria, as a tax-dodging crime.

On May 7 Wong was brought from Oakalla prison to Vancouver for X rays and examination by an eye, ear and throat specialist. The news reporter who got a glimpse of the young Chinese as he was hustled into the Birks Building described his "appearance of a very sick man"—gray pallor, a blackened eye, bloodless lips, and a bandage around his neck so ample that it hung over his collar. The same story reported that a physician had visited Wong while he was being held captive, the kidnapers having become nervous about the effects of the rough treatment they were handing out to the uncooperative houseboy.

The following day at the preliminary hearing of Wong's murder charge, in the Point Grey municipal hall, his lawyer J. H. Senkler at once challenged the police interpreter, Foon Sien, pointing out that this was the same interpreter brought in by the police for the inquests, a Chinese who had obliged the hearings with full answers though he spoke a different dialect from that of Wong and also did not understand the questions. Another veteran of the first inquest, expected to testify, was ex-Constable J. E. Green, who conducted the original police examination of the Baker home and had subsequently departed from the force. With such stellar attractions the murder hearing played to full houses, fashionably-dressed ladies arriving in autos while only two or three Chinese were admitted to the courtroom. The rest of the Chinese lined up outside, peering through the windows and hearing nothing. There is no evidence that they missed any milestones in the history of British jurisprudence.

The May 14 proceedings yielded two tidbits for lovers of the macabre. The first was Inspector Cruickshank's solemn account of ballistic tests he made with the murder weapon, firing bullets through the head of a pig, then through a human head. He did not immediately expatiate on the source of the human head. The second disclosure was F. L. Baker's admission that he was a member of a firm for which he negotiated a contract for $40,000 worth of drugs, including narcotics, while in Paris with his wife, child and Janet Smith. He testified that Janet knew nothing of the transaction, that there had been no party at the house the night before the murder, and that nobody in the house had ever tried to kiss or otherwise molest the nursemaid.

Rousing itself as from a long slumber, the bar association issued a statement condemning "in the most uncompromising manner" the abduction of Wong and the conduct of the whole investigation. Janet Smith's parents in London added comment, Mrs. Smith saying: "The secretary of the [Scottish] Society told us that they would not rest until they discovered Nettie's murderer, so that we knew all along that they were working on our behalf." Working on behalf of Wong, who had been committed for trial, the Chinese Benevolent Association offered a $3,500 reward for information leading to the arrest of Wong's kidnapers.

On June 7 a new area of bewilderment was opened for subdivision, with the report that a "mystery woman" had dictated a statement to the police. At the same time copies were received of a Scottish newspaper, the *Sunday Mail* of Glasgow, of which several columns were filled by the account of a Scottish crystal-gazer, detailing the case and its solution. Reliability of her story lay in her having had the same vision three nights running. She also had it for the Vancouver police, as she turned out to be the same Vancouver woman, a Miss Barbara Orford, who had made the "mystery woman" statement to the authorities. Under questioning Miss Orford refuted the crystal ball and declared that she had actually attended the party at the Baker home on the night before the murder. Her account, replete with the names of many prominent society people she said were present at the affair, was quite explicit about the unscheduled party game at the Osler Avenue house, begun by a dispute over the drug trade functioning between Shaughnessy and Chinatown, a brawl in which Janet Smith was killed.

In what must have been one of local journalism's most agonizing moments of frustration, Vancouver's two major dailies leaned over backwards to avoid repeating the potentially libelous statement. The Vancouver *Tribune,* however, printed the Orford story verbatim, and was promptly sued, in the person of editor J. S. Cowper, by F. L. Baker. Cowper in turn felt the ground shifting sickeningly beneath his feet when Miss Orford's story was proved to err in several details of fact—attributing mustaches to party guests who didn't have them, for instance—and Attorney General Manson dismissed the story as being without foundation.

On the same day, June 17, that Manson came to the rescue of the defamed, the *Province* hit the streets with an extra edition: Wong's abductors had been arrested. The list of suspects inspired awe. O. B. V. Robinson, head of the Canadian Detective Agency, was arrested that day, an assistant, V. W. Norton, and Robinson's son William being picked up June 18. All were charged with unlawful detention of Wong Foon Sing. In addition summonses were being sought against John Murdoch, chief of Point Grey police, H. P. McRaney, Point Grey police commissioner, Sergeant P. Kirkham, of the Point Grey police, David Patterson, president of the Scottish Society, A. S. Mathew and Mrs. F. H. Stratton, officials of the Scottish societies, and J. S. Cowper, editor of the *Tribune*. Norton was the informant, having become disgruntled with the amount of money he had been paid by Robinson for his part in the business. One piece of false economy doomed the workmanship of a truly baroque conspiracy.

The facts of the abduction now gushed forth, including a photograph of the house at 3543 West 25th Avenue where Wong was held—a sedate Dunbar district home about as far from the Kaiser's grand strategy as it was possible to get. Wong identified the room in which, he said, he had been threatened with a noose around his neck, and beaten till he suffered what the ear specialist confirmed to be a broken eardrum.

The dignitaries accused denied complicity. Norton elaborated on his first confession with the statement that he was told by his boss Robinson that the Victoria government was sharing costs of the abduction with the Point Grey police, and that he could expect a job with the Liquor Control Board, which had been his choice of government services to work for. At this point (July, 1925, the first anniversary of the murder) quite a number of trials were going on concurrently: Wong's trial for murder, that of various parties charged with Wong's abduction, and the Cowper trial for libel. The Janet Smith case was beginning to assume the proportion of God's plenty for Vancouver lawyers, or at least for those not in danger of being drawn into the widening whirlpool of arraignment. One who fell victim was M. B. Jackson, the Victoria lawyer in charge of the government inquiry into the Smith murder. Robinson implicated him, as well as another new personage, J. A. Paton, reeve of Point Grey.

These were by no means the largest pillars of the community to be caught in the mud slide. In reporting the Cowper trial testimony, the *Province* revealed for the first time that the Orford story involved the lieutenant governor of the province, Walter C. Nichol, as one of the guests at the Baker party that didn't happen. And in the course of the Wong trial, on November 6, Wong's lawyer Senkler implicated Attorney General Manson, as Norton's testimony was supported by Mrs. Donelly, Robinson's secretary, who testified that virtually every law officer of any distinction on the Lower Mainland had full knowledge of the abduction. The unlawful detention and physical abuse of the Chinese houseboy had been accompanied by a degree of collaboration between Victoria and the Terminal City such as has been rare since union of the colonies.

The attorney general was by now fully engaged in denying

complicity in the abduction. Yet, after Robinson and Norton had been found guilty and sentenced to the modest terms of, respectively, one year and nine months, Manson had enough impudence left to drop the charges against Jackson and the other luminaries involved. By now, Wong having been freed by the grand jury that found "no bill," and Baker having won his libel suit against Cowper and the *Tribune,* the action had moved to the main stage of absurdity: the provincial legislature. To opposition members' demands for a committee to investigate the entire Janet Smith debacle, Manson replied with a description of the ballistic experiments with the human head, explaining that the police had obtained an unclaimed corpse from the morgue at the Essondale mental hospital, with his sanction, and had fired bullets into its brain under provision of an act that permitted post-mortem dissection for medical research.

In December, 1925, the opposition flung itself into one final, hopeless debate of Manson's stay of proceedings against the accused, a legality known as *nolle prosequi.* The debate ended, and the house collapsed, with the question by member Tom Uphill as to who the devil was this "Nellie Prosskey" everyone was talking about.

With this fittingly farcical aside, the curtain fell on the Janet Smith case. The murder remained unsolved, but one more person had been shot, posthumously, by the police, in the course of an investigation which, for sheer community effort, for participation by various ethnic groups, illuminates the annals of crime with a light that never was, on sea or land.

The mind rebels at the thought that such a traumatic experience could have had no influence for the better on the city. It seems possible that some whites were shocked into a realization that their Chinese fellow citizens were something more than mere chattels, and that British justice meant something more than justice for the British. As for the Chinese, it seems likely that they absorbed a lesson in the desirability of learning to speak English, if only to improve their chances of getting a fair hearing in a court of law. Racial prejudice they could not expect to die, but it was at least a slightly chastened Vancouver that patronized the little neighborhood greengrocer whose shop could always be depended on to be open, and that bought fruit and vegetables brought to the back door by the indefatigable driver of the Model T Ford truck with the funny name (Lee Chew Fat, Wong Wing Bong) painted on the black van. Although it may never be known why Janet Smith died, she did not die entirely in vain.

In 1925 the municipality of Point Grey and the city of Vancouver were being drawn together not only by their sharing an acquired taste in law enforcement but also by the physical means of transportation. In a booklet published that year by the B.C. Electric Railway Company, *Twenty-nine Years of Public Service,* the company preened itself on having forty streetcar lines and four interurban lines serving a territory of 1,500 square miles, a figure comparable to the area of Luxembourg. The 408 streetcars, the interurbans, and the motor buses (the first of which had appeared on the Grandview route in 1923) were conveyance to most of the population of the Lower Mainland. The company also operated two gas plants and 256.1 miles of gas mains radiating from the gas storage tanks beside the Georgia Street viaduct, expansible silos complementing both the tidal flow and the panoply of smells of nearby False Creek. The patchwork of communities on the ridges between the Fraser and the inlet was now firmly laced together by single-track lines, on whose sidings one streetcar waited, engine thrumming impatiently, till its opposite number arrived and the motormen exchanged a block of wood in an occult rite whose meaning was lost on nonetheless enraptured children. Just as little boys of a later generation were to play spaceman with make-believe lunar modules, those of the twenties sat at their bedroom window on whose sill was affixed a stove grater for power and a hairbrush for brakes, and before which stretched an imaginary line of streetcar tracks on which no speed was impossible.

The story is told that in the early days of the Fairview line, when there were few automobiles and the streetcars stopped running at midnight, a doctor who lived near the carbarn was authorized, in the event of an emergency, wee-hours call, to requisition a streetcar and drive as close as possible to the address of the afflicted, taking the brass driving handle into the house with him to forestall joy riders. By 1925, however, the automobile had extended its functions well beyond medical crises. In that year the highway up Grouse Mountain was completed, the city paying the bill for this as well as for the chalet at the summit. Not the least spectacular part of the mountain drive was the ascent of the heat gauge on the radiator, and happiness was driving one's Ford, Chevrolet or Essex to the top without having to stop and release a geyser of steam from the shuddering blowhole.

The entire expedition was facilitated by the opening, on November 7, 1925, of the Second Narrows Bridge. Although the motorist shared the bridge with the railway and a lift span that could upset the schedule of an outing, this first solid traverse between the two shores of the inlet was hailed as a giant step in bringing Mohammed to the mountain.

The water that was borne across the inlet in the reverse direction was the subject of the setting up in the same year of the Metropolitan Water Board. The city would share the abundance of water with the surrounding municipalities of Point Grey, South Vancouver and Burnaby. One of the architects of this plan was Louis D. Taylor, who had come a long way since he wandered into town hungry and workless. L.D. was now in this third term as mayor of Vancouver, the two previous terms having been 1910–11 and 1915. A small, Chaplinesque figure with birdlike features unenhanced by circular granny glasses, wispy mustache and stubbly chin, L.D. looked like a country doctor who had mislaid his Hippocratic oath. In the archives are two red ties and an unsmoked cigar—his trademarks. Taylor's background suited him perfectly for the role of champion of the underdog, which was how Vancouver saw itself in the battle against the financial moguls of the East. With Harry Stevens, L.D. had fought for diversion of the grain trade through Vancouver, and he was to be the one who, during the Depression, pushed doggedly for a bridge across the First Narrows, against the opposition of the C.P.R. which did not relish the opening up of prime real estate in competition with its Shaughnessy Heights. Taylor also twisted the almost nerveless arm of the Canadian National Railways to make it fulfill its promise to build a major hotel in Vancouver.

L.D. was able to sustain these initiatives because the citizens of Vancouver elected him mayor 1925–26, 1927–28 and 1931–34, which with his earlier terms gave him the record eleven years as chief magistrate. Infinitely gregarious, he was the ideal mayor for the Vancouver of the late twenties, the counterpart of Jimmy Walker, New York's jaunty mayor. His popularity with the "little man" was merely strengthened by his once being almost evicted from office because he failed to fulfill the property requirement. Taylor's property consisted of a lot (No. 191) in Hastings Townsite that one of his foes found to be encumbered. The vacant lot was for many years the city's most distinguished piece of scrub land, particularly when, in 1934, Taylor built a $400 garage on the property to bring the assessed value over the $1,000 minimum for mayoralty candidates. Taylor had no car to put into the garage.

That many other citizens did have cars, and that Vancouver's busy streets were becoming even busier, was proved in 1927 when the hand-operated Stop-and-Go signs were replaced by the first controlled traffic lights. The city was approaching the crest of the greatest economic boom it had ever known. Smokestacks belched smoke from dozens of factories. Because the waterfront land had become too valuable for such a sprawling plant, in 1928 the Hastings Mill was consigned to be dismantled, despite its thousand employees and the annual payroll of two million dollars. The Vancouver Harbour Board bought the land and leased it to a variety of companies, the old mill that had nurtured the city being commemorated much later (1966) with a granite sculpture to mark the site.

To increase the amount of storage ground for the various sawmills, in 1928 three log barges and a floating grain elevator were towed to the North Arm of the Fraser and sunk to form a breakwater for the booms of logs. The jetty was later extended, but the name Wreck Beach clung to that part of Point Grey facing the open gulf, a quiet refuge for the students whose university bordered the cliff above.

Appeals in the legislature to preserve Point Grey and South Vancouver as separate communities were drowned out by the hammering together of new houses that kept pace with the raveling tram lines. In 1929 the two municipalities were amalgamated with Vancouver, forty-four square miles of city that licked its chops and looked around for more.

During the first few months of 1929 the employment index rose to 111.5, and Vancouver banks cleared nearly three billion dollars. Sales of the latest gadgetry, from radios to powerboats, soared to the special heights where only credit buying could breathe. Bursting its administrative britches, city council moved out of the old market building into "temporary" quarters in the Holden Building at 16 East Hastings, to remain there for the last seven years of the twenty-year wrangle about location of a new, permanent city hall.

In that wonderful, gluttonous twelvemonth of 1929, Vancouver had eighty-three millionaires, of whom not one, as Premier Duff Patullo remarked, had been known to give a cent to the university or any other community endeavor. Vancouver was a boorishly masculine city. The excess of male population, according to the *Canada Year Book* of 1927–28, was the greatest of any major city in Canada: 113.17 males per 100 females, as compared with Montreal's 94.75, Toronto's 92.62. The pervasive feeling that the Terminal City was muscled to put the effeminate East in her place was not without biological basis.

The gentler arts, performances not listed at the stock exchange, had run into heavy weather. Although the Vancouver Symphony Orchestra had been founded in 1919, its concerts were as sparsely attended as those of the artists who came to the Orpheum Theatre, as the Vancouver Opera House had become known. Impresario Lily Laverock had to sandwich Fritz Kreisler and Dame Nellie Melba between the dog act that concluded the matinee show and the soft-shoe dancer who opened the evening bill.

Vaudeville reigned at the box office. In November, 1927, the New Orpheum theater opened on Granville Street, stealing the name of its stately predecessor as well as its audiences, with programs advertised as "Ken Murray, with his big revue, and he is what is known in theatrical argot as a 'riot,' also a 'sensation,' likewise a 'find.' John Tiller's Eight 'Cocktail Girls,' who have been featured in many Broadway musical comedies, will be conspicuous in a series of pictorial dance divertissements." The New Orpheum typified the shift to Granville Street of Vancouver's popular entertainment, including cinemas, from Hastings Street where the Pantages theater had incubated vaudeville that became cock of the walk uptown, with the big-time Orpheum circuit. As for "Thespia's Temple," as the old Opera House was derisively called, it was entering the Dark Ages of legitimate theater in Vancouver that were to last, except for the dauntless though amateur Little Theatre, for more than a quarter-century.

This is not to say that Vancouver had deserted the Muses entirely. On August 25, 1928, in Stanley Park a statue was unveiled to honor the city's most revered poet: Robert Burns. Neither Pauline Johnson nor any subsequent local poet has come close to matching the adulation lavished on the Scots bard. The annual Burns' Night, on his birthday, was in that year exceeded for enthusiasm by the ceremony in the Park whose guest of honor was the British Labour Party leader, Ramsay Macdonald, and whose proceedings were published in a stoutly bound volume titled *Vancouver's Tribute to Burns.* The book modestly admits that it "fails to convey the remarkable enthusiasm that permeated the whole assembly, the fervour that characterized the singing of 'Old Hundred' and 'O Canada,' and the tense emotional thrill that passed through the assemblage when the cord was pulled and the figure of the Poet stood revealed in all its sublime dignity and simplicity." Also on the program were the "Address to a Haggis" and other oratory of an amount to test the sturdiness of pioneer stock, as well as the band of the Seaforth Highlanders. No domestic poet has created the kind of lyricism that can withstand accompaniment by the bagpipe.

Manly pastimes of the athletic type were equally vigorous in the late twenties. The tradition of a swim at English Bay on New Year's Day began during 1927–28, a form of mass dementia that later became known as the Polar Bear Club and that demonstrated the city's penchant for masochism as an outdoors activity long before the B. C. Lions football team arrived on the scene. The Coal Harbour side of the Park reverberated with the bloodythirsty roars emanating from the Denman Arena on Georgia Street, a ten-thousand-seat monster of a *palais de glace*, built by Frank Patrick of the Patrick brothers of hockey fame, and the second of the world's first two artificial ice arenas. The city's greatest moment of triumph came, however, at the 1928 Olympic Games at Amsterdam when Vancouver's Percy Williams won both the 100-meter and the 200-meter sprints. The city had proved that it could knock down anybody, on ice, or failing that could outrun him.

Perhaps it was an omen, a warning against excess of enthusiasm: in 1928, in the course of lending his presence to the inauguration of the B.C. Airways passenger service, Mayor Taylor stepped from the trimotor monoplane to shake hands with the welcoming party and was struck by a propeller that very nearly lopped off the back of his head. The mayor came close to dying. A year later, well into his sixties, he almost drowned on a five-week canoe trip of discovery up the Peace River with two cronies. The canoe was caught in an eddy and swept toward wild water, Taylor saving himself by a last-minute grab at overhanging branches.

L.D. used the evidence of his durability in the mayoralty campaign of 1928, but his readiness to shake hands with anybody had jeopardized his reputation as well as his health. He had become associated, in the public mind, with unsavory characters attracted to Vancouver by its homespun greed. The city was in the throes of one of its periodic cravings for reform. The clean broom that swept

Taylor out of office was W. H. Malkin, who was backed by the Christian Vigilance League. "New Town, Not Blue Town" was Malkin's campaign slogan, and his election in October, 1928, displayed a characteristic split of votes according to the geographical and economic partitioning—the East End voting solidly Taylor, the more affluent West End, Shaughnessy and Kitsilano backing Malkin. Upon the city's amalgamation with South Vancouver and Point Grey the following year, Malkin became the first mayor of the greater Vancouver. Somewhat contritely, the big city raised a gift of $5,000 for loser L.D. to enjoy a trip around the world.

Vancouver could afford to be generous to its checkered past. In its Sunday supplement of January 5, 1929, the *Province* sampled the city's assets: 42 banks and 256 manufacturers, 16 palmists (soon to suffer the wrong kind of handout) and 10 private detective agencies, 634 apartment houses, 245 lawyers, 232 practicing physicians, 36 chiropractors, 8 chiropodists, 41 master plumbers, 2,949 licensed dogs and an unknown number of vagrants, canine or otherwise. Six months later the newspaper noted a decline in churchgoing, blaming the radio and the automobile for the defection from Sunday observance compared to the time "when the downtown churches were so popular that it was a valuable asset to know an usher or a side-man who would let you in five minutes before the evening service started." The last-minute repentance that Malkin represented was both too little and too late. From the direction of New York City came the rumblings, the shaking of the earth whose local epicenter was at Pender and Howe—the Stock Exchange Building.

CHAPTER 12 1929–1939

Mecca for the Mendicant

The Crash, and the bum defined • Mighty Mouth McGeer to the rescue • The blow of the abdication of Edward VIII • Tin-canners and the Post Office riot • Pier D in flames, smoke over Europe

THE seismic tremor from the crash on Wall Street, in October, 1929, hit Vancouver almost at once. The first local industry to succumb to the economic quake was the building industry, which had extended itself to using 210,000,000 feet of lumber a year. The lumber industry, on which one Vancouver breadwinner in every half-dozen depended more or less directly for his livelihood, fell apart from woods to wharf. At the same time a world that could hardly afford to buy bread lost its taste for salmon, and the Vancouver offices of the canneries dismissed staff who joined the fishermen on the sullen gray streets. Shipments of grain from the prairies to coastal elevators tumbled by 17,500,000 bushels in a single year, and from the nearer hinterland that had funneled into Vancouver the products of mine and orchard came instead men out of work and mean of temper. "Relief" became the operative word in Vancouver, and was to remain so for almost a decade.

The Communists were quick to exploit the occupants of the bread lines outside the city relief office. On December 17, 1929, the office was stormed by workless men, and the following day several hundred unemployed paraded through the city, frightening nervous authorities into banning further parades and arresting two leaders of the unemployed as Red agitators. By January, 1930, the number of workless had increased threefold, with police arrests increasingly common when mass meetings were broken up on the Powell Street Grounds, a square of mud as desolate as men's hopes. The situation was not improved by the discovery that the chief city relief officer had accepted a rake-off on distribution of meal tickets. Rumors of the "Red army" taking over the city kept citizens at home by their firesides, which as often as not were the only warm places in the house.

Fuel or no fuel, Vancouver was still a warmer place to be than elsewhere in Canada. Every freight train from the East brought its shipment of human misery, more goods riding below the cars than in them, men "riding the rods," sometimes as many as 250 on a single train. By the autumn of 1930 Vancouver had 7,000 men on relief, with more arriving daily. One bread line queued outside the First United Church contained 1,252 individuals, while on False Creek and beneath the Georgia Street viaduct hobo jungles multiplied. "Shantytown" was the name given to the motley collection of shelters that began at Main Street and spread along the flats of the creek—sheets of tin, old boards, boxes, anything that kept a man dry if not warm. The rain jungle had been succeeded by the poverty jungle, whose fauna were mostly out-of-work loggers and fishermen who beachcombed the creek for firewood. Miserable though its conditions were, Shantytown was racially exclusive: no Chinese were allowed on the forlorn premises.

The residents were, however, unable to keep out the Vancouver health officer, whose duty it became to inspect the jungles for signs that the lack of sanitation posed a threat to the city's reputation for salubrity. As for damage to the spirit, the city was kept fully informed by the voice of its conscience incarnate, the Reverend Andrew Roddan, the fiery minister of the First United Church. With his church located in the midst of the tympanist section of empty bellies, and its door the head of the longest bread line in the city, Roddan had the credentials to chastise the more favored residents. His radio broadcasts, voiced with a Scots accent that shook every tube in its socket, became a Sunday scourge that gratified thousands of listeners. Honest burghers who had nothing but sympathy to offer to the indigent found that the best they could do was submit to the verbal flagellation delivered by the minister's tongue in the comfort of their own homes.

Roddan also published little books on the subject of the workless. He expatiated on the three classes of homeless men, who had been classified by St. John Tucker, former president of the Hobo College in Chicago: "A hobo is a migratory worker; a tramp is a migratory non-worker; a bum is a stationary non-worker." The hobo, though he rode the rods like other jobless, was often a hard worker, a pick and shovel man who lived in "Hobohemia" and was the real class among the impecunious. Commonly a remittance man or recent immigrant to Canada, he was too ashamed to write home for financial help. Many an old-country family thought that a son had been devoured by wild animals, when in fact he had fallen victim to the ubiquitous wolf at the door. He might also have fallen afoul of the "wolf" in the sense used in the jungles to describe an older man who wormed his way into the good graces of a youth and kept him for his own unlawful pursuits, ready to brawl with anyone that challenged his "ownership" of the unfortunate lad.

In his *Canada's Untouchables* Roddan listed no fewer than forty-seven of these highly specialized non-occupations. Everybody knew that the difference between a moocher and a panhandler was that the moocher went to the back door while the panhandler went to the front. More esoteric, except that every category was well represented on the streets and in the jungles that made Vancouver Canada's capital of the sans-culottes:

pillinger—solicits alms at stores, offices and homes
flopper—squats on side walk in business thoroughfares
stiffy—simulates paralysis
dummy—pretends to be deaf and dumb
wangy—disguises begging by selling shoelaces
stickers—disguises begging by selling court-plaster
timbers—disguises begging by selling lead pencils
sticks—train rider who has lost a leg
peg—train rider who has lost a foot
fingy or fingers—train rider who has lost one or more fingers
blinky—train rider who has lost one or both eyes
wingy—train rider who has lost one or both arms
mitts—train rider who had lost one or both hands
straight crip—actually crippled or otherwise afflicted
pokey stiff—subsisting on handouts solely

proper stiff—considers manual toil the acme of disgrace
bundle stiff—carries bedding
stew bum—hobo with cooking utensils
fuzzy tail—dregs of vagrantdom
grease tail, jungle buzzard—lower dregs
shine—colored vagabond
gay cat—employed as scout by criminal tramp
dino or dynamite—sponges food from fellow hobos
yegg—roving desperado
gun moll—a dangerous woman tramp
hay boy—a female stew bum
jocker—teaches minors to beg and steal
punk—boy discarded by a jocker

Most of the lingo, of which this is only a sampling, did not survive the conditions that gave painful birth to it. Equally mortal was the verse that poverty, like scenic grandeur, sex and prolonged imprisonment, seems to engender in men's souls. The lubricant for inspiration was canned heat, the drifter's sole escape from his circumstances. He spread it on bread and ate it as a sandwich. "It is cheap," wrote Roddan, "easy of access, gives a real kick, and makes a good finish when it kills them off."

Those workless who sought relief more militantly grouped for meetings almost as particularized as the beggars, meetings of jobless single men, of jobless girls, of jobless farmers, of jobless loggers, even of jobless jobless (unemployed who had never been employed). Instead of wealthy world travelers aboard the *Empress*es, a typical ship departure was that of a delegation of jobless headed for Victoria and a protest demonstration in front of the legislature. "Follow the birds," the traditional invitation to the capital, took on a strong connotation of vulture.

Free entertainment such as watching the ships come and go had much appeal for Vancouver citizens during these years of Depression. One such diversion relieving the gloom of the summer of 1930 was a sail past the old Hastings Mill store. At the last minute this oldest survivor of the Fire of '86 was rescued from the wrecking gang demolishing the mill. The Native Daughters of British Columbia raised both the funds and the energy to transport the wooden building to its last home, a journey described by the Daughters' Past Grand Factor, D. O. Reed Palmer:

> It was on July 28th, 1930, that Vancouver's oldest establishment—plainly, at that time, showing the passage of years—was hoisted aboard a large scow, and towed some five miles from Burrard Inlet, through Lions Gate and across English Bay to its new location. Brockton Point was crowded with interested spectators, and indeed it was a sight of tremendous historic value to citizens of Vancouver to see one of the first concerted efforts of its people gaily floating over the water, escorted by the Harbor Board yacht, *Fespa,* and other flotilla, while overhead through the clear blue of a summer day whirred and darted an aeroplane. Thus with all honor and ceremony did Vancouver's oldest pioneer go to its last resting place.

After all the thousands of feet of timber that were felled at Jerry's Cove and hauled to the mill on the inlet, the store was a shipment of prize timber in the opposite direction, to the grassy esplanade known as Pioneer Park. There the spruced-up store became a museum, a simple monument to the indestructibility of Commerce.

The next spring, on April 17, 1931, the city awaited another water-borne bit of free show, in the arrival of the king of Siam, Prajadhipoe, aboard the *Empress of Japan.* The king was the first ruling monarch of the Orient to visit Canada, and the city went to some trouble to ensure that the welcome would be more cordial than that accorded some of the previous arrivals from Asia. Whether or not His Majesty had been informed of the riots and other unrest being generated by the unemployed on Vancouver streets, he declined to leave the ship during the whole day that it was in port. Pleading a bronchial ailment, he was unable even to greet Louis D. Taylor, who had just been elected for his fifth term as mayor and was splendidly turned out to present the city's greetings to the monarch. L.D. was met instead by the king's father-in-law. As a final blow to Vancouver's self-esteem, the king and his retinue went straight from the ship to the train for New York.

Despite these slings and arrows of outrageous foreigners, Vancouver rode little waves of optimism such as that accompanying the opening, in 1931, of Sea Island Airport, and the construction of the Burrard Bridge across False Creek, a decorative span faintly redolent of the Tower Bridge, with coach-lamp pillars, and a center section that not only did not need to be opened to allow lowly tugs to pass beneath but also bore the engraving of the city's thoroughly belted coat-of-arms. By 1931, too, the city had seven grain elevators, which in the following year helped to set a new record for grain shipment from the port: more than 100 millon bushels. Lumber, copper, lead, zinc, paper, pulp, apples, salt and canned fish moved out with irregular activity that became somewhat better sustained by the Ottawa agreements of 1932, which gave B.C. products such as lumber, fruit and fish a preference in the British markets. During the same period U.S. monetary policy spurred the mining of gold and silver, producing a mini-boom in the Bridge River area and a spin-off of benefit to its supply center on the coast.

These sporadic gains did not begin, however, to offset the number of jobless continuing to swell the city's population—by 1931, one-tenth of it on relief—and the cost of supporting these unemployed, which for the same year amounted to $1.3 million. The setting up of relief camps in remote parts of the province, by the federal government, proved a very temporary easing of the pressure on the city's resources. During the winter of 1931–32 men embittered by conditions in the work camps converged on Vancouver streets to stage hunger marches that were broken up by the police. The siren call of socialism became clearly audible not only to the relief-campers but also to a considerable section of the public that was managing to make ends, however tattered, meet. The wintry months in Vancouver homes drew warmth from the impassioned radio oratory of Dr. Lyle Telford, local adherent of the newly formed Cooperative Commonwealth Federation. The C.C.F. contested the provincial election of 1933, and displaced the Conservatives as Opposition. Three seats, won by Ernest E. Winch, a veteran of the 1918 general strike, his son Harold Winch, and Mrs. Dorothy Steeves, were Vancouver ridings that accounted for an appreciable proportion of the 31 per cent of the total votes that had gone pink. Politically, the East End of the city was now closer to Moscow than to Point Grey.

The city as a whole, however, found another champion to joust with the times. His name was Gerald Grattan McGeer. He was the same Gerry McGeer who, in the nineties, with his three brothers and five sisters helped to deliver milk and cream before school, from his father's dairy farm on the Fairview outskirts of town. From his Irish immigrant father, who brought the family from Winnipeg when the boy was two, Gerry inherited both natural eloquence and a genial bellicosity. Father James McGeer spelled off his work at the milking stool by writing poems for elite literary publications in Britain. Aspiration flowed like butterfat in the family, and no youngster was better equipped to live the Horatio Alger story.

Gerry McGeer had quit school to apprentice as an iron molder at fourteen, working for Letson, Burpee & Co. for five years with a beginning wage of twenty-five cents a day, for a ten-hour day. He became an active unionist for the trade, and carried his union card to the day of his death. Having helped to organize a number of strikes, he observed that a lawyer earned as much in five minutes as an iron molder did in two days. He went out for law. A voracious reader, he deliberately patterned himself after Winston Churchill, as well as being a disciple of Lincoln, whose rise to power his own career resembled in miniature. Admitted to the bar of British Columbia in 1915, he entered partnership with his brother James and Gordon Wismer, later an attorney general of the province. McGeer was elected to the provincial house as Liberal member for Richmond, in 1916, then went off to war. During the twenties he was one of several ambitious lawyers who rode the freight rate issue as a high road to political popularity. In 1922 the brightness of his escutcheon was tarnished slightly by his submitting a bill of $77,000 for his legal services to the government as slayer of eastern dragons.

For the next ten years Gerry wielded a shorter sword as one of the back-room boys of the Liberal party. But being a gray eminence did not suit his coloration, which was ruddy and choleric. His ties with the city whose coeval he was became even stronger after his marriage to one of the Spencer girls. With Chris, owner of the big department store, as his father-in-law, Gerry could afford to tilt at windmills at the municipal level. He entered the lists of the 1934 mayoralty contest with the established renown of a crusader for lower freight rates, "the man who flattened the Rockies." The campaign afforded him full and glorious opportunity to spread the plumage of oration, the declamatory panache that caused one political foe to describe him as "intoxicated by the exuberance of his own verbosity," and another, more bluntly, to diagnose "inflammation of the vowels."

Vancouver was, however, in no position to look any gift, of the gab or otherwise, in the mouth. The pug-faced battler in the loud check suit may have smacked of Boston beans, but the city's stomach was growling for action. When he rose to attack the eastern brokers who were his favorite quarry, verbiage was no object. The Bank of Vancouver, which had gone into liquidation in 1915, had in 1934 finally wound up its shrouds and was being officially buried. Gerry stood over the corpse like Anthony avenging the dead Caesar, inviting the populace to dip its cloth in the red ink and wreak what justice demanded of the brutal countinghouses of the East.

The people responded by voting Gerry the biggest majority—34,521 votes—in the city's history. His opponent, L. D. Taylor, veteran though he was of garrulity warfare, was utterly routed, his charisma lying in ruins, his political career dead. McGeer had done for Taylor what Jimmy McLarnin, the former Vancouver newsboy, had done the year before in knocking out Young Corbett in the first round to win the world welterweight crown.

McGeer's spectacular performance as mayor of Vancouver began with his inaugural speech, described as the most devastating in the history of civic elocution. The new mayor's demand for provincial legislation reducing the city's debt by 50 per cent was merely one of the bombshells hurled at higher levels of government. To the extent that the Depression was a state of mind he launched against it projects none the less audacious for being equally fanciful. The province in general, and Vancouver in particular, were still crushed by the impact of the Kidd Report, the provincial government inquiry into finances, which in 1932 recommended economies that included, for instance, the suggestion that the University of British Columbia be closed down. Yet McGeer endorsed plans for a new and lavish City Hall. With the hay grown high on the Main Mall of the university for lack of funds for maintenance, and enrollment down to 1,606, the lowest figure of the thirties, the mayor in 1934 embroidered on preparations for the biggest party in Vancouver's history—the Golden Jubilee in 1936. McGeer's philosophy about the unemployed seemed to be that if people had no home but the streets they might as well be dancing in them. This kind of buoyancy sickened as many as it sustained. Vancouver people soon became split into those who adored "the Great Maverick" and those who muttered of jackass. "McGeer's Folly" became a stock name tagged on so many of the mayor's projects that it lost its value for inventory.

An occasion for impetuous action that many of his fellow citizens considered excessive was provided in 1935, when the almost-bankrupt city was invaded by 1,700 men from relief camps. One day in April these recipients of the twenty-cents-a-day dole handed out by the federal government organized a march which took them through

37. Lions Gate Bridge, viewed from Stanley Park toward North Shore mountains

38. Nitobe Memorial Gardens located on the campus of the University of British Columbia. The gardens consist of a rock garden and a landscape tea garden

39. Vancouver West End across Lost Lagoon

40. Lost Lagoon and the harbor

41. S.S. *President Roosevelt* on her inaugural visit to Vancouver, June 15, 1969

42. Kitsilano Beach, five minutes from City Centre, is only one of the many fine beaches in Vancouver
(Photo by William Bros. Photographers, Ltd.)

43. Skana, Stanley Park Aquarium's acrobatic killer whale

44. Flea Market, New Gastown

45. The Planetarium, with (right) the Crab Sculpture

46. Point Grey Campus of the University of British Columbia, English Bay, Stanley Park and downtown Vancouver in background.
(Photo by George Allen Aerial Photos, Ltd.)

47. Project 200 development of Vancouver waterfront

the warehouses of grocery wholesalers, after which they paraded up and down the aisles of the Hudson's Bay Company department store. When police arrived, the demonstrators indicated their displeasure by smashing showcases and scattering merchandise. Driven from the store, the men marched to Victory Square, where they chose a delegation to put their complaints to the mayor. McGeer was in no frame of mind to be sympathetic, as several policemen had been injured and he was convinced that Vancouver was the center of a plot to exploit the workless for revolutionary purposes. He had in fact threatened to name Brigadier Odlum as head of the "Citizens' Army" to maintain law and order. McGeer not only ordered the arrest of several of the delegation as they retreated from City Hall, but he seized upon the police chief's suggestion that he read the Riot Act. By this time the riot was over, and it was to men with all passion spent that McGeer addressed himself, in Victory Square, with the greeting: "Good morning, boys. You asked for it." The assembled jobless listened politely while McGeer advised them that their sovereign lord the king demanded their immediate dispersal upon pain of life imprisonment. They then marched off in orderly fashion, singing "The Red Flag." But the reading of the Riot Act, for the second time in the city's history, elicited a good deal of publicity in other parts of North America, and many Vancouver people blamed McGeer for overreacting.

Badgered by recurrent battles between the workless and police, by wildcat strikes and hunger marches, McGeer despaired of getting help from Ottawa and set about a program of public works, of which the new City Hall and the new Hotel Vancouver would be two, requiring financial assistance from outside sources that lay misted in vales of doubt. He also proposed that the four western provinces establish their own monetary systems, and in the course of a 1935 visit to Ottawa he threatened to throw the sheriff of Vancouver into the bay.

In the circumstances, namely straitened, the city might have been excused for observing its fiftieth birthday as modestly as possible. Gerry had no intention of excusing it. Instead he appalled taxpayers by endorsing a Golden Jubilee celebration that included the building of the Jubilee Fountain in Lost Lagoon and a party invitation to the Lord Mayor of London. The published details of the fountain, an elaborate, electrically programmed *jeu d'eaux* with rhapsodic changes of colored lights, caused mass boggling in Vancouver homes.

The watchdogs of the civic purse howled that the city could not afford to operate the fountain, let alone build it. Particularly incensed were the Native Daughters, who saw the fountain as desecration of the waters paddled by Pauline Johnson's canoe.

Yet, with the giddiness of people who know they are purchasing something wildly beyond their means, Vancouver bought Gerry's fountain. It also sang the Jubilee song, specially composed for the event. It conscientiously studied the plans, diagramed in the press, for spontaneous revelry in the streets, the same Granville and Hastings streets along which fifteen weighing machines were placed in doorways, a penny allowing members of a whole family to weigh themselves provided the heavier persons stood on the machine first. Above all, Vancouver basked in the expectation of receiving the Lord Mayor of London, once assured that the Lord Mayor would not be sending his father-in-law in his place.

To set the tone for the visit, Gerry dug out the mayor's official chain of office, formidable accouterment that had lain for sixteen years in a jeweler's vault, waiting for a paunch worthy of its heroic proportions. McGeer tried it on with his King's Counsel robes, but judged the garment inadequate and paid out of his own pocket $550 for a flowing black gown trimmed in purple and gold, together with a cocked hat, the total effect being described as "like a New York cop masquerading in the Pope's cassock."

To make it a real contest of ostentation, the Lord Mayor arrived with his entire retinue—the lord sheriff, the mace bearer, the sword bearer and the City marshal. In a ceremony so dazzling that it was optically safe to observe it only through a piece of exposed film, the Lord Mayor presented Gerry with a replica of the London mace. McGeer exhibited more pleasure at the gift than was indicated by his later comment ("Now what in Sam Hill would I do with a mace?")—but doubtless recognized a mace as a shillelagh that had been to college.

Other events of Vancouver's Golden Jubilee produced an equally unexpected aptitude for carnival. With the exception of one bad moment when the Jubilee Fountain was turned on, startling onlookers by sucking up small fish and spewing them into the lagoon, the Jubilee was a success, a bright interval in the gloom of the Depression, and its value as mental therapy almost justified the bill for expenses after the Lord Mayor departed with his entourage.

In 1936 two cities of the British Empire celebrated their golden anniversaries, the other being Johannesburg, South Africa. Johannesburg was a city built on gold, Vancouver a city built on water—as foundation less substantial, as resource more renewable. Vancouver's prosperity has risen and fallen with the Plimsoll lines of the ships loading in the harbor. The port in 1936 being desultory, the city seized on minor triumphs such as the return from abroad in October of the Kitsilano Boys' Band, a remarkable group of young musicians who, under the direction of Arthur Delamont, toured Europe to critical acclaim. The returning band was met by welcoming bands, including the Firemen's Band, and by a mayor who was also very strong in the brass section.

Two months later, however, the people of Vancouver were struck glum by the abdication crisis, the unbelievable choice by Edward VIII of "the woman I love," Mrs. Wallis Simpson, over the throne of the Commonwealth. To the thousands of Britons making up the preponderance of Vancouver's population the effect was traumatic. Nothing that was happening in Hitler's Germany or Mussolini's Italy stirred as much local hostility as the divorced American. To be part of an outpost of the Empire on which the sun never set seemed a sadly diminished role, second-best to a Yankee grittily referred to as "that woman." Even Gerry McGeer's formally unlocking the massive doors of the new City Hall, on December 4, could not compensate for the fact that somewhere six thousand miles away the doors had closed on the privilege of being a servant of the Crown.

Physically as well as mentally Vancouver was going through a period of adjustment. The new City Hall had been built, after passionate opposition to the selected site, at 12th Avenue and Cambie Street, the old Strathcona Park. Since 1912, when council began to talk about a new City Hall and approved a $750,000 plebiscite for a building on the Central School grounds (later the Vancouver Vocational Institute) at Pender and Cambie, the variety of sites ardently espoused by various factions had grown to include Thornton Park (opposite the C.N.R. depot on Main Street), Burrard Street, the Holden Building and Strathcona Park, not to mention buying the Marine Building. Alderman J. J. McRae clung tenaciously, a "voice in the wilderness," to the Strathcona site, and a three-member commission appointed by Mayor McGeer agreed that the wilderness was no longer all that wild, overruling those who had insisted that the city's head should be somewhere near its heart.

The fact was that in 1937 the geographical center of the city was shifting south and west. While the English Bay pier, constructed thirty years earlier, was being written off as nearing the end of its useful life, the opening of the Dunbar Heights subdivision, and the outspread of modest cottages from the 10th Avenue streetcar line, meant that more and more residents were adopting Spanish Banks, west of Jericho, for their promenading. Already the swank district of Shaughnessy was feeling its age, a severe blow to its prestige being an order from the fire department requiring the installation of fire escapes and fire gongs in mansions that had declined to boardinghouses.

Downtown the appearance of neon signs was transforming "Theatre Row," the stretch of movie theaters that began with the Colonial at Dunsmuir and ran up Granville to the Dominion, the Strand, opposite the Bay, claiming the carriage trade. "Town" was now something one went into, to work, to shop, to be entertained. On March 8, 1937, the city council banned all-day parking downtown, and the era of automotive restlessness began.

This was the era, too, of miniature golf, a means of obtaining the paranoia of the larger course without having to pay the green fees and with less chance of losing the ball. At the Georgia Auditorium another form of agony popular with the impoverished young was marathon dancing, couples staggering about for days in extreme stages of exhaustion in their effort to win cash prizes. A less debilitating spectator sport favored in Vancouver of the mid-thirties was the six-day bicycle race, particularly as the fans could admire the Peden brothers, Torchy and younger brother Doug, champions of the U.S. circuit and undoubtedly the fastest things to come out of Victoria.

Beyond the bright lights, however, lay the streets of ill repute. Main and Pender were the intersection of Sin and Wrong. Young bloods extracted awe from companions by telling that they had ventured, at night, into the alleys of Chinatown—Canton Alley, Shanghai Alley, Hong Kong Alley—each as sinister as imagination chose to make it. Trounce Alley was known to be the refuge of bootleggers, but the name that iced the spine with dread was Hogan's Alley, a cobbled lane east of Main so infamous that it did not have a signpost, in whose shadows huddled shacks whose inhabitants, as every schoolboy knew, combined the more disturbed attributes of Jack the Ripper, Count Dracula and Dr. Fu Manchu. The East Pender area was not improved by the *Province* report, March 5, 1937, of the first case involving marijuana, "which has become such a scourge in the United States," to come to the attention of Vancouver authorities. In the stomach of a man who had died under mysterious circumstances were found traces of hemp, of the cigarettes known to the nether world as Mary Warners.

To smoke even tobacco was, for girls, considered rather daring on the campus of U.B.C., where a new stadium was being built with student money and student labor that included among those wielding shovels a youth named Howie McPhee, who was to become a star sprinter and the greatest all-rounder produced by the province, till his untimely death during World War II. Among the students there was little active concern about the war clouds gathering over Europe. On the downtown street corners newspaper vendors like Newsie Jack —"Prov-ance, Suhn uh-dishun"—sold papers in which occasionally a city son wrote home of his adventures in the Spanish Civil War. Ernest Hemingway's serialized accounts of the struggle were so vivid as to make it seem like remote fiction. And Hitler was a rather comic figure, well suited to the talents of the *Province* humor columnist, Jim Butterfield.

People were listening at their radios—to Fibber McGee and Molly, Amos 'n' Andy, Alexander Woollcott. In 1937 the Canadian Broadcasting Corporation opened its Vancouver station, CRCV, which became CBR, later CBU, while private stations such as CJOR were attracting a talented group of very young performers—Bernard Braden, Fletcher Markle, Alan Young—who were to attain international stardom in the electronic media.

Such ripples of strife as reached Vancouver from the stormy Old World were pleasantly rewarding: Ottawa's increased defense budget made work in the city for improvement of the Jericho air base, for antiaircraft guns and searchlights. In June, 1937, a city factory was awarded a contract to build eleven warplanes, Blackburn Sharks. Japanese freighters loaded scrap iron at inlet docks. The city also welcomed Prince Chichibu, son of Japan's ruler, en route to London bearing gifts for the coronation of George VI. A flotilla of fish boats greeted his ship, and he toured the city through cheering throngs of the children of Japanese residents. The Japanese community was not to have another happy occasion for twenty years. A few months after the royal visit, Alderman Halford Wilson was urging the council to ask the federal government to ban Japanese women from coming to B.C. —"the peaceful invasion"—because of their high birth rate. Few Vancouver people took note that in 1937 for the first time a Japanese,

Suichi Kusaki, had won the governor general's medal as top graduate at U.B.C.

For the moment, however, Vancouver's war was, as usual, with the Chinese rather than the Japanese. While sympathy lay with China in the Sino-Japanese war raging in the Far East, the city was more emotionally involved with the local "Spud War," in which the Chinese truck farmers, the Potato Board and the Vancouver housewife were the combatants, or with the hiring of white waitresses by Chinese cafes. Three Chinese restaurants had their licenses lifted for employing white waitresses, and the new mayor, George C. Miller, was firm in declaring that he would in future close any such cafe. This was the city council's contribution to the campaign of the Chinese Benevolent Association to raise a "foreign legion" to fight the Japanese invading China. The demons of race prejudice that attended the Janet Smith case had not been entirely exorcised.

The city's running war with the Near East (Victoria), and the threat of a taxpayer's strike, subsided under the build-up of excitement about the coronation of George VI. For weeks before the great moment of pageantry, May 15, 1937, other news was crowded from the front pages of Vancouver newspapers. After the blow of Edward's abdication, a massive transfusion of publicity was required to restore color to royalty's image. It worked. Much of the success was due to publication of the first news photos to be flown across the Atlantic, pictures of the ceremonies in the Abbey which, as the *Province* noted proudly, "left London two days ago."

A week after the coronation it was announced that Trans-Canada Airline pilots would be trained at Vancouver Airport. The government-owned airline was preparing to carry airmail. A few days later, the Imperial Conference named Vancouver as Pacific air terminal for flights to Honolulu. The Sea Island base had graduated to an international airport. Adding excitement to Vancouver's emergence into the commercial air age was the first attempt, by a Soviet aircraft, to fly nonstop from Moscow to San Francisco. The plane's flight plan was to bring it over Vancouver, and many Vancouver residents were watching the June sky when word came that the Russians had landed in Vancouver . . . Washington. That the other, smaller, American Vancouver should steal the attention of the world put the city's nose out of joint only briefly. In July the first trans-Canada flight, by a T.C.A. Lockheed monoplane bearing Transport Minister C. D. Howe, landed at the Vancouver Airport, after a "daylight-to-dark" crossing of the country. Almost every subsequent edition of the newspapers reported the opening of a new air route or the crash of aerial pioneers. Vancouver's boosters had talked of trans-Pacific dirigibles, a vision that was abruptly obscured by smoke from the fiery death of the *Hindenburg* at Lakehurst, New Jersey, early in May, 1937.

More domestically, in 1937 the Vancouver stock market, still decidedly fragile from the Crash, took additional lumps with disclosure of the Hedley Mine scandal, a classic demonstration of ore salting. Although the investigation found the exchange itself to be not guilty, the degree of enterprise shown by the crooked promoters hit local brokers like a karate chop. Not to be outdone by private industry, the police station reported the loss of bail money from a room, the key to which was hung on a nail beside the door. Again, it was difficult to establish culpability.

Police morale was not improved by the standing order to arrest "tin-canners," unemployed begging on the streets. The city had set a policy of "no work, no relief," requiring the able-bodied to earn their pittance. As one of the works programs the city was cleaning up the Indian reserve squatters' shacks at Kitsilano and planning improvement of Spanish Banks Beach. When two hundred relief men failed to answer the call to bear shovels, however, the jails filled rapidly with mendicants, and in October Victoria announced that it would open a special prison camp for panhandlers.

For the jobless woman the situation was no better. The city was reputed to be a major recruiting center for white slaves, prairie girls unable to find jobs. Prairie people were invading Vancouver in unusually large numbers as the result of special excursion rates on the railway. On one weekend five trains landed two thousand flatlanders in Vancouver, a rail-borne plague that alarmed the natives.

The one visitor that Vancouver coveted, as he had accepted an invitation to visit Victoria, was Franklin Delano Roosevelt. F.D.R. was an appreciably bigger catch than Harding, but Roosevelt sent his regrets—"I wish I could see Vancouver too"—and the city was left with its memory of an outdoor production in Stanley Park of *Midsummer Night's Dream.*

Although the city did not receive the world's most famous polio victim, it did take delivery, on October 13, 1937, of its first iron lung. Polio was at its peak as the dread of parents. In that same month another threat to life and limb was challenged when the attorney general announced that he was considering the establishment of a speed limit for motor vehicles, in Vancouver and elsewhere on provincial highways. Increased horsepower of the automobile was facilitating and multiplying the number of quite spectacular accidents on Vancouver streets. Collisions were not as notable as grand solo leaps from bridges and the wrapping of cars around telephone poles. Despite the demonstrated need for restraint, Vancouver's motorist clung stubbornly to the British tradition of *laissez aller* like blazes on the public thoroughfare. Nor were tempers assuaged by Victoria's added insult of compulsory driver's tests, and the threat of auto testing as well. Hitlerian curtailment of freedom had spread to the Lower Mainland and the democratic function of the gas pedal.

A more serious limitation was that announced by President Leonard Klinck of U.B.C., in January, 1938, setting enrollment of first-year students at 450 to hold total enrollment to about 2,000. The university had accommodation for 1,500, and the 2,289 students enrolled in 1937 created a bulge in classrooms "unfair to students." In downtown Vancouver business schools were growing too, as parents recognized the critical importance of some kind of training for young people if they were not to join the glut of unskilled labor.

Or to qualify as cannon fodder. The deterioration of hopes for peace in Europe was brought home to Vancouver people by the St. John Ambulance Corps' announcement that training in the use of gas masks would begin as soon as the masks arrived, shipment being delayed by the heavy demand in Britain. Also, in January plans were revealed for the fortification of Point Grey and Stanley Park (at Ferguson's Point), two batteries of six-inch guns at each headland, to guard the entrance to English Bay. In its original assignment as military reserve, Stanley Park was grimly resuming its duties.

To add to the chill of the winter month, a Vancouver man was found to be involved in a plot to blow up a Japanese liner docked in Seattle. The would-be frogman had been paid by San Francisco Chinese to plant a charge of 369 sticks of dynamite against the hull of the ship—a macabre perversion of west coast commerce.

Vancouver people, or at least the young set, tried to drown out these disturbing rumbles of war with the sounds of the big bands. While vaudeville did its soft-shoe dance into the wings of oblivion, with only the Beacon—the old Pantages theatre on Hastings Street —presenting a bill of tired acts, Vancouver's big ballrooms were bouncing. The Commodore on Granville for private galas of debutantes and the university's Greek societies, the Palomar on Burrard Street for the visiting bands of such as Sammy Kaye and Glenn Miller, made dancing a participation play. The popularity of the cabaret was directly related to the custom, born of British Columbia's Neanderthal liquor laws, of smuggling a bottle of liquor into the night club. Since consumption of alcohol in a public place of entertainment was prohibited, the patron put his bottle on the floor under his table so that in the event of a police raid he could disclaim ownership. The cabaret provided the mixer and waiters who were extraordinarily agile in executing the slalom between "crocks" on the floor. The booze-under-the-table custom was one of the local mores which more than any other bemused visitors from lands where beverages were dispersed above floor level. Thanks to a succession of provincial premiers who were either teetotalers or supporters of Queen Victoria's misgivings about leaving the consumption of spirits to the discretion of the natives, Vancouver was to practice this curious ritual for another quarter of a century, before licensing of premises made it unnecessary for a night-club patron to enter exhibiting the false pregnancy of the bottle stashed under the coat.

In 1938 the police intimated that they would wink at drinking in hotel rooms—also a violation of the law—provided the parties were not too numerous or too noisy. All the auspices of the law conduced to consumption of a whole bottle with a minimum of grace and gaiety, and the peace was that of the passed out.

In June, 1938, the city was to get more sobering proof that the veneer of civilization was not too firmly glued. The month before, on May 11, about sixteen hundred unemployed men, whose ranks had been swollen by arrivals from the prairies, organized themselves into compact units, ten men and a leader to each platoon, and marched into occupation of the Post Office, the Art Gallery and the Hotel Georgia. When the city offered to pay five hundred dollars in temporary relief, the group in the Hotel Georgia marched out in orderly fashion, but the men in the other two buildings held out for "money from Ottawa." The "sit-downers," as they came to be known, held concerts and organized sports days in the cavernous halls of the Post Office. They also published *The Sitdowners Gazette*, putting into print their rejection of Premier Patullo's demand that they evacuate the buildings at once.

On June 15 the premier renewed his warning to what he called "the stay-inners," adding that it was useless to send a delegation to Victoria and that it was deplorable that Vancouver people were contributing funds to the cause of lawlessness. He also blamed the single men from the prairies for not staying there and for refusing the offer of free transportation home.

On Sunday morning, June 20, the sit-downers were still in residence when Royal Canadian Mounted Police, on orders from Ottawa, stationed themselves around the Post Office. It was 5 A.M. At the same time the Vancouver police led by Chief Foster arrived in front of the Art Gallery. Both the hour of the dawn attack and the call for surrender had been chosen to discourage a violent response. After giving the men twenty minutes to evacuate the buildings, and allowing an additional ten minutes' grace, each contingent of police fired a tear-gas bomb.

At this point events at the two buildings took different turns. C.C.F. member Harold Winch intervened at the Art Gallery to plead with the men there to leave, which they did without further trouble or bloodshed. At the Post Office, however, resistance was urged by a young radical leader named Steve Brodie. Somebody threw a chair through a window, and quickly every pane of glass on the ground floor was shattered by flying furniture. The RCMP waded into the building, laying about freely with their quirts. They sought out the known ringleaders for special attention, and Brodie's very conspicuous orange sweater became both a rallying point for the embattled incumbents and a primary target for police clubs.

The RCMP had the building cleared in minutes, but the enraged rout poured down Hastings Street smashing windows of Spencer's and Woodward's department stores and doing about $30,000 worth of damage. Because of the early start, there remained plenty of Sabbath for further disturbance. Encouraged by a meeting of C.C.F. leaders who, shortly after noon, denounced the eviction of the sit-downers as "a ghastly, inhuman, brutal course of action," the workless and sympathizers met at 2 P.M. at Powell Street Grounds and marched, two thousand strong, to the police station to demand release of those arrested earlier in the day. They broke some windows before being sedated by promise of a hearing in Victoria. The delegation that proceeded to the capital found the parliament buildings locked.

Vancouver people were incensed at having their safety jeopardized by two higher levels of government, namely Ottawa whose RCMP broke a lot of heads, and Victoria whose policy and premier had emulated the ostrich in face of probable violence. Ten mothers who joined the trek to Victoria on behalf of the bruised and battered were particularly vocal about being received by locked doors. The main consolation was that the Art Gallery, which had opened in 1931, suffered no damage to any of the pictures—art, at that time, being such that it was possible to tell.

At that time, too, there was less understanding of the relationship between civil strife and the long, hot summer. The summer of 1938 was one of the most torrid in the history of the Lower Mainland. Fierce forest fires raged on Vancouver Island, and the overcast of smoke drifting across the gulf to Vancouver was a reminder of that earlier June when the city incinerated itself. Nor was the city to be deprived of an even more comparable spectacle. On July 27 a pillar of black smoke billowed upward from the C.P.R.'s Pier "D" on the waterfront. Connoisseurs of fire-watching agreed that the blaze that swiftly destroyed the million-dollars' worth of pier was vintage holocaust. Not only did it occur in daylight, adding body to the huge crowds that impeded firemen trying to reach the scene, but it consumed property belonging to the C.P.R., making of the bouquet pure delight. Although no lives were lost, several firemen pumping water from a raft under the pier came close enough to tragedy to substantiate the city's renewed demand for a fireboat. The failure of the Harbour Board to provide a fireboat was interpreted by some citizens as indifference on the part of Ottawa as to whether the port facilities were burned out or otherwise. And there was real concern that the next waterfront fire might destroy something belonging to Vancouver.

A few months after the fire Burrard Inlet was again the center of attention with the opening, on November 12, 1938, of the Lions Gate Bridge. Since the start of its construction, the bridge across the First Narrows had splintered public opinion in Vancouver, as the approach causeway through Stanley Park necessitated the felling of trees. Developers who tore down churches met little opposition in Vancouver, but the Park was sanctified ground. It was freely predicted that motorists who used the swath of concrete desecrating the natural forest would bear a curse—a prophecy which proved entirely accurate. The three-lane cut was to be the most unkindest of all, to future commuters caught in traffic backups.

Criticism was, however, largely offset by the prospect of acquiring a suspension bridge billed as the longest in the British Empire. "Painted in International orange and Veridian green," descanted a brochure published by the First Narrows Bridge Company, "nature's own colors, making a perfect setting that nature herself would seem to have designed with cunning eye for this stately creation of human engineering triumph." Also, the developers who built the bridge in order to open up the large tracts of land bought on the North Shore (the British Properties) were at least a change from the C.P.R. The major stockholder was the Guinness family. There was historic continuity in the fact that an alcoholic beverage was extending the purlieus of Gassy Jack's pub crawl.

In December, 1938, the man responsible for keeping alive the memorabilia of Jack Deighton's village, Major J. S. Matthews, took on the Vancouver city council in one of the livelier battles of a long-running war. The major, invariably described as "doughty" by an enraptured press, had been appointed city archivist in June, 1933, in official recognition of the fact that he owned most of the archives. In 1936 Mayor McGeer called the archives "a lot of junk"—junk that was to be supplemented by Gerry's splendid robes of office—and far from being *cordiale* the *entente* between council and the major had been characterized by recurrent closures of the archives, at the major's displeasure, and threats of probes by frustrated aldermen. In every confrontation the mayor's men learned a painful lesson in the tactics of trying to outflank a military man who held the deed to the battlefield. On December 29, 1938, Major Matthews surrendered title to the archives to trustees appointed by the council. The council then discovered that nobody else was willing to act as custodian, and that for want of other accommodation much of the archives resided in the major's basement. It was decided to return the key to Matthews as official custodian, making his *de facto* status entirely *status quo*. It was to remain *status quo* while trustees chosen to outlive the major followed one another to the grave, and twenty years later, at the age of ninety-plus, Major J. S. Matthews was still chamberlain to the treasures of early Vancouver.

As the last full year of peace closed out, Vancouver sought a new broom to be mayor. The city elected its first socialist mayor in Dr. Lyle Telford, said to be one of the city's wealthier residents, who swept into office as a reformer bent on evicting vice. Mayor Telford set the tone for the New Year with his January announcement of a purge of bootleg joints, "vice dens" and other establishments in bad odor. He blamed the beer parlors for nourishing social disease, the Gentlemen section failing to offset the Ladies and Escorts as the trysting place of pickups. In scheduling (on a Friday the thirteenth) the crackdown on bawdy houses, the socialist mayor was not without compassion for the inmates. "I don't want to turn the girls out," he said. "It is not fair to send them to Revelstoke, Calgary, Winnipeg and these other places. It is up to us to do something for them." This threat alone was enough to send many of the girls running for trains and buses.

As usual with Vancouver's periodical grappling with corruption, the mayor's campaign was reduced to an investigation of the police force, which also as usual proved that the police were almost entirely on the side of law and order. The Vancouver policeman's lot has never been an altogether happy one because he has never been able to establish his identity, which lies somewhere between the impassive rectitude of the British bobby and the U.S. sheriff's folksy firepower. This has made the Vancouver policeman emotionally insecure, a condition that successive administrations have read as moral flaccidity, till proven wrong.

More decisive than his trying to make the streets safe for virtue was Mayor Telford's driving the first car through the city's motor vehicle testing station, opened March 6, 1939. Other minor triumphs that helped to salve the city's abraded morale were the air shipment, in April, of daffodils to Ottawa on the newly inaugurated transcontinental service of Trans-Canada Airlines, and the opening of the new Hotel Vancouver. In the new hotel, Vancouver at last had a man-made eminence to complement the Marine Building, the lonely facsimile of New York's Chrysler Building and souvenir of the soaring twenties. Jointly operated by the C.P. and C.N. railways, the massive new hotel occupying a half-block at Georgia and Burrard was of "16th century French design," a press description of the attempt to combine the architecture of a Bourbon king's château with more bedrooms than even François *Premier* could have serviced. Vancouver was properly impressed, nevertheless, by the stately ballrooms and the murals in the lobby depicting scenes of exploration apt to intimidate triflers headed for the elevators.

The hotel had been rushed to completion so that the opening, on May 25, would coincide with the royal visit, the keenly anticipated arrival on May 29 of King George VI and his Elizabeth, still radiant from coronation. In preparation Vancouver had swept its economic mess under the rug, shined its worn shoes and erected a huge floral arch at Hastings and Burrard. "The greatest day in the city's whole history," headlined the *Province*. Especially gratifying was the influx of Americans, filling the hotels, a tonic to the till and a mercy to monarchists. Window space along the parade route sold fast, prices ranging from one to five and ten dollars including refreshments. The one fear possessing the city was that the parade might be assailed by one of the May showers that in Vancouver could resemble a monsoon season. On the Sunday before the morning arrival of the king and queen many people prayed for sunshine, and were astounded to see their prayers answered. The royal party toured the city under smiling skies, and if the cheers were not as vociferous as on earlier royal visits, by the Prince of Wales for instance, it may have been because the Depression had diminished the youthful exuberance of the populace. In any event the people drew sustenance from King George's farewell comment: "I think Vancouver is the place to live." Thereafter, among the citizens of Vancouver, the perspicacity of the monarch was never in question.

The royal pair departed for Victoria with a destroyer escort that included H.M.C.S. *Ottawa.* In September, 1942, the *Ottawa* would be torpedoed, among the lives lost those of six Vancouver men.

CHAPTER 13 1939–1946

Dit, Dit, Dit, Dah

First casualty of World War II: butter • Air-raid precautions • The loss of sawdust • Pearl Harbor, the blackout and the darkness of despair for Vancouver's Japanese • V-E Day Cocktail • The Greenhill Park *explosion • War brides, and Vancouver re-evaluated*

MOST people sensed, if they did not know, that the royal visit had the purpose of strengthening the ties of the British family of nations against the inevitable war looming in Europe. As Hitler's panzer units pushed into Poland, and the world waited for Neville Chamberlain to mobilize his umbrella, the hulk of the old Hotel Vancouver sitting closed and dark seemed to symbolize the end of an era, the assignment to demolition. Word of Britain's declaration of war reached Vancouver on the same Sunday, September 3, 1939, with most people clustered around their home radio sets. Although Canada did not officially declare war till September 10, considerable numbers of Vancouver men had already responded to the call for volunteers, spurred by news of the torpedoing of the British passenger liner *Athenia,* September 4, with 434 Canadians aboard. Within weeks trainees were saying their farewells to relatives in the railway stations, before entraining for the army camp at Vernon; and by December, the first troops from Vancouver were on their way overseas.

After the "phony war" of the first few months, reported with occasional photos of Vancouver soldiers, sailors or airmen missing in action, the new year brought lengthening casualty lists. Promoted to major general, Victor Odlum took the 2nd Canadian Division to Britain, but was shortly transferred to Australia as high commissioner. Vancouver chafed for action. The only noticeable change in the physical appearance of the city lay in the harbor, where canvas-hidden sections of the stern or bow of merchantmen marked the addition of cannon or antiaircraft guns. The inner man was, however, beginning to register some of the ravages of war. In 1939 butter had been in such abundance that the city gave it away to the needy, but in 1940 the supply shrank to the dimension of a butter famine. Stomachs were also unsettled by the putting into effect of national registration. As of August 19, every Vancouver person over sixteen was required to carry a registration card, on penalty of fine or imprisonment or both, the only exceptions being cloistered nuns, members of the armed services on active duty, and persons confined to mental institutions.

The fall of France and the Battle of Britain were suffered vicariously, by Vancouver people, as the player on the bench feels anguish that his team on the field is too busy to be aware of. The city was grateful for any word that brought it into the picture of ordeal, as when a resident, Mrs. Fitz James, received a postcard from George Bernard Shaw saying: "So far we have not budged a step, and shall not unless Hitler pushes us out by the scruffs of our necks. In that case we shall certainly come to Canada, as we have a joint annuity there to die on. And Vancouver is the pick of Canada. . . ."

An additional boost to coastal spirits was the August visit of the British entertainer Gracie Fields, welcomed by crowds second in size only to those of the royal visit the year before. Between moments of being able to relate to the group on the war front, Vancouver doggedly bought its Victory bonds, and renamed Little Mountain as Queen Elizabeth Park, and elected a non-nonsense mayor, J. W. Cornett.

The mayor helped to organize the city's Air Raid Precautions unit (A.R.P.), in emulation of the fire wardens who were helping London and other British cities survive the blitz. Stirrup pumps, scoops and buckets took their place in the basements of a good many Vancouver homes, usually those of veterans of World War I. On April 27, 1941, plans were announced for a test blackout of the city. This raised a number of problems, such as what to do about the numerous beehive burners of hog-fuel at Vancouver sawmills, rosy beacons to any airborne enemy. It was decided that in a real emergency wardens would throw water on the burners and hope that the clouds of steam blended with the smog. For the May 22 test, however, it sufficed that citizens doused their house lights. The test was judged to be a success, within its terms of reference.

Reliefers still paraded in the streets, but their numbers were being eroded both by enlistment and new jobs available in Vancouver area shipyards. In October Ottawa was formulating plans whereby the yards would construct 150 seagoing wooden ships, freighters and Q-boats to combat enemy submarines. Between the outbreak of war and 1943, 168 freighters would be built locally, and Vancouver once again dreamed of postwar construction of ocean liners. Unfortunately the high wage demands of the shipyard workers and the costs of assembling materials foreclosed the phantasy, except for the building of ferries and scows.

To conserve power for war industries, and after several years of controversy, Vancouver adopted daylight saving, or "War Time" as it was called, to help subdue the Fraser Valley farmers whose milking schedules were deranged. Doing its best to identify with the V that was for Victory, Vancouver threw itself into the Milk for Britain fund drive. A July meeting attended by six thousand persons endorsed a demand for conscription for war service, an issue seen as more clear-cut than in cities closer to Quebec. From the brave disaster of Dieppe Vancouver salvaged pride in a wounded hero, Colonel Cecil Merritt, commanding officer of the South Saskatchewan regiment, who was awarded the Victoria Cross for his part in the raid.

During the latter months of 1941 the city that had been looking anxiously toward the old country felt the breath of war on the back of its neck: Japan was drawing together with the other Axis powers. The 1941 census for Vancouver gave ethnic totals of English, 150,688; Scottish, 78,050; Irish, 40,177—and Japanese, 9,299. By far the largest fleet in the waters around Vancouver was the Japanese—1,100 fishing vessels. Thus no city in Canada watched so uneasily the sparring match going on between Japan and the U.S. to see which would land the first blow. The November press report that the Canadian troops sent to reinforce Hong Kong had landed and were "looking forward to their first rickshaw ride" merely made Hong Kong seem much farther from Vancouver than Vancouver was from Tokyo.

In that same month U.B.C. opened its new armory for the officers' training corps, and the quiet residential streets of University Hill resounded to the marching boots of uniformed students whose C.O. was Colonel Gordon Shrum. "Shrum's a bum, Shrum's a bum" was the chant that kept the cadence in columns to the rear.

The city's call for volunteer fire fighters to handle incendiary bombs was ironical in view of the sawdust shortage that threatened Vancouver homeowners with a winter of fireless furnaces. At that time most Vancouver homes with central heating were served by a sawdust burner, whose voracious hopper was fed from a large bin that occupied much of the basement. Vancouver was a ship drifting into battle with no fire in her boiler.

Japan attacked Pearl Harbor on December 7, and in a matter of hours the tidal wave of terror rolled over all the cities on the Pacific coast. Officially declared to be "on a war basis," and with all leaves canceled for troops in the area, Vancouver began the roundup of "dangerous enemy aliens." On December 8 the Japanese language schools and the city's three newspapers printed in Japanese were closed down. The fingerprinting of all Japanese was hastily completed, the Japanese fishing fleet immobilized, while Chinatown noisily celebrated the extension of the Sino-Japanese war. Thousands of Vancouver people who had never before given the matter any thought suddenly felt required to distinguish Japanese from Chinese, and the recognition guide (longer name, shorter eyesight, lower cheekbones) was anything but foolproof. There were also one or two awkward episodes of native Indians being accosted as dangerous aliens.

On December 9 a total blackout for Vancouver came into force. Citizens rushed to buy tarpaper with which to cover windows, batteries for emergency lighting. The blackout entailed early closing for industries and offices not blacked out, and the shutting down of radio stations from 5:30 P.M. Automobiles moved only with headlights covered except for a horizontal strip on each lens not wider than three inches and not more than one inch deep. Lightless streetcars groped through fog, and on the tenth occurred the first of several tram collisions. When darkness descended on the city it became a silent state of apprehension, the fog being further reminder, if any was needed, of the London that lay blitzed. For the first time in its history Vancouver was physically engaged in war, and the novelty brought no joy.

A city can hold its breath only so long. After three nights, the blackout restrictions were relaxed slightly, and by January 7 a semi-blackout was in effect that banned porch lights, lighted store window displays and billboard lighting. But mitigation of the initial panic did not, unfortunately, affect the public agitation for removal of all Japanese from the coast of the province. On January 3, 1942, the city council gave official voice to the clamor by recommending that all Japanese be sent to communal work camps east of the Rockies. On January 14 Ottawa ordered the exodus of twenty-four thousand Japanese from the west coast, classing them all as enemy aliens with the exception of those, such as veterans of World War I, who were granted special permits by the police.

The order struck despair into that part of Vancouver's Powell Street called "Little Tokyo," particularly as the federal government was vague about compensation for abandoned fish boats, and loss of businesses and homes, many of which belonged to Japanese who had never seen Japan and who were genuinely loyal to Canada. Reacting to treachery in the Pacific and fear of treachery in the Gulf of Georgia, Vancouver citizens succumbed to the mob psychology that gives justice a very low priority.

In February—the same month in which the great gray hulk of the *Queen Elizabeth* appeared mysteriously in English Bay, the ship having been converted to the world's largest troop carrier, with an appointment in Esquimalt dry dock—general evacuation began of Japanese to inland camps and towns. On the whole the Japanese accepted their lot with good grace, but in May those held in the Vancouver immigration building rioted in protest against being held for two weeks behind bars while the federal government made up its mind where east of the Rockies to send them. The "troublemakers" were interned, and the building was patrolled by military guards with fixed bayonets.

Lending credence to the belief that the city's Japanese were in the toils of the fatherland, reports circulated about the "Black Dragon Society of Japan" that was intimidating, at long range, the Japanese in B.C. A commission investigating this plot produced a great deal of smoke and no fire whatever. As crowning indignity heaped upon injury, the 1942 sockeye salmon run was the biggest in a generation, a bonanza which the dispossessed Japanese fishermen were obliged to watch being hauled in by whites.

The harsh treatment of Japanese citizens would have been made to seem more justifiable had Japan attacked Vancouver in force. Stern measures presupposed strong provocation. It was not till June that Japanese troops occupied Kiska and Attu in the Aleutians. But on June 20, 1942, the city was galvanized by the news that a Japanese submarine had pumped a couple of shells at the lighthouse at Estevan, on the west coast of Vancouver Island. It was not much, in terms of bombardment, but Vancouver seized on it with a thrill of alarm. For the first time in two world wars enemy shells had landed on Canadian soil.

The armed forces of Japan failed to follow up, however. It was not till September that the full calamity of war was brought home to the people of the city. Ottawa ordered chlorination of Vancouver's public water supplies, to protect the troops in the area. This bomb dropped squarely on the Vancouver Water Board, the emotive equivalent of a direct hit on St. Paul's. The water board responded with a high-velocity jet of opposition directed at the nation's capital. Mayor Cornett, a former chairman of the water board, delivered a Churchillian address vowing defense of Vancouver's water to the last drop. He had behind him a citizenry that rose as one man in face of the outrage, the impugning of the purity of water as virgin as any Belgian maid ravished by the Hun. Here was a wartime atrocity that would also violate the water rates. Therefore residents previously neutral girded themselves for battle with the minister of health, Ian Mackenzie, when he released the explosive charge that Vancouver water contained bacilli in an amount above international requirements.

Vancouver quickly counterattacked, to hurl back the allegation that germs had infiltrated the watershed, lying behind a natural fortress of mountains and guarded by fences respected the world over as unassailable. Ottawa riposted with the argument—as preposterous as it was bizarre—that the watershed had been fouled by sea gulls flying over it and dropping into the reservoir lakes bits of rotted food picked up in the harbor. In all its anticipation of aerial bombardment, Vancouver had foreseen nothing as diabolical as its own gulls dropping garbage into the drinking water. The city produced witnesses, watershed workers, who swore that they had never seen a sea gull, with or without a mouthful of refuse, fly that far back into the mountains. But the will to fight had been sorely wounded. In spite of a valiant rearguard action by the Anti-Chlorination League, early in 1943 Vancouver surrendered to adulteration of its water supply. "It will be Ottawa that has the bad taste in its mouth," muttered the *Sun* editorially, "before this chlorination business is all washed up clean again." The message was not lost on those elements of the Resistance that had already switched to beer.

However, further calamity fell at once upon those who rejected the Vichy water: during the winter Vancouver suffered a beer drought. The liquor ration allowed a guerrilla forty ounces of hard stuff a week, and two dozen pint bottles of beer supplied one dozen at a time. But agents of oppression had also set the hours of sale in beer parlors as well as drying up stock in the liquor stores. Tom Uphill rose in the legislature to deliver an impassioned plea for the working class, brandishing a bottle of beer and declaring it to be "as necessary to workers as milk to a baby."

Sale of another dairy product, whipping cream, was prohibited as of January 1, 1943, and gasoline rationing curtailed even the mild intoxication induced by speeding on the highway. Many of the thousands of Vancouver people who planted victory gardens in the spring of 1943 did so because there was no way of getting to greener fields.

Aside from her sons, Vancouver's contribution to the military war effort was being made by workers in the shipyards and the aircraft plants. At the Sea Island Airport a Boeing factory employed thousands to turn out parts for the B-29 Superfortress, workhorse of U.S. bombing raids. On the waterfront, the activity in the shipyards spurred the city to order two commando-type fire barges. The barges had limited mobility, but they did float, and with any reasonable amount of cooperation from a fire they could be towed within range.

The blaze of battle, however, remained remote. On September 21, 1943, a submarine was sighted off the coast, apparently charging its batteries, but the fishermen who sighted it completed their fishing before returning with the report, to the considerable disgust of local naval officers. The following month survivors picked up from a Japanese sub sunk in the South Pacific identified their ship as the one that had shelled Estevan lighthouse. This knocked out the first and last enemy force to show an active interest in tangling with the armed might based in Vancouver.

In November, emboldened by the defeat of Italy, the Vancouver City Council demanded that chlorination cease at once. The council's terms were that the chlorination machinery should be used only in the event of an attack, by Japanese or bacilli. Meanwhile the onset of winter was inflicting real hardship on members of the Resistance, men and women in the line, the long, thin column that stretched, foul weather or fair, from the liquor store to ever-increasing distances around the block. The liquor ration was down to one quart of spirits per month, or three dozen pints of beer, or one gallon of Canadian wine, or two bottles of imported wine. Nondrinkers of both sexes could not be sure whether they were being loved for themselves or for their unused liquor ration. A girl tested a man's sincerity by telling him that she drank like drains, and sons traveled long distances to be with an abstinent mother at the beginning of the ration month.

The "dim-out" to conserve power wrought less havoc than the strictures on bottled illumination. Subdued lighting was in fact a prerequisite of the performance by Miss Faith Bacon at the Beacon Theatre. Co-claimant with Sally Rand to the title of inventor of the fan dance, Miss Bacon represented both the demise and transubstantiation of vaudeville as burlesque, as well as the moral permissiveness engendered by war. Boys too young to enlist tested their manhood in the front rows of the Beacon, sitting beside elderly Chinese from nearby Chinatown whose patient inscrutability caused many a visiting top banana to wither in the bunch. The semidarkness of the theater was more benign, however, than that of streets where seamen and off-duty soldiers brawled with gangs wearing a new uniform: the zoot suit.

The invasion of Europe clearly dooming Hitler's hopes of victory, rumors of peace conferences drifted across the Atlantic. It was typical of Vancouver's center-of-the-universe syndrome that the city, through the press (the *Sun*, September 29, 1944), should ask: Why not hold the peace conference in Vancouver? It was a last-gasp effort to be an identified participant in the drama of World War II, a gesture soon lost in the ungrateful Wehrmacht's counterattack and the Battle of the Bulge.

Vancouver took what comfort it could from the end of tea and coffee rationing, after two years, and the removal of security guards from the bridges. In its concern for wartime navy the city did not at first grasp the historic significance of the slipping into the harbor, October 16, 1944, of a diminutive RCMP supply vessel, the *St. Roch*. The *St. Roch* was completing its east-to-west journey through the Northwest Passage, having made the west-to-east trip two years earlier, the first vessel ever to accomplish the feat that was the dream of the explorers who first charted the west coast. One hundred and fifty years after Captain George Vancouver probed the inlets, *St. Roch* skipper Sergeant Henry A. Larsen proved that there was another way to go home.

On October 18 Vancouver launched another ship, built of stone and designed to go nowhere: H.M.C.S. *Discovery*, on Deadman's Island. The old Indian massacre ground, the scene of Ludgate's Last Stand, perpetuated its military history as a naval training base. Elsewhere in the city the housing shortage, aggravated by a spectacular rise in numbers of marriages and births since the start of the war, found the city deficient two thousand units needed as family dwellings—and the war veterans had yet to return home.

The prospect of that homecoming grew brighter with each passing day of the new year. The city's morale was lifted not only by its record of sons decorated for heroism in battle but also by the totally unexpected distinction won by one of its young women: Miss Yvonne de Carlo was chosen by Hollywood, after a long and strenuous campaign of publicity for the film *Salome, Where She Danced,* as "The Most Beautiful Girl in the World." The link with victory in the Middle East, though tenuous, was welcome.

On the eve of victory on all fronts Vancouver was jolted by a disaster that echoed—mercifully without the terrible force of the original—the 1917 *Mont Blanc* explosion in Halifax harbor that killed more than two thousand people. On May 6, 1945, when the downtown business offices were emptying of employees headed for their butterless lunches, a shock wave struck from the explosion of the freighter *Greenhill Park,* docked at Pier B, at the foot of Burrard Street. Loaded with flares and explosive material, the *Greenhill Park* caught fire at once and threatened to unleash a second blast more catastrophic than the first, which had been powerful enough to shatter hundreds of windows in the downtown area, the flying splinters injuring dozens of people. Eight men working about the ship were killed by the first explosion. No one knew how much remained unexploded of the 94 tons of sodium chlorate packed in 1,783 steel drums, 2 tons of calcium silicide, packed in 328 drums, 7½ tons of distress signals, packed in 265 wooden boxes, 50 barrels of whisky, and other combustible materials such as varnished cotton cloth.

At some peril, harbor tugs closed in to pick up survivors of the blast, and when the tug *Kyoquot* threw a towline on the burning *Greenhill Park* the ship's crew remained aboard to assist in the agonizingly slow towing of the freighter away from the pier, out of the harbor to Siwash Rock at the extremity of Stanley Park, where she was beached and allowed to burn out. When the blaze had died down, the ship was towed back to Ballentine Pier, where she split almost in two, the amidships area having been virtually demolished. The *Greenhill Park* was later removed and rebuilt, but the evidence of the subsequent inquiry was less simply put together. The fifty barrels of whisky were, it appeared, the most volatile substance aboard. Justice Sidney Smith's report concluded: "We think the true explanation of the speedy spreading of the fire was that whisky escaped from one or more of the barrels, spilled into the surrounding combustible cargo, and was ignited by a match carelessly dropped by a longshoremen in the vicinity." The operative words were "whisky escaped." The method by which whisky escaped from the barrels was hinted at by the report, which noted the discovery of lunch pails specially soldered to carry liquid in bulk, and of longshoremen's jackets into which hot-water bottles had been sewn, an odd way of insulating the body during one of the milder months of the year.

Vancouver did not wait for the official V-E Day, May 8, 1945, to give vent to jubilation. As soon as the news arrived on May 7 that Germany had capitulated unconditionally, downtown streets filled with conga lines of people serpentining joyfully, bellowing the inevitable "Roll Out the Barrel" to off-key accompaniment by auto horns and ships' whistles. The city was drunk with release from tension. It also drew strength from the "V-E Day Cocktail," the recipe for which, because of the liquor rationing, was circulated as:

> Three bottles of soda pop
> Two jiggers of canned heat
> A large bottle of the best after-shave lotion

The recipe did not bear the good housekeeping seal of approval of Mayor Cornett ("Ninety per cent alcohol, worse than the flavoring extracts"), and a magistrate deplored that police were determining degrees of impairment by the perfume of the lotion used in the drink.

For the ordinary mother, father and sweetheart, however, intoxication enough was the thought of return of son or lover, after as much as five years far from home. With the returning veteran a new word entered the popular vocabulary—repat—than which no sound fell sweeter on the ear.

The war in the Pacific had yet to be won when in June a new

tremor of anxiety was caused by Japan's radio broadcasts that threatened suicide raids against the west coast, by piloted, bomb-carrying balloons. While the kamikaze balloonist seemed a somewhat peculiar offensive weapon, Vancouver had heard enough about the dauntlessness of Nippon's airmen to take seriously the prospect of an armada of balloons drifting toward the city upon some Japanese Current of the sky. When residents spotted an airborne object floating cross-town on the twilight air, police sirens wailed, two RCAF squadrons of Kittyhawks scrambled, and thousands of phone calls jammed civil defense switchboards. The object proved to be a box kite, Canada-based.

Japan did, however, attack North America with small, unmanned balloons, incendiaries ingeniously designed to sail several thousand miles across the Pacific, then fire-bomb the highly susceptible summer forests of the Northwest. Discovery of the first of the balloons, landed near Minton, Saskatchewan, occasioned excitement and muted skepticism about the balloons' operational range. Subsequent finds indicated release of hundreds of the balloons, which were constructed of tough paper, thirty-three feet in diameter and carrying nineteen thousand cubic feet of hydrogen gas. The balloons were built to stay aloft a week. If they fell below the proper height for approach of the coast, a device automatically released sandbags. And each balloon carried a bomb triggered by contact with the ground. Although no major damage was attributed to the Japanese balloons, they were taken seriously enough for the RCAF to designate aircraft to intercept them. It is probable that a fair number of the bombs that landed on the coast remain undiscovered.

All lesser bombs became duds, so far as concerned continuation of the war, with the burst of the atomic bomb. When Japan surrendered in September, V-J Day was almost an anticlimax to the awesome repercussions of Hiroshima and Nagasaki. The end of armed hostilities in no wise mellowed sentiment toward the Japanese interned in Canada. Well into 1946 the public demand for deportation of all Japanese to their homeland received sympathetic attention from Ottawa, and as late as May, 1946, the attorney general for British Columbia, Gordon S. Wismer, was asking for legislation more legally binding than the order-in-council to deport Canadian citizens of Japanese origin. It was not till January, 1947, that the deportation order was finally lifted, and some of the Japanese citizens returned to Vancouver to try, with slight success, to salvage more from their expropriated belongings than what passed for official compensation.

As for the city, it may or may not have been a hint of shame, at being able to identify with Nazi consignment of citizens to concentration camps, that the color bar was removed at the Crystal Pool. It was a memorial, of a sort, to Joe Fortes, who had patrolled the adjoining beaches of English Bay for so many years before his death in 1922.

For a time it appeared that those same beaches would be the only accommodation for some of the thousands of repats rolling out of discharge centers around Vancouver. At the university, where enrollment jumped from 2,900 (1944) to 7,300 (1946), the administration bypassed proper channels, "liberating" dozens of old army huts from units in the vicinity, hauling them bodily to the campus and having just time to nail the loosened boards before the huts were engulfed by veterans, and their families, taking advantage of educational benefits. By no means all the returning veterans were fortunate enough to qualify for higher education. "Invest in a Veteran" was the slogan intended to stimulate the hiring of men and women no longer employed in saving civilization. The homeless heroes became particularly restive at the news that the old Hotel Vancouver, with its hundreds of empty rooms, was about to be demolished. In January, 1946, the New Veterans seized the hotel, seven hundred registering after the peaceful *putsch* had been consolidated. For law enforcement officers, a more awkward situation could hardly be imagined and the entire city breathed more easily when the Citizens' Rehabilitation Committee offered to take over the hotel and run it as a hostel for veterans and their families. Vancouver's returned soldiers had recaptured the heart of the city without bloodshed.

Over the most wicked of her foes, however, the city was denied victory. As soon as the main conflict concluded in September, 1945, Vancouver pushed for the end of chlorination of her water supplies. Provincial health authorities recommended that the city retain chlorination, the kind of advice to be expected from Victoria. The Greater Vancouver Water Board in March, 1946, at the instigation of Mayor Cornett, announced its decision to expunge chlorination and dispose of the abominable equipment. With victory thus almost within grasp, the city reeled from repulse on a totally exposed flank: in November, the Great Northern Railway operating the service between Seattle and Vancouver was ordered by the U.S. federal government not to take Vancouver's unchlorinated water into its trains for cooking purposes, as the water was "not fit for human consumption." Coming from Ottawa, this preposterous categorization could have been scotched, but from Washington—a body blow. Other railways threatened to follow suit. Vancouver's tourism was menaced. The last tattered flag was hauled down with the *Province* editorial of November 21: "There remains, then, only one thing for Vancouver to do. She believes in her water. She must bring others to believe in it by removing its purity altogether beyond the field of controversy. She must chlorinate. It may hurt her pride to do so. But it will do no other damage." Henceforth Vancouver's boast would be that her drinking water was minimally chlorinated, like the girl who was only a little bit pregnant.

Girls pregnant and otherwise began to arrive in batches from Britain—war brides, the tangible proof that Vancouver's soldiers, sailors and airmen had been fully occupied in absorbing the glories of the Old World. A new sprinkling of English and Scottish accents dappled the more nasal drone prevalent in the multiplying supermarkets. The war brides were by no means universally beguiled by their new environment. For some, the primitive liquor laws in particular, and the sedate pace after wartime Britain, dulled the gloss on the portrait of Vancouver that their husbands had painted for them. A number went home, taking with them the scarifying experience of seeing what could happen to a pub when it was called a beer parlor.

Most remained, however, and with husbands who had seen something of the graces of civilization while overseas added their voices to those of people who, for the first time, viewed their city critically. This spirit of passionate analysis found expression in a new breed of artistic cat like poet Earle Birney, who newly returned from war service was writing poems such as "Man Is a Snow":

> I tell you the wilderness we fell
> is nothing to the one we breed. . . .
>
> . . . Beauty goes
> or stays and we do not know it.
> Man is a snow
> that cracks the trees' red arches.*

* "Man Is a Snow" from *Street of Anian* by Earle Birney, reprinted by permission of The Canadian Publishers McClelland and Stewart, Limited, Toronto.

Veterans who had seen *les grands boulevards de Paris* observed that their home town, a brooch of humanity in a great shawl of natural forest, had treeless, ugly streets gridding a downtown gone shabby. Voices were heard, incredulous that there were no licensed restaurants or sidewalk cafes, that regulations made it illegal both to drink standing up indoors and to drink sitting down outdoors.

As one improvement in appearance the city was prying up its old streetcar tracks and covering the cobblestoned ruts with blacktop. Trolley buses were on their way, the first one-way street was yet only a gleam in a traffic engineer's eye, and the city undertook the planting of boulevards with trees other than the forest maples, for each of which it had formerly paid a homeowner one dollar if he planted one in front of his lot, only to find that no tree has roots more energetic in heaving pavement and choking drains.

This cosmetic treatment of a sick countenance did not satisfy the young architects and town planners appearing on the scene and claiming the city as their ward. One of them went so far as to call Vancouver "disgusting." Even hardened city longshoremen had never heard this kind of language applied to the belle of Canadian cities. Capping the criticism, in 1946 came the first intimation that Vancouver's beaches were polluted. Decidedly, the bloom was off the skunk cabbage.

CHAPTER 14 1946–1959

Onward if Not Upward

The Diamond Jubilee · Gerry goes home · A show called Fred · TUTS, P. & O. and the B.E.G. · The B.C. Lions and other problems of survival · Flynn died here

THAT the city's boosters still held preponderance over the knockers was evidenced in the planning for the Diamond Jubilee celebrations. The sixtieth birthday party was to be the most grandiose of all, the apotheosis of narcissism coinciding with the recognition that the face that launched a thousand scows was developing unsightly wrinkles. The city hired a Texas-born American, John Harkrider, as "director-general," to come to Vancouver and produce an extravaganza, the biggest spectacle since the place burned itself down. One of Harkrider's early suggestions was, in fact, that the great outdoor show at Brockton Oval, in Stanley Park, be climaxed by setting fire to the North Shore mountains as a replica of the original inferno. He was dissuaded only when it was pointed out that the finale might wipe out the communities across the inlet and be difficult to restage after opening night.

While the director-general was modifying his program, an old stager of the Vancouver scene quietly took his last curtain call. L. D. Taylor died June 14, 1946, in reasonably comfortable poverty, in a flat whose rent was unpaid but never demanded, at Robson and Granville, from which point "Mr. Vancouver" could see the Hotel Vancouver that he had helped to bring into being. After a last abortive try at election to City Hall in the late thirties, Taylor had sadly sold the celebrated vacant lot in Hastings East, and the garage for which he had no car. Vancouver gave its forgotten man a big civic funeral, however, at which several thousand citizens paid their respects to the grizzled little veteran of political wars.

A couple of weeks after the funeral, the city registered a more literal shock. The June 23 earthquake was the severest in its history, stopping the clock atop the Vancouver Block at fourteen and one-half minutes after 10 P.M. Not the least of the surmise with which the temblor was received was that it had been arranged by Harkrider as the overture to the Jubilee Show. The July 2 opening of the show was preceded by a parade that drew 250,000 people, at least half of whom saw something of it. Vancouver was in such a magnanimous mood that the judges awarded Victoria the prize for the best float.

Nor did the city stint in its attendance of the show—cast of five thousand—staged at Brockton Point. Sparing no expense, the director-general had hired opera star John Charles Thomas to sing the parts of Captain Vancouver and Van Horne in the pageant of Vancouver's history, ethnic variety, and politer pursuits of pleasure. American comic Eddie Cantor was to be conveyed by jeep from the "wings" to the mid-point of the 515-foot outdoor stage. During the fashion parade that was to grace the show's slam-bang finish, patrons in the several hundred yards of specially built bleachers would breathe perfume sprayed by the gallon from large, mechanical musk glands.

The one factor overlooked by the director-general, possibly because he derived from an arid section of the U.S., was what a typical Vancouver midsummer downpour might do to this mighty spectacle open to the skies. On opening night, the skies too opened. The director-general tried valiantly to rally his units, jeeping from the orchestra pit, where the fiddle section was adamant about compounding damage to soggy strings, to the exasperated John Charles Thomas whose powdered wig was running down his face, and to the thousands of extras waiting damply beyond the rise of the cricket pitch, before moving forth in waves to portray Vancouver's sportive delights of tennis, skiing, baseball and other pastimes. Only those representing swimming were costumed to meet the weather. Not without some difficulty the performance was halted and rain checks issued to the scattering audience. Successive performances were more fortunate climatically, but the spectators tended to be outnumbered by the cast, which was swollen by interlopers sneaking in "backstage," and the Indians in the cast grumbled threats to go home because they were affronted by the cheap totem poles decorating Vancouver streets, and because they were missing the fishing season.

Also in July the city was treated to the spectacle of labor violence, around normally tranquil Victory Square. A strike by International Typographical Union workers, in sympathy with eastern work stoppages against Southam newspapers, had forced the Vancouver *Province* to cease publication on June 5. On July 23 the *Province* resumed publication with an edition printed by its supervisory staff and, allegedly, outside help. Members of the striking local responded by intercepting the trucks loaded with newspapers, overturning one of them and creating a glut of street copies outside the Province Building. The mayor ordered police to supervise distribution of the newspapers. Although these events resulted in no serious injuries to persons, the schism opened between the city's senior newspaper and the working community was deep and deleterious to both. After almost two years of litigation, the courts judged the strike to be illegal and fined leaders of the union local $10,000, but the damage done to the *Province* exceeded many times the cash value of the judgment. The Vancouver *Sun*, which started as a morning daily in 1912 and which, under publisher Robert Cromie, in 1926 absorbed the Odlum family's *Evening Star* to move into the evening field and into direct, bitter competition with the *Province*, picked up the canceled subscriptions and quickly outstripped its competitor in circulation if not in respectability.

The July riot did not endear Mayor Cornett to the East End of the city. In the December, 1946, civic election campaign the "down-to-earth" mayor who refused to wear Gerry McGeer's robes of office, and who had presided over the council for six years that included the adversities of wartime, stepped down. The twenty-fifth mayor of the city, who admitted to being no orator, yielded the podium to the candidate whose forte was the untrammeled flow of words: G. G. McGeer. Senator McGeer had been elevated to Canada's upper house in 1945, as reward for his long and faithful backbenching in the Commons and his stumping for the Liberals in the Maritimes. When his appointment to the Senate was announced, the Vancouver Chamber of Commerce sent him a bottle of sleeping pills, and he received a wire saying: "Paths of glory lead but to the grave." The top hat, morning coat and striped trousers did not suit Gerry, whose attempts to give Senate debate mouth-to-mouth resuscitation came too late. His fellow senators were only mildly roused by his ringing declaration that Vancouver youth had no recreation but movie theaters and beer parlors. "It is a long way to Ottawa, but it is ten times as far from Ottawa to Vancouver," Gerry complained, and he returned to his old stamping ground to run for mayor and "beat the C.C.F.," represented by candidate Tom Alsbury.

Despite his being leveled by an attack of peritonitis on the eve of the election, or perhaps because of it, and with his vocal salvos diminished not at all for being fired from a bed in St. Paul's Hospital, McGeer won back his right to wear his resplendent robes. A city hungering for color and excitement after the war's austerity gave him a record majority. The victor received the press in flaming red pajamas, in harmony with the simultaneous extension of the Art Gallery to provide accommodation for its Emily Carr collection. Vancouver had had enough of the conventional arts.

Postwar, the population of the city was not so much a melting pot as a furiously tossed salad: ex-servicemen, some of them from other parts of Canada, and the world, who had visited Vancouver on leave or in transit; their brides, and their brides' relations; Europeans like the Czech Koerner brothers, who had fled Nazism to become timber magnates and grateful patrons of both the university and other cultural endeavor; Germans who were "Austrian"; and Japanese former residents claiming $3 million for expropriated property. The influx helped to raise the 1947 population of Vancouver to 354,000. "Everywhere," commented the *Province*, "the civic clothing is bursting at the seams." The city council was budgeting for new sewers, new parks, new water mains, while bickering over the future of the Vancouver International Airport, which was so busy that the city couldn't afford to run it. The proposal to sell the airport to Ottawa ran afoul of fierce possessiveness strengthened by the suspicion that if Ottawa was willing to buy it, there must be something wrong with selling it.

In the whirling schemes and dreams for an electronic-era Vancouver the nucleus was a civic center. Mayor McGeer was campaigning vigorously for this focus of social energy, and had just returned from a visit to Nelson, when he was found, on the morning of August 11, on the sofa in the den of his home at 4812 Belmont, having died peacefully in his sleep. He had lain down to rest after working late, giving his family orders not to disturb him. A heart attack completed his appointments. Hundreds of his fellow citizens filed past the coffin in the rotunda of the City Hall that was his monument, and more than twenty thousand jammed the streets to watch the funeral cortege to Christ Church Cathedral, paying their respects to the man who more than any other had worn his heart on his sleeve in his love for his native city.

Another death that grieved the city was that of Rabbi M. M. Pastinsky, February 16, 1948. As spiritual leader since 1919 of Vancouver's Jewish community, he had done much to help immigrants, to establish scholarships, and to give the community an unobtrusive cohesion. He helped to foster patience with the discrimination that protected some of Vancouver's private golf and businessmen's clubs from being linked with humanity. In a city as religiously fragmented as Vancouver, patience was bound to outlast bigotry. As attested to by the growing assortment of architecturally diversified synagogues, Sikh temples, Lutheran churches, evangelical halls and other places of worship, it is fortunate that Vancouver is God's own country. The message would arrive badly garbled if He lived out of town.

Vancouver lost its second mayor within a year when Charles Jones, elected in December, 1947, succumbed in his sleep September 1, 1948. His successor as chief administrator was Charles F. Thompson, who during his two years in office called for tenders on a new Granville Street Bridge to replace the arthritic swing span dementing increasing numbers of motorists. Thompson was also head of the council that won selection of Vancouver for the British Empire Games (1954), that instituted the first low-rental housing plan for veterans, and that initiated plans for a new public library and for the Capilano baseball stadium near Queen Elizabeth Park. Thompson's tenure coincided with record arrivals of tourists—a major industry worth $30 million to the city in 1948. Some concern was expressed that many American visitors were merely passing through Vancouver on their way to Vancouver Island or the B.C. interior. The knowledge that Victoria had retained a charm, as a little bit of old England, that was being dissipated in the pace and pollution of Vancouver nagged at the city's tourist bureau, which urged all citizens to exercise courtesy as an antidote for having to direct visitors to the Island ferries.

The other cross that Mayor Thompson had to bear was that of another investigation of the police department and the crime wave that had crested with wide-open gambling, bootlegging and bookmaking. Major crime had to contend with Inspector (Honorary)

J. F. C. B. Vance, for forty-two years the famed director of the health department sleuths and of the lab in which several sensational murders were solved. But lesser offenses, such as armed robbery, were mocking the men in blue. The police chief, Walter Mulligan, had enjoyed the admiration of the community for some years, but eyebrows began to levitate when, on September 13, 1948, he phoned the police station from a bank saying that he had held it up. Mulligan was testing his new radio prowler cars. He "robbed" two banks in all, a performance that took on a symbolic significance during the subsequent probe into alleged misdeeds of the constabulary.

As a further routing of the forces of darkness, downtown division, the David Spencer department store on Hastings Street was bought, in December, by the East's T. Eaton Company. To see the popular department store, which had become something of an institution since its opening in 1926, swallowed whole by Eaton enterprise was a shock to city pride. But, in addition, the rigid moral principles of founder Timothy Eaton were immediately applied to the new branch store. The tobacco counter, an aromatic atoll amid the treacherous currents of women shoppers, was closed, plunging thousands of smokers and chewers into a deep snit. In addition, all the store's show windows were equipped with shades, so that there might be no display advertising on Sundays. Christmas, 1948, came to Vancouver with a supplement of beatification from Toronto the Good.

The setback was, needless to say, only temporary. On the campus of U.B.C. the new student residences afforded expanded opportunity for pantie raids, under the tolerant eye of President Norman A. M. MacKenzie. Installed as head of the university in 1944, "Larry" MacKenzie brought a deceptively casual mien to administration, strolling about the campus in clothes that presented no threat to the list of Canada's ten best-dressed men, accompanied by an old, one-eyed collie, and chatting with students who not infrequently thought they were addressing a member of the grounds staff. Yet the MacKenzie regime was energetic enough to witness expansion of the university's traditional Arts and Science with five new faculties—Law, Medicine, Pharmacy, Forestry, and Graduate Studies—between 1945 and 1951.

On September 4, 1949, the academic community and the city lost one of its most brilliant teachers—G. G. Sedgewick, former head of the university's English Department. An outstanding Elizabethan scholar and champion of civil liberties, the peppery Dr. Sedgewick joined the staff in 1918. For the next thirty years, till his retirement in 1948, his classes in Shakespeare and Chaucer filled the amphitheater, despite the amiable tyranny with which he dominated his students. "G.G." seated the football players in the front row so that he could emphasize points, and perhaps penetrate a massive skull, by pounding their brows with his small fist. A superb performer well aware that he was a loss to the stage, he was a master of timing, his voice spellbinding a huge class so completely that he could lecture seated or, on one occasion, reclining on a table. During the period when legitimate theater was in the doldrums, Sedgewick blew up a storm for more than a generation of students, with a mere wave of the handkerchief he deliberately drew from his jacket cuff when clearing his throat for another soliloquy.

With Sedgewick died a good deal of Vancouver's active concern for civil liberties. The outbreak of the Korean war in 1950, and the witch-hunts in the States for which Senator Joseph McCarthy was chief inquisitor, found Vancouver not wanting in readiness to panic about Communist undermining of the city. Mayor Thompson announced that all civic employees would be screened for Communist sympathies. Civil defense was reactivated, and the air-raid sirens were tested frequently enough to negate any value as a warning. Tension in the Pacific was also implicit in the fact that in 1950 the port of Vancouver still hosted only one regularly scheduled liner, the R.M.S. *Aorangi.* The seventeen-thousand-ton ship, the first large passenger vessel powered by oil-fired engines, since her maiden voyage from Vancouver to Sydney in 1925 had been a sentimental favorite of Vancouver people who liked to go down to Stanley Park to watch her cleave the Narrows. The surviving C.P. *Empresses*, subsidized before World War II, did not return to service after the war. A troopship during the war, converted back to a passenger liner, the *Aorangi* in December, 1950, was reported to be on her last trip from Australia to Vancouver.

Perhaps to relieve the pressure of another war that could be the last, the city treated itself to a new mayor, Fred J. Hume, in an election that reflected the endorsement of candidates by the Non-Partisan Association, a group begun at least partly out of apprehension about socialists in the city's seats of power. In the same December election votes defeated the proposal of Open Sunday, but not so emphatically as on previous submissions. Hume, the grandson of one of Colonel Moody's Royal Engineers, was born in Sapperton and played center for the New Westminster Salmonbellies lacrosse team while his older friends escaped to the relative tranquillity of World War I. He had an attractively checkered career, working as a power lineman and founding one of the first radio stations in British Columbia—CFKC. Hume was owner, manager, announcer and disc jockey for the station, but as he had no commercials it did not pay, and he sold it to those who changed the call letters to CJOR. He became an electrical contractor, prospered, served for nine years as mayor of New Westminster, and became owner of the Vancouver Canucks hockey team. A florid, genial person, an immaculate dresser who was naked without the red rose in his buttonhole, Fred Hume became mayor with the promise of "neighborly" policy. As an effulgent example his home on Sentinel Hill, on the North Shore, celebrated Christmas each year with a dazzling display of colored lights, a beacon of goodwill.

Not the least of Hume's charm lay in his being a millionaire serving Vancouver as a dollar-a-year man. For his second year in office Fred took his full pay, having discovered the high cost of being convivial at the mayoral level. He helped to endear himself to the populace by greeting Princess Elizabeth and her husband, on their 1951 visit to the city, with his arm in a sling. The popular account of the accident was that he broke his arm practicing bows, and fictional though this was, Mayor Hume did prove to belong to the accident-prone class of chief administrator epitomized by L. D. Taylor. In August, 1952, having gone to London to return the visit of the woman who was now Queen, he wrenched his back in a tumble in an English tub, and a few months later damaged his nose by walking into a door at the City Hall. Hume had a real, physical gift for making his fellow citizens feel that they were relatively fortunate.

Under the aegis of this cordial mayor Vancouver diverted some of its anti-Communist animus towards the Liquor Control Board, in Victoria, which adamantly ignored the city's pleas for more enlightened laws regulating drinks with meals, licensed cabarets, and beverage rooms whose tempo of guzzling was set by waiters who seized an emptied glass before the suds could settle. The increasingly cosmopolitan population of the city, and the experience of its young people touring Europe as part of their postgraduate education, were creating a demand for wine with dinner in a restaurant. The L.C.B., however, continued to think in terms of the wino with his jug of throat abrasive. With visible reluctance it stocked its liquor stores with better marks and vintages, and feigned not to notice the consternation of the New Canadian who saw his bottle of Château Pontet Canet being handled by the clerks like a juggler's pin. Not till 1952 did a liquor probe commissioner recommend legalizing drink-with-food in public eating houses.

Vancouver's other local villain, circa 1951, was the Marpole Bridge. This ancient structure linking the city with Sea Island and the International Airport, dated from Horatius and had even more success in holding up traffic. During the airport's busy seasons the bridge could be depended on to lose an argument with a scow and subside into the North Arm of the Fraser. Because the bridge was outside city limits, other levels of government were to be persuaded of the need for a replacement. According to a legend of the time, when a senior government dignitary was scheduled to be driven from the airport to the city, a high-masted vessel manifested itself and obliged the swing span to yawn open, effectively delaying the official party. It was never proven that the ship was subsidized by the city.

More publicly supported by municipal funds was the Children's Zoo in Stanley Park, opened in 1950. The baby goats and other junior beasts added their voices to the off-stage effects that were part of the popular summer entertainment of Vancouver's adults: the Theatre Under the Stars, in the park's Malkin Bowl. TUTS, as the seasons of musicals were known, had developed from amateur beginnings in 1939 to productions having professional polish and importing established stars. The outdoor theater was entirely at the mercy of the elements, and performances of *The Desert Song* sometimes suffered from a credibility gap created by precipitation. Producer Bill Buckingham schooled his directors in the desirability of musical or dramatic crescendo to contend with the firing of the Nine O'Clock Gun at nearby Brockton Point, but guests sopranos never really adjusted to finding themselves singing a duet with the C.P.R.'s *Princess Louise* blowing for the First Narrows. But on a fine August evening, to sit with one's young lady sharing a blanket across the knees, listening to Victor Herbert melodies heightened by a semiquaver of ducks orchestrating the sunset—such were delight's simple means.

From the direction of the sunset came, in the later months of 1951, a strange complication born of the war in Korea. It was revealed that Vancouver's Chinese community was being blackmailed by the Communist regime of mainland China. Threatened with vengeance against families in China, some Vancouver Chinese were transferring sums of money to Red agents. One withdrew his life savings from a bank, another hanged himself. Also as a result of the extortion, Vancouver Chinese gave up the custom of shipping home the bones of their dead every seven years for burial in China. Thus the Korean war indirectly helped to integrate the Chinese community with the rest of Vancouver, and to conciliate the remains of much-abused pioneers with Canadian soil.

A cultural attraction that drew together whites and Orientals, the State burlesque theater on Hastings Street lost its license in January, 1952, because of the "suggestive movements" of the strippers. This area centered by Hastings and Main was now the main intersection of the errant, the Skid Road at its sleaziest, the resort of loggers on leave, drifters, ladies of easy virtue (too many of them Indian girls snagged in the human debris of the white man's civilization). On Pender Street the night clubs owned by impassive, pragmatic Chinese gave the white thrill-seekers what they wanted, while exploring the limits of the law. Not far from the gaudy signs of the Mandarin Gardens, of the excellent Chinese restaurants, darker streets hid flophouses, and beer parlors vomited their drunks onto the sidewalk. In 1952 Earle Birney's *Trial of a City* was published, a poetic indictment of the smug metropolis. A witness for the prosecution, Long Will of Langland, testifies:

> Yea, then I moved to my hill's margin
> and saw a soft middleclass swaddled in trees,
> in unfrequented churches and fears not a few.
> Chained as fast to profits as poorer folk to wages,
> roofs and hopes high, yet higher still their mortgages.
> Some knew nobleness and neighbourly lived;
> some had milk in morning to melt their belly's ulcers
> and rode alone to office, an ego to an auto.*

In February, 1952, the ego's morning paper, the Vancouver *News Herald*, was sold to Roy Thomson. The tabloid daily had developed a reputation for quality, thanks to talented journalists such as Jack

* From *Trial of A City* by Earle Birney, reprinted by permission of The Canadian Publishers McClelland and Stewart, Limited, Toronto.

Scott and Barry Mather. The purchase was to prove to be one of press lord Thomson's rare mistakes of acquisition, however, as the advertising dollar was about to be sundered by the impact of a new medium: television. In December, 1953, the Canadian Broadcasting Corporation opened its Vancouver TV station, CBUT, and the fate of a third daily newspaper was sealed.

By December, 1952, Vancouver was once again serving as a repat depot for Canadian troops returning from the Korea conflict. Not all the maritime activity was keyed to war, however. In November, 1952, the letter *N* painted boldly on the funnels of its cargo vessels marked the entry of a new fleet servicing coastal points out of Vancouver: the Northland Navigation Company. The immediate purpose was to create a lifeline for the instant town of Kitimat and its Alcan project, but in time Northland took over much of the former role of the Union Steamships (which discontinued passenger service in December, 1957) and C.P. coasters. In addition Northland provided passenger accommodations on ships cruising the passages north to Alaska.

As for ships on the trans-Pacific run, a last reprieve for the *Aorangi* expired in 1953, when the gallant old thoroughbred returned to the Clyde, her birthplace, and the knacker's yard. But her blue-water path to the Antipodes was picked up by P. & O. ships like the *Oronsay* and the *Orcades,* brand-new ships whose pork-pie funnels and stocky physiques took some getting used to, among Vancouver ship-watchers. On February 13, 1955, the *Orsova* arrived from Australia, the largest liner to have entered Vancouver harbor. Each visit of a P. & O. ship being worth several hundred thousand dollars to Vancouver in provisioning and tourist trade, the big white vessels became lovable in their own way. Also, as the ships varied their runs to include voyages to Britain via Panama, Vancouver had available a luxury cruise to California, though subject to the vicissitudes of weather off Cape Flattery.

Many of the Vancouver people who boarded ships, or planes, in the spring of 1953 were on their way to witness with their own eyes the coronation of the Queen who, like her father, was a personal friend of the city. At Lansdowne Park, on Lulu Island, loyal subjects thronged the racetrack that June for the special Coronation Day races, proceeds from which went to bolster the British Empire Games fund. But the royal pageantry was being played out against the background of an obscene purple: the mushroom-shaped cloud of Soviet Russia's hydrogen bomb. That test evoked another in Vancouver, the test of an air-raid alert, June 20, 1953, the same day that Julius and Ethel Rosenberg went to the electric chair as spies for the U.S.S.R. "Operation Beware" was intended to familiarize the populace with diving into buildings designated as air-raid shelters, and into home basements. The "death" total after the test was placed at fifty, the main disappointment to civil defense authorities being that the sirens did not deter a rush of food bargain hunters on a downtown wholesale warehouse. The "enemy bombers" were, however, driven off by Vampire and Mustang fighter planes of the RCAF, while these lasted.

Vancouver authorities were also concerned, in 1953, about improved technology as it related to the oldest profession. The traditional streetwalker was being displaced by the call girl, summoned by telephone, transported by cab, and virtually impossible to charge with other than jaywalking (which had recently become a traffic offense). Not only had the call girls percolated into apartment blocks of the West End, which put them on the polite side of the Stock Exchange Building, but their growing number included women from various stations of life, many of them housewives. Police Chief Walter Mulligan expressed himself as being decidedly disturbed by the ruining of another profession by amateurs in unknown numbers, and some quiet nostalgia was felt for the old-fashioned brothel, such as that storied stew raided by the police during World War I and found to be furnished with bedroom furniture supplied from the store owned by the mayor.

Flying squads of Mulligan's police were kept fully occupied handing out tickets to pedestrians either too absent-minded or too precipitate to observe the WALK and DON'T WALK signals installed in time for the Christmas shopping rush. Further evidence that the city's moral fiber was fraying badly was provided by the *Tobacco Road* case. This courtroom drama held the town in thrall from the night that the cast and director of the earthy play, produced at the old State Theatre, renamed the Avon, by a company called The Everyman Theatre, were arrested on a morality charge. With the play's author, Erskine Caldwell, on hand to testify on behalf of theatrical freedom, the definition of obscenity was hungrily gnawed down to the bone, which was cracked and the marrow extracted. When the players' appeal of the conviction was reversed in March of 1953, both justice and the box office were seen to have triumphed. From that day forward, censorship in Vancouver was not so much a judgment of Solomon as of Mammon.

For more wholesome drama based on sex the city depended on the Park's new penguin pool, opened in 1953, where reproduction was attended by mass egg-watching, and each try at the rarity of a penguin born in captivity was avidly reported in the press and invariably addled in the shell.

As an occasion between penguin eggs, 1954 provided the February 4 opening of the new Granville Street Bridge. The third of its line was not only Vancouver's first eight-lane bridge but also the most purely functional, an open arch of steel cresting in the middle, branching into tentacles of access ramps which expedited the desire to get off it. Mayor Hume presided at the opening, in the van of a procession that included a 1909 Cadillac driven by Mrs. Arthur Brydone-Jack, who was one of two women drivers among the first to cross the bridge's predecessor when it was opened in 1909. The new Granville Street Bridge eliminated the bottleneck of the swing span, but helped to fill more quickly the downtown area—a bottle that was rapidly becoming all neck. In a few years Granville Street would be the only remaining two-way street between Burrard and Beatty, and difficulties of Morton, Brighouse and Hailstone in threading the wilderness to False Creek began to look more trivial.

From the new bridge the city's attention was turned, for much of 1954, toward the Hastings Park area that was to be the site of most of the events of the British Empire Games (July–August). The Empire Stadium rose there with a disregard for expense that was a tribute to the city's resolve to outdo Hamilton, a previous host of the B.E.G. Up to the moment when Percy Williams turned the first sod, the location of the big stadium was the eye of a hurricane of controversy, as was that of the Empire Swimming Pool at U.B.C. Having reconciled themselves to facilities placed at opposite poles of the city, however, the citizens looked forward with lively anticipation to the games and their feature event: the race that brought to the same track the world's two greatest milers: Britain's Roger Bannister, first man to crack the four-minute mile, and John Landy of Australia, holder of the world record for the event.

The city preened itself on the presence of the Duke of Edinburgh and Field Marshal Earl Alexander, as guests of honor for the games, as on the winning of gold medals by Vancouver's Doug Hepburn, world record holder for weight-lifting, and by the U.B.C. rowing eight ("Sink mighty England!"). But suspense was building to the big day, August 7, which proved to be warm and bright, ideal for the running of the Miracle Mile. The two major rivals did not let the crowd down. In one of the most exciting moments known to sports, Bannister, after trailing Landy to the last turn of the track, turned on the winning kick that caught the Australian looking over his left shoulder while Bannister flashed by on his right to win in 3.58.8 minutes, Landy at his heels with 3.59.6, the first time two men had broken the four-minute barrier in the same race.

Barely had the cheers died down when elation turned to horror. Through a gate on the stadium track staggered the front runner of the twenty-six-mile marathon, Jim Peters. The heat of the afternoon as well as the distance had drained from him all but the will to continue, and while thirty-five thousand people watched appalled, Peters fell, struggled to his feet, reeled and fell again. With his English teammates urging him to get up, and with pleading cries of "Stop it!" from the stands where women stood in tears of anguish, a man who was clearly out on his feet literally crawled the remaining distance to what he thought was the finishing line. The actual tape was halfway again around the track, but in the view of the world watching the event on television the raw courage of Jim Peters ("the world's greatest loser") had won a medal whose substance was more precious than gold. It is doubtful that the annals of sport record an afternoon as emotionally exhausting as that Saturday in August, 1954, in Vancouver's Empire Stadium.

The city had not, however, lost its flair for going from the sublime to the ridiculous. Into the stadium for their debut as members of the Canadian Football League marched the British Columbia Lions professional football team. "Lions roar in fifty-four" was the invocation, which proved to be something less than prophetic. Despite the first of many dismal seasons during which the Lions explored the cellar of the league, the football team quickly proved that a large segment of the citizenry had an appetite for witnessing marginally controlled violence in an outdoor setting.

One reason why the management of the football club had no trouble selling twenty thousand season tickets was that the Vancouver area had an increasing density of population to draw upon. Burnaby, the North Shore and the Lulu Island district of Richmond were taking the overflow from a city whose population by 1954 was close to 400,000. With the greater concentration of human beings came the problems of the big city. In January, 1955, at a Vancouver hospital a baby was born as a drug addict. The mother had passed on to the child the symptoms of narcotics addiction. In February the press named Vancouver "the key market center" for international drug traffic, some of the seven murders committed in the city in 1954, and the popularity of golf courses for disposing of bodies of unsuccessful traffickers, being linked to the new industry. As further embarrassment to the city's law-enforcement officers, an RCMP inspector was appointed to examine the evidence produced by the Tupper commission inquiry into charges of criminal laxity and corruption in the Vancouver police department. In the course of the inquiry a "mystery witness" in the shape of a veiled brunette woman told tales of pay-offs by gamblers to policemen, and explained her relationship with police chief Walter Mulligan as that of a friend who typed his speeches for "clubs, churches and so on." During assessment of the evidence Mulligan left for California without announcing any plans for his return, and another investigation into police corruption ended inconclusively.

A number of older residents expressed the conviction that the breakdown of law and order could be attributed to the fact that in 1954, policemen were granted permission to doff their tunics in warm weather.

The deteriorating regard in which the constabulary was held by some sections of the public was amply demonstrated in the riots that accompanied the city's playing host to the 1955 Grey Cup game. Not even the November 22 rainfall, which was a record (3.15 inches) for a twenty-four-hour period, damped the mob spirit flaunted in front of the courthouse. Having dutifully deplored its conduct toward an event involving two outside teams, the city a few days later voted the majority needed to legalize Sunday sports as of 1956. The bill for riot damage was quietly added to the deficit for the B.E.G., as Vancouver's contribution to athletic activity.

The city remained in excellent shape to pay for its excesses. In 1956 the value of property within city limits topped one billion dollars for the first time. During the year $68 million was spent on construction, much of it large buildings. Of these major structures rising downtown the most visually striking was the B. C. Electric Building, at Burrard and Nelson, known as "Grauer's Tower" after the exceptionally able head of the company, Dal Grauer, whose personality was reflected in the building's bold design. The building dominated the senior churches across the street. Henceforth the power, if not the glory, was vouchsafed as 110/120 volts, and eternity was measurable in kilowatt hours.

The streets increasingly shadowed by these new tall buildings bore heavier traffic of motor vehicles, thirty-nine thousand new autos being sold in 1956. City Hall was beginning its long travail of traffic engineering, to companion such older bugaboos as the illegal suites which, as a housing problem, were a war souvenir of 1939–45. To reduce the weight of its responsibilities the council instituted the Board of Administration, which, like the defunct ward system, proved to be a cure for which the disease had to be invented.

One council innovation that proved to be an unqualified success was the opening of the Aquarium in Stanley Park, June 8, 1956. The Aquarium's director, Dr. Murray Newman, lost no time in effecting his program of presenting living tableaux of as many varieties as possible of the fish of B.C. waters, not excluding the largest. His quest for a killer whale led to the capture in July, 1964, of Moby Doll, the first of her species to cavort as a zoological exhibit. When Moby Doll expired, an improved pool was built for the longer-lived Skana, whose medical needs were supervised in part by Dr. Pat McGeer, nephew of the former mayor and a U.B.C. professor of neurology. From interpreting the messages of the intelligent killer whale Dr. McGeer went on to become leader of the provincial Liberal party, a more complicated problem in communication.

The medical needs of the human population, too, were growing, requiring expansion of the city's hospitals. St. Paul's Hospital opened its new wing in June, 1955, and Vancouver General was becoming the largest hospital complex in the country. As might be expected, the Catholic hospital was noted for its maternity ward while VGH pioneered open-heart surgery and other ramifications of WASP stress.

A malaise less easy to diagnose was that developing among Vancouver's lovers of the arts. The city's best-loved novelist, Sir Walter Scott, had been vaguely threatened by the presence, in a shack on the beach of nearby Dollarton, of novelist Malcolm Lowry. The success of the Stratford, Ontario, festival aggravated the sensation of inadequacy, and the fact that Vancouver was a city of roughly the same size and latitude as Edinburgh, site of another very prestigious festival, was not lost on the sufferers of cultural itch. Something about putting numbers of Scots near open water causes their community to break out in a rash of military tattoo and allied arts. It should also be remembered that the Salish Indians of prehistory practiced frontal lambdoidal cranial deformation, binding pads of cedar bark to apply pressure to the front and back of the infant's head: Vancouver's first highbrows.

In any event, the city no longer felt culturally fulfilled by the Pacific National Exhibition, the country fair begun in 1910 in Hastings Park as perpetuation of the fun and games of New Brighton. Although the fair had grown to attract about a million people to the grounds each late summer, ranking it among the top ten fairs of North America, there was no question that the cultural tone was set by the swine, goats and girlie shows.

Accordingly, Vancouver threw together a committee that announced plans for the first Festival of the Arts, to be held in 1958 in conjunction with British Columbia's centennial celebrations. The festival committee promised importation of artists of global celebrity. Little doubt was expressed that the festival productions, added to the existing seductions of the city in summer, would draw tourists from all parts of the world and take some of the wind out of Auld Reekie's sails.

More typically, Vancouver had greatness thrust upon her, as in November, 1956, at the summer Olympic Games in Melbourne, when the U.B.C. rowing four won the gold medal for the event. The rowers' chances had been judged so minimal that the Olympic committee had been reluctant to pay their way to Australia. Similarly the U.B.C. eight, which finished second to the U.S., had practiced under coach Frank Read in the debris-littered waters of Coal Harbour. "Cinderella team" has been a much-used sobriquet among Vancouver sportswriters, nonetheless busy trying to jam the glass slipper on the wrong foot.

Another trait of the city—the readiness to adopt a waif—was displayed during 1957 in the Christian Hanna episode. Hanna, whom the press quickly described as "the man without a country," jumped ship and sought sanctuary in Canada. After a year of playing dodgem with immigration authorities and winning the sympathy of a fair part of the world, Hanna fell afoul of the law in other ways and returned to sea, still without a passport. Other ship jumpers, notably Fijians, have also flattered the city with illegal entry. No less welcome was a sizable batch of Hungarians fleeing Russia's quashing of the abortive revolution in their country. Led by a group of forestry students who were helped to adjust to a new language in courses at U.B.C., the Hungarians added their own special seasoning to the cosmopolitanism being accentuated by the arrival in Vancouver of more and more Australians, Germans, Italians, South Africans, and darker-skinned natives of Commonwealth countries.

The social nexus of the newcomers was Robson Street—Robsonstrasse. From Howe Street west toward the Park the small shops were transmuted into a Continental bazaar: delicatessens festooned with fancy sausages whose ingredients would have shocked earlier Vancouver as an insult to the flag; curio shops whose clerks wore saris and whose merchandise wore nothing whatever; schnitzel houses and European cafes whose tablecloths were stained with the gravy of genuine goulash; magazine and phonograph record shops in which the spoken language was *Deutsch* and the background music *biergarten*—all these cheek by jowl along a few blocks of pavement crowded with cheerfully conglomerate natives of elsewhere. Such was Robsonstrasse, and Vancouver was pleased to discover it as a bright ribbon to wear in her hair.

The ethnic geography of Vancouver was becoming even more checkered than in the city's beginnings, but with varying degrees of conspicuousness. In 1951, of Vancouver's total population of 344,833, only 244,528 were of British origin. Of the remainder, two of the larger minority groups, the Scandinavians and the Slavs, were rather unobtrusive. The Icelanders, Finns, Norwegians and Swedes naturally gravitated to the woods and coastal waters during the work season, their residence in Vancouver manifesting itself mostly in the trim Lutheran churches scattered throughout the city. The Ukrainians, removals from the Canadian prairies, lost much of their communal impact through similar dispersion throughout the districts. Even more assimilated were the Baltic groups, the Netherlanders, the Spanish. The Greeks were just beginning to show an affinity for West Broadway, where by 1970 they would have several restaurants and a resident belly dancer. The Jewish community, with some centralization in the Cambie Street–41st Avenue area of Kerrisdale, with community center and synagogues, had their homes in all parts of the city. One of the more sizable ethnic groups, the Germans, recovering from the opprobrium of two world wars, began to make their influence felt not only on Robsonstrasse but in the trades, particularly the construction industry, which also absorbed most of the influx of Italians, post-1950. The Italians created both the youngest and most homogeneous group in the city, to the weekly distress of soccer referees. *Les Canadiens*, at first a negligible factor in Vancouver's population, had to wait till the late sixties before becoming more cohesive, with introduction of the lively French-language weekly *Le Soleil* and the CBUF-FM radio station broadcasting *la belle langue.* Finally, there was the gradually increasing incursion of Americans, mostly university teaching staff, or those in flight from U.S. foreign policy and the draft. Many of these were dismayed to find themselves the victims of a new kind of persecution in the form of neighbors practicing lawn and garden worship, and retreated back to the States to escape the terror weapons: lawnmower and bug bomb.

As perhaps the most convincing sign that it had at last discarded its xenophobia, the city in 1957 elected to parliament that body's first Chinese, Douglas Jung, a young Vancouver lawyer and graduate of U.B.C. And the city's new generation of Chinese women, their slim figures setting off the latest styles in Western dress, gave quietus to the old childhood chant, "Me Chinese, crooked at the knees."

As the center of the city took on new shadings of ethnic character, the periphery continued to radiate population, so much so that in 1957 the city accepted chairmanship of the Greater Vancouver Metropolitan Planning Committee. The congestion of traffic on the Lions Gate Bridge, where commuters from North and West Vancouver were failing to enjoy their protracted view of the Park afforded by backed-up columns of cars, amplified the demand for a second crossing at First Narrows. Opening of the new Oak Street Bridge across the North Arm of the Fraser, in the summer of 1957, evoked a different and typically perverse demand: because the new crossing was a toll bridge, the announcement by the provincial government that it intended to dismantle the sixty-eight-year-old Marpole Bridge, long a thorn in the city's side, but free of tolls, produced an outcry of protest. The sagging nuisance suddenly took on a rustic charm. A Save-the-Marpole-Bridge committee was formed. Enshrinement of the miserable object as a historic site was averted only by the removal of tolls from the Oak Street Bridge. Then execution was swift.

None of these bridges was included in the escape routes defined by the booklet *Evacuation and Survival Plan for Greater Vancouver Target Area*, published by the Vancouver civil defense authorities in 1957 and delivered to every householder. The booklet, official acknowledgment of Russia's development of nuclear weapons and of the new era of intercontinental ballistic missiles, counseled Vancouver citizens to get beyond the twenty-mile radius of the city, if they had a car, otherwise to "walk to the nearest playground or dock" and think positively about being picked up by a truck. A study of the evacuation routes having been coordinated with knowledge of the time available in the event of ICBM attack, many Vancouver people discovered new virtues in their basements. Some actually stocked cellar shelves with canned goods, in compliance with Ottawa's recommendation in *Eleven Steps to Survival.* Vancouver was learning to live with the balance of terror that was the cold war.

The only catastrophe to strike the city in 1958 was a grim tragedy of its own making. On June 17, at 3:40 P.M. of what became known as Black Tuesday, the new Second Narrows Bridge, whose steel spans jutted uncompleted over the treacherous current, abruptly collapsed. Fifty men working on the bridge plunged 212 feet into the water, many of them fastened to girders by safety belts that suddenly became death traps. Eighteen died, the city's worst disaster since the Fire. In the attempt to recover bodies pinned in the wreckage, a diver was lost, bringing the total to nineteen. A subsequent investigation indicated that the temporary scaffolding supporting the outermost of the steel spans was too weak to take the weight, and its collapse triggered the chain reaction of plummeting sections of the new bridge. The accident stunned the city and ended its charmed life in contention with a rugged environment.

A more pleasant reminder of Vancouver's efforts to domesticate the wilderness was provided by the events of the centennial year, the hundredth birthday of the founding of the Gold Colony. As its contribution the federal government opened, in March, 1958, the "mail palace" that was the new Vancouver Post Office. The $13 million, block-square structure at Georgia and Hamilton streets was officially opened by Mayor Hume and unofficially described by Vancouver artist Jack Shadbolt as a monumental eyesore, a fine example of the school of architecture known as Ottawa Utilitarian. The government had supplied much improved facilities for moving mail, without altering the old post office's atmosphere conducive to riot. The new post office was in fact immediately picketed by jobless.

The bad taste of bureaucracy was forgotten in the visit of the queen's sister, Princess Margaret. At local garden parties girdles creaked like Spanish galleons in the battle line of curtsies, and hands that had touched the royal glove remained unwashed for days. Those who were not invited to meet royalty found solace in the opening of Sundays to commercialized sports, a relaxation of the blue laws that made perdition as available to the working class as it was to the Sunday golfer and yachtsman.

All classes answered the call of the summer's premier event: the first season of the Vancouver Festival of the Arts, now titled the Vancouver International Festival to obviate any suspicion of parochialism. Foreign music-lovers were expected in such numbers, it was said, that several hotels had their spittoons tuned. Music critics were also coming from the wide world, astonished that anyone in the region played anything but a salmon. The Festival box offices were rewarded with clamoring queues, only slightly lengthened by the closing of Vancouver beaches for the first time because of pollution.

The temperature also rose to the occasion. With most of the plays and musical events performed in the barnlike Georgia Auditorium, the Orpheum Theatre and the old Lyric (Vancouver Opera House), the hottest summer in years combined with the V.I.F. to convince Vancouver people of the artistic values of air conditioning. Many patrons went home after an evening performance and watered their lawns, in the moonlight, wearing formal dress, because a shortage of water in the mains had required restriction of sprinkling to the hours between midnight and noon. Some of the more revealing scenes of the season were played out on back lawns by neighbors flitting about in night clothes and garlanded with garden hose.

The festival provided a splendid occasion for some of the last public appearances of Professor Francis, one of Vancouver's several distinguished eccentrics. A tall, gaunt figure of thoroughly disreputable aspect, ever clad in a tattered overcoat, a long-deceased flower in the buttonhole, and hugging a rolled-up newspaper, the Professor was for years the most dependable patron of every stylish concert held in Vancouver. Spurning paid admission, he somehow gained entrance to any theater he cared to crash, despite the most elaborate preventive measures of the theater manager, and swept up and down the aisles like a superbly gracious scarecrow, quickly zeroing in on the most distinguished patron—he particularly relished a lieutenant governor—to engage that worthy in conversation no less animated for being one-sided.

The legend was that Professor Francis had been a pianist of great talent, whose career on the concert stage was blighted by an unhappy love affair that also stilled his interest in regular shaving.

He turned his artistry to the magic of materializing in the middle of a theater whose entrances were all carefully guarded. On one occasion, having been ejected twice from the Lyric, he reappeared for a third curtain call, and was asked by the frankly impressed manager how he had got in.

"Through the coal chute," replied the Professor, without malice, and set off to launch his grubby apparition at the loge containing dignitaries. Toward the end of his career, theater managers gave up the unequal contest and looked upon the Professor's arrival as a good omen for the performance, the theatrical equivalent of a stork nesting in the chimney. Appropriately, Professor Francis died in public, of a coronary while giving an impromptu concert after the regular musicians had left the Johann Strauss Coffee House. He bequeathed, to nobody but the phantom of the opera, fourteen bank books totaling $20,000, and a mystery quite intact.

Candor requires that it be noted, here rather than *passim*, that Professor Francis was only one of a continuum of town characters dating from the genesis of Vancouver. The same soil that favors the nut-tree has nurtured other oddities such as Crazy George, Whistling Texas, the Russian General, Tarzan and Canada's first town fool, Joachim Foikis. The first clipper ship to bring London cargo direct to Vancouver, the bark *Titania*, on July 25, 1889, was skippered by "Dandy" Dunne, a mirror of fashion irreparably shattered when the departing captain stepped off the wharf without connecting with the gangplank, landing head-first on a log below.

Crazy George, of the same period, was a Vancouver hermit who heard voices. "In spite of his being 'crazy' we recognized that Crazy George had been reared in culture to be a courteous English gentleman," wrote Dr. Gladys Schwesinger, recalling her childhood in a pioneer Vancouver family. Crazy George was an extreme case of the English remittance man finding himself with no peer group and obliged to converse only with himself.

Whistling Texas, a longshoreman who for forty years seemed to have no home but the waterfront docks, communicated in a somewhat different way. He sat on the wharf stringers and whistled at ships, notably the Union ships, as they pulled out. After a long career of perilous perching over the piles, Whistling Texas was killed in 1936 by a fall from a fire hall.

He was contemporaneous with the Russian General, a small, fierce-looking person who wore a Balaclava helmet, and faded but scrupulously clean tunic and breeches, as he strode the downtown area, clipping his jack boots with a riding crop.

Whereas the Russian General was clearly on the march against some nameless foe, Tarzan reveled in the elements, delighting in drawing shocked looks from shopping crowds by loping along the downtown streets in rain and freezing sleet with his chest bared by the unbuttoned shirt, which, pants aside, was his only concession to covering.

Unconventional behavior in public attained the status of a profession, in the late sixties, with the self-appointment as town fool of Joachim Foikis. Aided by a Canada Council grant, Foikis capered in his red-and-blue jester's costume, beating his drum in various processions of flower children, to his ultimate destination of police court. Again, Vancouver had shown itself equally compatible with king, queen or joker. Possibly the omnipresence of the massive aberrations of mountain reminds those who live here of the puny stature man owns in creation. Where else in Canada would it seem appropriate, in the same year that man landed on the moon, for a group of young, chanting monks, heads shaven and wearing saffron robes, to play finger cymbals and intone Hindu rhymes for the edification of shoppers entering the Bay? Vancouver has never given up in the effort to prove that Columbus was not altogether wrong when he assumed that he had reached India.

In 1958 the strangest cultists of all, Vancouver football fans, convened to give the Grey Cup game the largest crowd ever to have witnessed the event in Canada: 36,629 persons, who watched the Winnipeg Blue Bombers defeat the Hamilton Tiger Cats 35–28. The B.C. Lions' record for the season was three wins, thirteen losses. The team got a new head coach and was on its way to a record for going through more coaches than a C.P.R. trainman.

The other loser as the year ended was Fred Hume, defeated after eight years as mayor by Tom Alsbury, the schoolteacher favorite of the East End of the city. Vancouver was expressing one of its periodical returns to rectitude after free-spending conviviality. Although the city's Playland amusement park had inaugurated the biggest roller coaster in the country, not all of the giddiness of '58 was innocuous.

In 1959 Vancouver went back to work with the slight peevishness that sometimes follows a night on the town, the dark brown taste in the municipal affairs, and the industrial headache of strikes that reduced the logging industry to a chip on the shoulder. Labor strife filled the newspapers with the clash of claim against claim, battle cries of company and union spokesmen, and the thud of the court injunction against picketing. The year saw the consolidation of an enduring antipathy in leaders of unions whose headquarters were in Vancouver, toward the Social Credit government of Premier W. A. C. Bennett in Victoria, which passed legislation that labor viewed as distinctly unfriendly. The labor newspapers published in the city painted a picture of Bennett and his ministers as a cabinet only slightly less sinister than that of Dr. Caligari.

The mood of the city was not noticeably improved with the opening, a year late, of its centennial project: the Maritime Museum at Hadden Park, Kitsilano. The museum opened in April with no staff and no exhibits, a situation that even the most charitable recognized as disadvantageous. The expired funds were resuscitated, and in time the Maritime Museum acquired not only a worthy collection of salty memorabilia but also an adjoining shelter, completed in 1966, for the RCMP vessel *St. Roch.*

Equally embarrassing was the May madness of the Fireboat That Couldn't Go. After many years of nagging various levels of government for a fireboat, Vancouver had at last obtained one. But when fire broke out aboard the freighter *Ferngulf* outside the First Narrows, the fireboat did not answer the call for help. The reason given for this reluctance was that the fire was outside the fireboat's frame of flammatory reference, and that to go to the freighter's assistance would have left the waterfront unprotected. The city responded by beginning a campaign for a second fireboat.

After this undistinguished beginning, the year gained some luster with the visit of the queen and the Duke of Edinburgh. The primary purpose of the royal visit to Canada was to meet President Eisenhower and grace the opening of the St. Lawrence Seaway, but in the view of the Vancouver planning committee the pivotal event was the queen's presiding over the opening, on July 4, 1959, of the new civic theater-auditorium that had been named after her. The weak spot in the projected itinerary of the royal couple was identified as the problem of parking their train for the night. After a day of passing through the spectacular scenery of the Fraser Canyon, the royal coach was scheduled to be shoved onto a desolate siding under the Pattullo Bridge, from which point Elizabeth and Philip would have an unimpeded view of the B.C. Penitentiary across the river.

The theater for which the queen and her husband were the first star performers was fitted with the latest equipment for staging spectacles too large to be played at the City Hall. The great stage easily contained any opera regardless of the numerical strength of its spear-carriers, and though the acoustics were found to be faulty and the murals enigmatic, the plaza fronting the theater was widely admired for its attempt at an urban fountain, the first play of water in the downtown area and the direct result of the discovery, by civic officials, that part of the charm of European cities was controlled precipitation, centrally located.

The QET, as the theater came to be known, was in fact well provided in its first summer with everything except audiences. The second season of the Vancouver International Festival took it over for five weeks of opera, symphony concerts, Japanese dancers and an all-Canadian deficit, a dazzling display of ambitiousness outstripping budget. The festival was successful, however, in administering the *coup de grâce* to the Theatre Under the Stars. TUTS staggered on for one more season, but rained-out performances and competitive attractions doomed what had become a popular if soggy institution. Gradually there was borne upon the boosters of the arts the hard truth that Vancouver people were neither sufficiently numerous, nor readily enough deterred from sloping off to summer cottages and campsites, to realize the vision of Salzburg the Younger.

The most flamboyant demise of 1959, the one that put the name "Vancouver" on the lips of millions who had never before pronounced it, was the sudden passing on the premises of film actor Errol Flynn. Flynn was visiting the inlet in the company of a blonde lady friend, a circumstance that in no way detracted from the sensation created by his death. Although there was no explicit evidence that the hard-living actor had chosen Vancouver, like Naples, to see as the consummate experience before expiring, residents took a quiet pride in sharing the last moments of a life dedicated to pleasure.

Flynn was one of a number of Hollywood stars who were beginning to visit Vancouver less finally, though often in passing, en route to salmon fishing up the coast. Bing Crosby, John Wayne, and Eddie Albert were some of the regulars escaping the more strident tones of California, while from eastern Canada more and more head-office executives found it necessary to make a visit of inspection to their Vancouver branch offices after eastern winter had closed the golf courses around Toronto and Montreal. The merits of the city's evergreens were dramatized by Stan Leonard, the Vancouver-born professional who won three major U.S. tournaments, was eight times Canadian professional champion, and was named international Golfer of the Year in 1959, as well as outstanding Canadian athlete of the year.

To complete a year of notable visitors, on December 27 the largest passenger liner to have visited Vancouver in commercial activity, the P. & O. liner *Arcadia* (29,734 tons), added her lights to the harbor's festive mood. But at night all waters look unpolluted. Vancouver was entering the sixties with new sources of disquiet ("Are We Most Beautiful?" was the querulous head of a *Province* editorial). And the mirror on the wall no longer returned an unequivocal response to the question of who was the fairest city of all.

CHAPTER 15 1960–1970

A Touch of Megalopolis

The Beastly Electric slain by the many-headed Hydro • Hurricane Frieda, and fresh wind at City Hall • Hippieville • The New Gastown

VANCOUVER made no special plans to celebrate the city's seventy-fifth birthday. The bills for earlier birthday parties were still outstanding. More significant, perhaps, was that the city had reached the size where there was less natural enthusiasm for a familial celebration. In spite of the relative austerity, and the absence of the Grey Cup game, in 1960 Vancouver recorded 11,500 arrests for drunkenness. Of that total 7,690 arrests were made in a small area of fifty square blocks, bounded on the west by Richards Street, on the east by Gore, on the south by Pender, and on the north by the waterfront. This was alcoholism's ghetto—the unsteady Skid Road—to which gravitated the walking wounded from the hinterland: the chokerman crippled by a log, the failed fisherman, the prospector finding his last glint of gold in a bottle of bay rum. By nationality, the highest proportion of arrested drunks were Irish, Scottish and native Indian, but the fights they engaged in were more impersonal than in the days of the Deighton House, and when a man fell from a flophouse window the extra height was usually fatal.

It was clear that the city was suffering from cirrhosis of the livability of a vital part of its mid-section. Plans were prepared for $100 million slum clearance, with public housing to replace the old buildings sheltering both dipsomaniacs and the desperately poor.

The program at once ran afoul of the residents of Chinatown, most of whom were older citizens to whom the rapport of their community and unity of family, however numerous, were to be preferred to the antiseptic blocks of concrete set apart from Chinatown. City planners were faced with the anomaly that Chinatown was one of the better-behaved corners of the city's badlands, whereas some of the worst riots of youthful hoodlums occurred in the solidly upper-middle-class districts of Kerrisdale and Dunbar. The sixties brought the dawn of understanding that poverty had no monopoly on the raw material of antisocial behavior.

Another expectation rudely deflated was that the delayed opening of the ill-starred Second Narrows Bridge, August 2, 1960, would relieve the pressure of traffic across the Lions Gate Bridge. North Shore commuters adhered stubbornly to the overburdened suspension bridge, and even the removal by the provincial government of tolls from the new bridges did little to divert an appreciable amount of traffic through the East End.

As for public transit, its faltering wheels were made more wobbly still by the earth-shaking event of 1961: the taking over, by Bennett's provincial government, of the B.C. Electric Company. The May announcement struck the populace into the same awe with which earlier natives observed an eclipse of the sun. Although the threat of public ownership had hung in the air for years, few of those whose formative years were shaped by the imperative clang and rattle of the streetcar, whose earliest reading was the *Buzzer*—a pink paper found among the ads for Player's Navy Cut cigarettes and Lydia Pinkham's pills—could believe that the giant had been evicted from his castle. The $700 million price paid by the provincial government hardly covered the trauma of having the Devil exorcised without the promise of an adequate replacement. The expropriation was followed by a year of litigation in which the company fought the arbitrary conditions of its execution, a struggle which the people of Vancouver watched with the mixed emotions of the man who sees his mother-in-law drive over a cliff in his new car. The prospect of swearing at buses that were, in effect, one's own, depleted the satisfaction. On the other hand, the prospect of a lower rate for domestic users of electricity put many normally stout capitalists on the side of public ownership. The matter was finally settled in March, 1962, by an act of the legislature that merged the B.C. Electric Company and the B.C. Power Commission into one colossus: the B.C.

Hydro and Power Authority. Henceforth, in these utilities, the public was its own worst enemy.

To this tumbling of idols the fallout across Canada of Soviet nuclear bomb tests added disquiet. In four weeks of September, with word that Russia had developed the hydrogen bomb, the Greater Vancouver civil defense headquarters received ten thousand inquiries for information on fallout shelters. Vancouver gardeners worried about strontium 90 even as they inhaled large quantities of DDT from their spray cans. The Lord's Day Alliance also suffered damage, in the *angst* of that summer, the attorney general yielding to the demand that laundromats be allowed to open on Sundays, and the agitation in Vancouver for Sunday movies assuring the parting of the last strand (April, 1963) of the city's ties with Presbyterian conscience.

What should have been a happy event for Vancouver's lovers of legitimate theater, namely the opening in 1961 of the small playhouse built back-to-back with the Queen Elizabeth Theatre, lost its dulcitude in the row about choice of name for the place. A highly vocal body of citizens wanted the playhouse to be called the Pauline Johnson, in honor of Vancouver's first professional trouper, but the suggestion was resisted by an equally articulate group who wanted a name with less connotation of old canoe and a chain of candy stores. As was its wont, the city council chose a name that satisfied nobody: the Playhouse. Once the raised hackles had subsided, the name proved entirely serviceable to the Playhouse Theatre Company, which took it over for the production of Vancouver's first professional theater seasons in some time.

As a culminating emotional disturbance for the city, after years of wrangling the council accepted Ottawa's offer of $2.75 million for purchase of the Vancouver International Airport. The fact that the city could not afford to build the expanded runways and other facilities required by the jet age was at once forgotten in the soul-searching stirred by dread that the federal government had got a bargain.

Perhaps as a result of this temporary state of stress the council chose, once again, to challenge Major Matthews on the matter of who owned the archives. A 1957 court order that had named the city sole trustee of the archives pinged harmlessly off the major's well-armored personality. When, in 1959, the visible portion of the archives was moved from the City Hall to the new public library building on Burrard at Robson, the major went along with it and consolidated a position as impregnable as ever. Nevertheless, in a renewal of what the *Province* termed "the Thirty Year War," new and brash Alderman William Rathie tried to motivate Matthews to produce historical items believed to be kept in his private vault, and instituted action for council to take over custodianship of the archives. The major routed the attack with customary ease, but the bold if foredoomed gallantry of Alderman Rathie did not go unperceived by Vancouver citizens. A year later (December, 1962) they elected him mayor.

Without doubt the most exceptional occurrence of 1962 was Hurricane Frieda. Vancouver, the city with no previous experience with Mother Nature gone to extremes, on the night of October 12 took the last, angry flick of the tail of a great typhoon that swept out of the Pacific and, totally unexpected, raced up the coast from California, devastating Oregon and Washington shoreline before hitting Vancouver with howling fury a little after midnight. Unlike the coconut palms of the tropics that are pliant before the gale, the big conifers of the Northwest remained rigid as they toppled over, wrenching huge roots out of the soil. Over the Lower Mainland the sky was lit by strange flashes, some caused by lightning that accompanied the driving rain, others by trees falling across power lines at split-second intervals. In Vancouver people stood at their windows enjoying the rare phenomenon, too ignorant to take cover below ground, and failing to identify the rippling sound overhead as rows of shingles being stripped off the roof.

Traffic was paralyzed by fallen power lines. Some houses caught fire, but the downpour helped to extinguish the blazes. The less lucky individuals were those caught on the Stanley Park causeway at the height of the hurricane. In pitch darkness, and with some of the region's biggest Douglas firs and hemlocks crashing all about them, passengers of forty cars sat trapped and helpless, waiting to be killed by the city's oldest living things. One woman died and several persons were injured in the nightmare scene, before the storm hit its peak gusts of 87 mph at 2:43 A.M. and the rain mercifully tapered off as hundreds of homes lay open to the sky.

During the days that followed, many Vancouver householders were fully occupied covering roofs laid bare, and the shingle manufacturers enjoyed to the full the homily about an ill wind. Thousands of people spent as much as two weeks without electric light, heat or telephone, and damage to homes was placed at ten million dollars.

The more lasting mischief wreaked by Frieda was that in the Park. Although the old men were at their accustomed play on the oversize checkerboard the Saturday morning after the hurricane, the storm had cut wide swaths through stands of magnificent timber that deserved a more leisurely return to the earth. The cleanup operation of the parks board brought tears to the eyes of the city's old-timers and West Enders. Necessary though it was, it destroyed perhaps forever the wilderness character of much of the Park, the tangled wonderland of rotting giants, brilliant green ferns and saplings springing up willy-nilly amid the bird-filled underbrush. Frieda was a vagrant that despoiled the last part of the city that was kin to innocence.

Vancouver's chance to buy another park was lost in the December election that won the mayor's chair for William Rathie. The voters turned down a proposal to buy from the C.P.R. the old Shaughnessy golf course, property become too valuable to be shared with divot makers. On the other hand Sunday movies were approved. Provision of breathing space for the future was of less concern than means of escape from a wet Sunday at home, particularly as the Lord's Day Alliance was less expensive to deal with than the C.P.R.

These electoral issues were barely settled before the new mayor flummoxed the indigenes by announcing that he would make no public speeches for at least three months. The purpose of the self-imposed silence was that of getting on with the job, but the statement was nonetheless unsettling to a populace accustomed to seeing press photos of the mayor lending his presence to everything from a soapbox derby to the annual rose show. Rathie was the first of a new model of mayor: the successful and wealthy businessman whose interest in the job was that of the managerial executive rather than the breezy politician. But Vancouver people were slow to appreciate this flesh-and-blood proof that the city's problems had grown so serious and complex that they required all the chief magistrate's attention. The old concept of the mayor as a jolly and somewhat bibulous uncle, direct descendant of Pollyanna, died hard.

Very soon after bringing this hardheaded *modus operandi* to his desk, Mayor Rathie was faced with a situation that could hardly have been less amenable to a businesslike solution. In the latter months of 1962 several hundred members of the Sons of Freedom sect of Doukhobors began a three-hundred-mile trek from their homes in the Kootenays to Agassiz, in the Fraser Valley, where a number of the sect had been placed in a special jail because of acts of violence in the interior. In January, 1963, the small army of men, women and children dressed in their traditional Russian garb moved down from the camp at Hope to hold protest meetings in Vancouver's Victory Square. To the growing alarm of civic officials the numbers of Sons encumbering the streets around the square approached a thousand. Although the protest took the form of hymns, sung with a natural harmony that was by no means unpleasant, the Doukhobors attracted large throngs of "Son-watchers," as the press called them, who helped the stoutly shod visitors in churning up the grass of the square and turning most of the surface of the area into sleazy muck. The Canadian Legion complained bitterly to Mayor Rathie that the cenotaph was being desecrated by a peaceful demonstration. Fortunately the mayor turned a deaf ear to the voices calling for forcible expulsion, and after several weeks the tuneful anarchists melted away, moving back to Agassiz and building a hut camp, there to wait out the sentences of the imprisoned.

Other huts, those of the students overcrowding the University of British Columbia, were part of the conditions that moved the university's new president, John Barfoot Macdonald, to produce in January, 1963, the report aimed at reorganizing facilities for higher education in the province. Among the sweeping changes recommended by the report was the establishment of a second university, by upgrading the existing Victoria College, and establishing four junior colleges immediately, four more by 1971, as well as a four-year degree-granting college in Burnaby. The provincial government subsequently built the Burnaby campus as a full university, Simon Fraser, and took over the old King Edward High School as the Vancouver City College. In 1970 the City College moved into new buildings on the former Langara golf course, and Vancouver at last had an institution of higher learning, within city limits, to which it could point without a wince of shame.

While the Macdonald report was serving the intellect, the B.C. Lions were stimulating lovers of the physical by winning the Western Conference play-offs of the C.F.L. and playing host, November 30, to the eastern champion Hamilton Tiger Cats. The Grey Cup game at Empire Stadium was attended by 36,465 fans who watched in consternation a late tackle by Hamilton lineman Angelo Mosca that concussed Willie Fleming, the Lions' star halfback. The visitors went on to win 21–10, a decisive demonstration of the toughness of the steel town over the mild western metropolis. The theory was enunciated, by sportswriters, that something about the soft air, or water, of Vancouver caused professional athletes to become languid contemplators of the lotus. Football players imported by the Lions from even the flintiest towns of Pennsylvania risked permanent injury to the will to maim, if they remained on the west coast for more than a couple of seasons. Some escaped in time, to the National Football League in the States, but more stayed in the city's thrall, opening restaurants in which they became happily corpulent, or becoming salesmen for local wineries and general agents for perdition.

What the football players lacked in desire, in the destructive sense, was manifested by Vancouver fans. On the Saturday night following the '63 Grey Cup game six to eight thousand frustrated followers of the chronic losers milled about downtown, brawling and throwing bottles, with 319 arrests. The following year the Grey Cup game was held in the East, the Lions won it, and Vancouver's merchants were as grateful as the coach.

The social structure of Vancouver also had to adjust, in 1964, to the integration of its beer parlors. A Liquor Control Board ruling of the previous December had tumbled the wall of Jericho separating men from women or couple. Henceforth a woman was permitted to enter, unescorted, that part of the beverage room reserved by law for men only. A sizable portion of the city's male population was at once plunged into mourning. The law that had been decried as primitive was found to have many silent supporters, under the generic grouping known as That Old Gang of Mine. The men's-club atmosphere of the beer parlor, with its unmodified choice of vocabulary, was defunct, and many a tear dropped into a glass of lager held by the older man to whom the beer parlor was a refuge from womankind. Once again Progress was shown to be a double-bitted ax whose sharper blade severed a man's peace.

The take-over by women of the hotel's licensed premises was paralleled by that of hotel management by Americans. Vancouver's newest and most prestigious hotel was now the Bayshore Inn, near the site of the old arena. In December, 1963, came the announcement from the C.N.R. that it was turning over management of the Hotel Vancouver to the Hilton interests, who would also renovate the *grande dame* of railway châteaux. The effect of this news on the community was comparable to that of hearing that the queen mother was to have her face lifted by a Hollywood make-up artist.

The community could and would, however, forestall that foreign element based east of the Rockies. The city hungered for a coliseum to accommodate visiting spectacles too expensive–such as pop music's rock groups–or otherwise un-housebroken–such as the circus–for the Queen Elizabeth Theatre, as well as to house the city's aspirations to membership in the National Hockey League. But when Stafford Smythe, president of Toronto's Maple Leaf Gardens, offered to build the coliseum for the sum of one dollar (given the land, two blocks of property opposite the QET), the citizens closed ranks and rejected a bylaw that had the support of the council, press and much advertising. Five years later Smythe was cited for income tax evasion and temporarily ousted as director of the Maple Leafs club. Once again western virtue was triumphant.

The buoyant economy of the city was reflected in not only the season ticket sales for hockey and football games (the latter over twenty thousand each year, despite a team gifted with new ways of losing), but also such luxuries as winter holidays in Hawaii. During 1965, Canadian Pacific Airlines increased its service to Hawaii to eight jets a week and carried forty thousand passengers between Vancouver and Honolulu. A blow to the airline was the sudden death, on June 20, of its president, Grant McConachie, while holidaying in the U.S. McConachie, who had started flying while a student at the University of Alberta in the twenties, had became a pre-eminent member of the fraternity of bush pilots. He had then taken over C.P.A. when it was still a fly-by-the-seat-of-the-pants operation and built it into one of the world's major airlines, with its base in Vancouver, pioneering the international air service to the Orient and the Antipodes.

Local air traffic, too, augmented the throngs churning about in the totally inadequate Sea Island terminal. Pacific Western Airlines, B.C. Airlines and charter services of float planes popularized the direct route between remote coastal or interior points and the bright lights of Vancouver, the logger and the miner enjoying quicker immersion in the city's simmering fleshpots. To add to the problems of the airport control tower, the Vancouver area in the mid-sixties underwent a population explosion of European starlings, the huge flocks veering over the Lulu Island berry farms by day and roosting by the tens of thousands under the Cambie Street Bridge. Fauna of the Old World, including the marsh crane fly, had joined the common rat as companions of *homo Vancouveritus*.

Also during the summer of 1966 many citizens were incensed by the loss of the magnolia trees, long an embellishment of the lawns fronting the courthouse, to human predators in the form of the provincial government. The works minister in Victoria had promised a fountain to replace the landscaping, as the government's Canadian Centennial project. Although the courthouse properly belonged to the provincial government, Vancouver people naturally felt proprietary about the only bit of greenery in the center of the city. As the trees were hauled away and the lawns dug up, local tempers were not improved by secrecy on the part of Victoria about the design of the fountain. The opinion was general that any fountain whose sculpture was approved by the provincial works department would be, by the laws of bureaucracy, a watery blot.

The contractor surrounded his hole in the ground with a half-block-square fence, built high enough to discourage sidewalk superintendents. Called "the Great Wall of Chant," after the works minister, the fence became the world's longest uncoordinated mural as dozens of amateur artists staked out a panel each and painted a picture each according to his own whimsy. Credit for originating the "paint-in" was given to a visiting night-club comedian named Pat Paulsen, who on August 5 appeared in traffic court. He was charged with obstructing pedestrian traffic on Davie Street by painting a canvas on the sidewalk with his head while hanging by his feet, in front of the coffee shop where he was appearing as an entertainer. From his brief career as a cranial abstractionist Paulsen went on to even more distinguished work in the United States, including an unsuccessful but wildly popular candidature for the presidency. The art form that he helped to stimulate was hailed as not only unique in the known world, but also indicative that the city was capable of a spontaneous outburst of creativity.

In October the fountain arrived in three wooden boxes, to be assembled behind a double screen that confirmed suspicions that it was a secret weapon of the higher level of government in Victoria. On December 16 the official unveiling of the Courthouse Fountain took place, in the midst of a torrential downpour. When the fountain was turned on, the combined volume of water gushing out of the sky drenched the official party headed by Premier Bennett and evoked screams of "Don't turn it on! Shut it off!" A few hours later an unofficial critic of the statuary added detergent to the fountain's circulating system, and the fountain choked in a cascade of suds.

The great washout was one of the last official occasions for Mayor Rathie, who had been defeated earlier in the month by the mayor-elect, Tom Campbell. Rathie had run City Hall in forthright fashion, but had alienated many voters, shortly after his election, by obtaining a new mayoral car that cost $18,000 and by ordering even more costly renovations of his office at City Hall. To those who grumbled at the expense the mayor replied that it was necessary to "think big," a philosophy that did not sit well with citizens who admired a certain shabby gentility in their mayor—unless the money he spent was his own. Despite the backing of the Non-Partisan Association, Rathie lost to Tom Campbell, who ran as an independent. Like Rathie, Campbell was a wealthy businessman, a promoter and owner of apartment buildings. Campbell's campaign slogan was "City government is a big business." He too rejected, or seemed to, the homespun image of the leader of the city's government, saying: "The mayor is the president of a corporation, not a social leader who spends half his time in things like meeting the first shipload of Japanese oranges."

In the battle of the businessmen Campbell showed more flair for showmanship, enlisting go-go girls to illustrate his progressivism and proposing to put up a prize of $1,000 or an all-expenses-paid trip to Hawaii in a contest designed to attract voters to the polls. The contest was called off as illegal, but Campbell still had caught the eye of enough voters in the East End, where he was born, to win access to the mayor's chair.

Defeated along with "the administrator's administrator" was the bylaw to fluoridate Vancouver's public water supplies. The lost virginity of the drinking water since chlorination notwithstanding, enough people cherished its purity to reject fluoridation, and did so again two years later, when Tom Campbell was re-elected mayor.

One of Mayor Campbell's first duties in 1967 was to welcome to Vancouver, on April 27, Emperor Haile Selassie of Ethiopia. The Lion of Judah was en route to Expo in Montreal and was accompanied by a pet chihuahua named Lulu, which in the course of enjoying the freedom of the city that included a tour of the Faculty Club at U.B.C., demonstrated how quickly the informal atmosphere of Vancouver put visitors at their ease.

Some of the wisdom of the Solomon that was Selassie's ancestor was required to deal with the much larger number of visitors, during the spring, who gave to Vancouver the title of "Hippie Capital of Canada." To the indigenous population of young people who had rejected the values of society were added runaways from most of the other provinces. Like the workless men of the thirties, the hippies were attracted by the milder climate and the beaches on which they could sleep outdoors. The center for their social life was a stretch of Fourth Avenue west of Burrard, handy to older houses that were converted into communal havens for the lank-haired, bizarrely-dressed couples, to the considerable disgust of the Kitsilano Ratepayers Association. By day the hippies hove to the courthouse fountain, where they presented the legal problem of distinguishing loitering from lingering. On Sunday, March 27, 1967, about a thousand hippies took part in the "Human Be-in" near Second Beach in Stanley Park, dancing to the god of love as their Easter rite. Brandishing the usual placards ("Make Love, Not War," "Burn Pot, Not People"), and dancing to electric guitars, the "UFP" (Unidentified Flying People) wore vestiges of Indian garb. It had taken the Park just one hundred years to come full circle back to the savage beat and the pagan worship of the Squamish village of Chay-thoos.

The flower children had their own newspaper, *Georgia Straight,* sold on downtown corners by vendors of even more weird aspect than the old-timers who chalked their own editorials on boards beside the heaps of *Sun* and *Province.* The two major dailies had merged their physical plants and moved into new premises at Sixth and Granville, under the name of the Pacific Press. An abortive attempt to unseat them was made in the mid-sixties by a new newspaper, the Vancouver *Times,* one of whose directors was General Odlum. The *Times* fought a brave fight to overcome the strength of the established papers, but went keel up, to the dismay of many small investors who had pinned their hopes to its masthead.

The migration of the Pacific Press from its old home on Pender Street was symptomatic of the withdrawal from the area around Hastings Street, Cambie and Carrall. In April, 1967, a last-ditch effort to save the Majestic Theatre—the old Pantages and Beacon—from demolition, a fight led by a lawyer named Shakespeare, lost out to plans for a parking lot. The city's business center of gravity had moved inexorably southwest, into buildings whose prestige was measured in nearness to West Georgia Street. City planners were considering a freeway plan to link the North Shore with the new Trans-Canada Highway section via Port Mann Bridge, one plan including an overpass flanking Chinatown and menacing the community with the final indignity of trespass by motorized madness.

Although the total cargo handled through the port of Vancouver in 1967, more than 23 million tons, put the city ahead of Montreal for the first time, and the opening of the new Pacific Coliseum in Hastings Park, January, 1968, led to the city's winning a berth in the National Hockey League in 1970, the misgivings of growth continued to attract more attention than the physical evidence of prosperity. "A city without a heart," a professor of architecture called it. "The city without a soul" was the even more severe diagnosis, as suburban shopping centers such as Oakridge and Brentwood spirited away the smarter shops, including the genus known as *boutique*. Yet the downtown streets became increasingly congested with the wrong ingredient: vehicles, instead of people. The central intersections were places to drive through rather than to. Automobiles thwarted at these main junctions spilled into the overtaxed streets of the West End, where high-rise apartments skied higgledy-piggledy on a peninsula of buggy-lane access. "Like a monk's head, bald in the middle," a critic said of the development. Elsewhere, too, in the city whose vacant land was virtually all used up, or priced beyond the practicality of private houses, apartments and townhouses had sprung up in such numbers that by 1968 the balance was tipped from homeowners to a preponderance of tenants, with all that this meant in sociological terms of loss of wholesome environment for children, the loneliness of the human termitary, the impersonality of violence on the streets and the rest of the sorry inventory attached to megalopolis.

The civic neurosis gave rise to an entirely new and debilitating condition: envy of Toronto and Montreal. The architectural renaissance of the eastern cities, typified by Toronto's new City Hall and Montreal's Place Ville Marie, deeply disturbed Vancouver people living with the fact that the main intersection of their city, the spiritual center, was occupied on one corner by a parking lot, on another by a drugstore, and on the remaining two by an aging department store and an office building equally long in the tooth. After some acrid arbitration the city obtained the two blocks on Granville Street northwest and southwest of Georgia, and the Pacific Centre moved off the drawing board. No one was grieved to see the parking lot disappear, in 1969, but the demolition of the old Vancouver Opera House adjoining raised the dust of remembrance. The wreckers moved onto the stage that supported the piano of Sergei Rachmaninoff, into the dressing room from which was carried the then-crippled Sarah Bernhardt to enthrall a Vancouver audience, and through the Animal Room where waited the horses of a live production of *Ben Hur,* with its chariot race on thundering treadmills.

The motion-picture houses remaining on Theatre Row sold tickets to a much different type of patron from the one that lined up at the Opera House to see the Marx Brothers or Katherine Hepburn. The veteran manager of the Orpheum, Ivan Ackery, described a person over forty on Granville Street on a Saturday night as almost an excuse for a sociological study, so youth-oriented had films become. In order to dress up a street that had become a rendezvous for no-goods, the businesses along Theatre Row between Robson and Smithe on Granville renovated the pavement, street lamps and store fronts, but the effect was still well removed from Pall Mall.

In other, major plans for the downtown area, such as Project 200 that would restore the waterfront to the people of the city as a promenade with noble vistas of inlet and mountain, and the midtown civic square that would humanize a density of high buildings, there appeared the gleam of a beginning of understanding among the city fathers and their town planners of such concepts as perspective and relation of structural dimension to the mental health of the urban individual. A bright spot on an otherwise badly blotted copybook was the Centennial Museum, opened October 26, 1968, on the land taken over from the RCAF depot on the old Indian reservation at Kitsilano Beach. Beside the museum was built the Planetarium, a gift of lumberman H. R. MacMillan, and a small gem of architecture—"Taj Mahal on the Creek" the *Sun* called it.

Also in 1968 the upper reaches of False Creek were the subject of a proposed apartment-housing development by a C.P.R. realty affiliate, involving a land swap with the city, but after almost half a century of dealings with the company the city had become rather wary of its schemes. In addition to the density of residents in proportion to open breathing space, the plan had the objectionable feature of renaming the area "Edgewater Park." Major Matthews was one of the first to snort that it was False Creek and False Creek it would remain, regardless of whatever subdivisional silk purse was made of the old sow's ear.

A mortality that was almost a relief to Vancouver was the last gasp, in 1968, of the Vancouver International Festival. After two disastrous years the festival had slung around its neck a tastefully stuffed but still very dead albatross in the shape of a $236,687 deficit, with creditors in all the lively arts. With the festival died a naïve aspiration to the grandiose. At a time when bathing beaches were being closed because of pollution, when smog was dense enough to make visitors from Los Angeles feel uncomfortably at home, when downtown traffic was approaching the point of ultimate congealment, international eminence as a festival city was less pertinent than Vancouver's survival as a habitable environment. The *Sun*, which a few years earlier had run glamour photos of development in the West End, now ran articles describing "the sweet life turned sour for would-be swingers," and "lonely people living lies, and blank faces peering from balconies."

In microcosm—a somewhat large microcosm—the city's physical disorders were duplicated on the campus of U.B.C., now hyper-pituitary to the extent of more than twenty-two thousand registered students, and administrative problems that defeated two successive presidents in as many years. Walter Gage, a veteran of the student-faculty wars, was appointed president till his retirement, but there was no mistaking that the real authority on the campus was that of the power shovel and the bulldozer setting the tone for activism over the traditional atmosphere of study and contemplation. The university, like the city, was now a multimillion-dollar "plant," a good-sized city of commuters like those whose occupancy of apartments in the city was increasing by eight thousand people annually.

Notwithstanding an assessment of land values that in 1969 topped one billion dollars, Vancouver was experiencing a crisis of self-confidence.

Metropolitanism, as the solution to some of the more basic problems such as sewage treatment, evoked the proposal by Burnaby reeve Alan Emmott of amalgamation of the district with Vancouver. Vancouver balked, in keeping with the unfailing dedication to self-interest that characterized all the districts of the area euphemistically called Greater Vancouver. The population of that area was now close to one million, of which a little less than half (410,357, according to the 1966 census) lived in Vancouver city. The extra-urban elements were favored in their rugged individualism by the area of Greater Vancouver—531 square miles compared to Metropolitan Toronto's 240 square miles. Regional planning for the Lower Mainland remained the kind of contemporary music that dispenses with harmony.

Concern about the complexity of the big city's ailments having penetrated the younger, professional groups in Vancouver, representatives of these formed a new organization in 1968, The Electors' Action Movement (TEAM). Its slate of candidates in the December civic election was largely defeated, including its mayoral nominee, Alan Emmott. Tom Campbell, who had won over to his side a section of the population by harassing the hippies via the prosecutor's office, was re-elected by what some called "old ladies in tennis shoes." But the door to more enlightened civic government had been wedged open slightly. Even the aldermen whose ears picked up nothing beyond the sound of their own voice were coming to understand that the forces jeopardizing larger cities all over North America required measures more sophisticated than the ban on back-yard burning that they bravely implemented in 1968.

Everywhere on the continent the cult of bigness, the super-city, was being scorched by riot. Conflict with higher levels of government, in which the special problems of the city had no priority, was generating restlessness with the whole hierarchy of governmental power. The desirability of resurrecting the city-state was seriously discussed, as inappropriate prologue to the 1971 centennial of British Columbia's joining Confederation.

Partly as a reaction against the cereal-box skyscrapers, partly because attention was directed to that part of the city by the Project 200 transformation of the waterfront, a remarkable and encouraging phenomenon occurred as Vancouver entered the seventies: the restoration of Gastown. Some of the impetus behind the movement stemmed from a group called the Improvement of Downtown East End Society (IDEAS), whose object was to rehabilitate Skid Road, but more consequential was the enthusiasm of individual entrepreneurs, young architects, artists and university students, who looked at the sturdy old buildings dating from 1887 to 1900 and saw that beneath the shabbiness lay possibilities for a variety of enterprises that would profit from interiors warmed by the old wood and brick, and by the full-blooded if not altogether gracious history of the Victorian hotels, saloons, office blocks and warehouses.

With active support from the city council, and with the publicity of walking tours sponsored by the Community Arts Council, a new generation discovered the tarnished charms of old Gastown in such parts as Trounce Alley and Blood Alley, Maple Tree Square (Water Street at Carrall), and the flatiron Europe Hotel. One of the first renovations was that of 8 West Pender, unofficially credited with being the narrowest office building in Canada, by a couple of youthful architects. The "Gastown Shoppe" became a smart address for boutiques, a flea market, an art gallery. Young businessmen converted an old warehouse into studios and flats. The opening of a fashionable men's clothing boutique was graced by the presence of one of London's foremost fashion designers, wearing a creation that would have stunned Gassy Jack and did flabbergast some of his alcoholic heirs who gaped at the proceedings from the sidewalk. Unreconstructed tenants of the rooms above the boutique lowered empty wine bottles on strings, to be filled with punch, which they were, to the satisfaction of both salons.

CHAPTER 16

Discovery the Second

The options: the garden city gone to greed, or the finding of beauty that is wise

THE rescue of Gastown from squalor might or might not be a lasting deliverance. The shoulder-rubbing of rubby-dubs with the concerned ladies of the arts council symbolized the schismatic character of the choice facing Vancouver as the city entered the latter decades of the twentieth century. The city's history from the beginning has been a contention between the agents of greed to whom the site was first and foremost a piece of prime real estate, and the people who cared about the city as a place in which to live in company with the beautiful. Only by translating their concern into action could these people retrieve from megalopolis the qualities of life that had attracted them to Vancouver since it was a clearing, and in such numbers as to make it the instant city.

A writer for the New York *Times* once described Vancouver as "one of the 'gardeningest' spots of our northern continent. . . . The people of Vancouver nurture the fine British tradition of gardening, and other folk who settle there are soon infected. Motor mechanics, business men and professional people are proud of their plantings, whether small or large, and as a result the whole town looks like a flower seed catalogue." The *Times* man was wrong. In Vancouver gardening has been more than a contagious disease. It has been a religion, indeed *the* religion, the Sabbath observed on the knees in the rockery, or in the pew of a row of carrots to be thinned. The

Devil was a worm, and Vancouver people had some faith in prayer but more in peat moss.

Evidence was abundant, however, as the city entered the seventies, that the garden city was luxuriant with *fleurs du mal:* the national capital of drug addiction, of alcoholism, of divorce, of suicides (officially 18 per 100,000, twice the national average and probably closer to the 26 per 100,000 of San Francisco, sometimes known as the suicide capital of North America).

To be called "the San Francisco of the North" had become faint praise with an annual increment of damnation. Like the California city, in her youth Vancouver was a natural beauty, the belle of the continental ball. The cities east of the Rockies were the big, strong men of Canada's economy, the home of the masculine industries of steelmaking, auto manufacture, grain and oil production. To Vancouver fell the feminine role of the not-so-big, the milder (and more easily moved to tears), the physically exciting. This was the city that made husbands leave homes in Toronto and Montreal, to dally with her delights. Now, the bloom of youth gone, Vancouver had the choice of becoming either a blowzy slut or the kind of charmer to whom the passing years add only graciousness.

It is not too late. Vancouver is still a pretty girl who uses the wrong make-up. Young, endowed by nature with charms to a degree that to many a crowfooted prairie eye has bordered on the indecent, she dresses herself with an odd assortment of buildings—metropolis gone Auntie Mame.

Her streets are too busy. She hasn't learned how to walk. And like many of today's young matrons, she's getting overdeveloped toward the south.

But, crack the facade of cheap cosmetic, the rouge of neon lights, let the sea breeze wash her face, and Vancouver sits as fair as any maid in her bath. She is the kind of city a sailor wants to marry. Stanley Park still swings like a plush green purse in the city's hand, and the children still laugh at the penguins doing their endless imitation of waiters in a restaurant recently involved in a multiple food poisoning.

Nothing, however, accelerates depreciation of a great beauty more quickly than her trying to satisfy too many admirers. And if it is true that each man kills the thing he loves, Vancouver has never wanted for lovers. One of the city's senior swains, L. D. Taylor, bequeathed to her nothing more valuable than the advice: "Don't try to grow too big. A big city is no place to live. You don't know your neighbors." What L.D. failed to mention was that what makes a city too big, and unlovable, is not entirely the size of the population. Paris, Rome, Edinburgh are cities of large population, but the disposition of the cities themselves is such as to make them seem less big than, say, Windsor, Ontario. Montmartre is full of people to whom the Sacré Coeur by moonlight is all the neighbor they need.

For the first century of growth, Vancouver's Sacré Coeur was the dramatic basilica of mountain, beyond the cobbled strait flecked with droppings of the dray-horse sun. The city's faith in the prospect was consummate. Arrested in Toronto in 1937 for buying a fifteen-cent package of tobacco on a Sunday, a Vancouver man said: "I don't think Vancouver would do that to anybody. Their vision is too broad. You can't be petty amid such grandeur and beauty."

Little by little the grandeur and beauty were cut off, diminished, lost to view by rising towers of concrete, by smog, by a pace of living that caused even the highest North Shore peaks, Sheba's Breasts indeed, to vanish in the fumes of frustration. For Vancouver, "the site in search of a city," the hunt was leading into ever more labyrinthine problems of environment. Penetrating these problems would require a class of civic administrator blessed with extraordinary ability. On this subject Gerry McGeer said: "We have lacked leadership in keeping with the enormous possibilities of achievement that are ours to accomplish." The successors to the men at City Hall whose first thought was to preserve the wilderness of Stanley Park had lost that genius for bold strokes, had become myopically fascinated by the graphs of tax revenues and rentable floor space.

In 1969 a group of leading citizens began to promote the project of reproducing Captain Vancouver's ship *Discovery*, as a floating exhibit. Laudable though the venture was, the task of exploration confronting the inhabitants of the place that the captain merely scanned called for a craft of greater complexity. The charts of the city's future were as enigmatic, as perilous, as the west coast inlets appeared to the rowers of the captain's bark. If the hand on the tiller remained that of the developer, if the rudder responded only to Captain Silver Dollar, the city would founder.

Vancouver entering the 1970's was on collision course with the slow black ship gutting a fish-scale sea. On the navigational skill of those aboard Burrard Peninsula, and on their understanding of what buoys the quality of life, would depend Vancouver's attaining safe harbor among the great cities of the world.

BIBLIOGRAPHY

ADAMS, JOSEPH, *Ten Thousand Miles Through Canada.* London, Methuen & Co., 1913.

BIRNEY, EARLE, *Trial of a City.* Toronto, Ryerson, 1952.

BRADLEY, A. G., *Canada in the Twentieth Century.* London, Constable, 1905.

BRITTAIN, HARRY, *Canada There and Back.* London, The Bodley Head, 1911.

BROOKS, F. G. H., *Vancouver's Origins.* B.A. Thesis, University of British Columbia, Vancouver, 1952.

BURWASH, E. M. J., *The Geology of Vancouver and Vicinity.* Chicago, University of Chicago Press, 1918.

CAMERON, RONALD LLOYD, *Social Conditions of Skid-row.* M.S.W. Thesis, University of British Columbia, Vancouver, 1964.

CAMPBELL-JOHNSTON, R. C., *The Story of the Totem.* Vancouver, Ryott, 1924.

COPE, M. C. L., *Colonel Moody and the Royal Engineers in British Columbia.* M.A. Thesis, Department of History, University of British Columbia, Vancouver, 1940.

CORNWALL, IRA H. B., *A Geographical Study of the Port of Vancouver in Relation to Its Coastal Hinterland.* M.A. Thesis, Department of Geology and Geography, University of British Columbia, Vancouver, 1952.

GOMERY, DARREL, *A History of Early Vancouver.* B.A. Thesis, Department of History, University of British Columbia, Vancouver, 1936.

HAMILTON, J. H., *Western Shores.* Vancouver, Progress Publishing Co., 1933.

HOBSON, J. A., *Canada Today.* Vancouver, London, 1906.

HOWAY, F. W., and SCHOLEFIELD, E. O. S., *British Columbia from Earliest Times to the Present.* 4 vols. Vancouver, Clark, 1914.

JOHNSON, EMILY PAULINE (TEKAHIONWAKE), *Legends of Vancouver.* Toronto, McClelland & Stewart, 1961.

LIONNET, JEAN, *Chez les Français du Canada.* Paris, Plon, 1908.

LOGAN, HARRY T., *Tuum Est, A History of the University of British Columbia.* Vancouver, Mitchell Press, 1958.

LOPATIN, IVAN A., *Geography of Vancouver.* M.A. Thesis, Department of Geology and Geography, University of British Columbia, Vancouver, 1929.

McEVOY, BERNARD, *From the Great Lakes to the Wide West.* Toronto, Biggs, 1902.

MILDMAY, AUBREY N. ST. JOHN, *Sea-room, a Vancouver Empire Song.* Toronto, Biggs, 1910.

MORLEY, ALAN, *Vancouver: from Milltown to Metropolis.* Vancouver, Mitchell Press, 1969.

NATIVE SONS OF BRITISH COLUMBIA, *Romance of Vancouver.* Vancouver, 1926.

ORMSBY, MARGARET A., *British Columbia: a History.* Toronto, Macmillan, Vancouver, Evergreen Press, 1958.

RODDAN, ANDREW, *Canada's Untouchables.* Vancouver, Clarke & Stuart, 1932.

ROY, PATRICIA E., *The Rise of Vancouver as a Metropolitan Centre, 1886–1929.* B.A. Thesis, Department of History, University of British Columbia, Vancouver, 1960.

ST. MAUR, MRS. ALGERNON, *Impressions of a Tenderfoot during a Journey in Search of Sport in the Far West.* London, Murray, 1890.

STAINSBY, DONALD, and KUTHAN, GEORGE, *Vancouver: Sights and Insights.* Toronto, Macmillan, 1962.

VANCOUVER, CAPTAIN GEORGE, *A Voyage of Discovery.* London, Stockdale, 1801.

WALHOUSE, FREDA, *The Influence of Minority Ethnic Groups on the Cultural Geography of Vancouver.* M.A. Thesis, Department of Geography, University of British Columbia, Vancouver, 1961.

YOUNG, C. H., and REID, H. R. Y., *The Japanese Canadians.* Toronto, University of Toronto, 1938.

BROCHURES AND PAMPHLETS

ARCHIVISTS' CLUB, *Vancouver, a Short History.* Vancouver, 1936.

THE BRITISH COLUMBIA CENTENNIAL COMMITTEE and B. C. LIONS FOOTBALL CLUB, *The British Columbia Sports Hall of Fame.* Vancouver, 1967.

BROWN CARS, *Vancouver, B.C. What to See and How to See It.* Vancouver, 1917.

DOMINION ILLUSTRATING CO., *Greater Vancouver–Illustrated.* Vancouver, 1908.

FREER, K. M., *Vancouver, a Bibliography*. Thesis, University of London Diploma of Librarianship, London, 1962.

GREATER VANCOUVER PUBLICITY BUREAU, *A Thousand Facts About Vancouver*. Vancouver, 1931.

HODGE, G., and ROBINSON, I. M., *Jobs, Transportation and People* (Report to the Metropolitan Joint Committee, Table IVA). Vancouver, 1960.

KING, WILLIAM LYON MACKENZIE, *Report on Losses Sustained by the Chinese Population of Vancouver, B.C., on the Occasion of the Riots in That City in September, 1907*. Ottawa, 1909.

LORT, ROSS, *Old Houses and Buildings in Vancouver* (Address to the Tuesday Club of the Vancouver Public Library). Vancouver, 1960.

MATTHEWS, J. S., *The Cenotaph*. Vancouver Archives, 1963.

MATTHEWS, J. S. (ed.), *The Founding of the Salvation Army, Vancouver*. Vancouver Archives, 1962.

MATTHEWS, J. S. (ed.), *The Naming, Opening and Dedication of Stanley Park*. Vancouver Archives, 1964.

MCGEER, G. G., *Vancouver, City of Destiny*. Vancouver, 1936.

MCLACHLAN, C. W., *History of Vancouver up to 1900*. Paper submitted in History 11, Summer School, University of British Columbia, Vancouver, 1935.

NICOLLS, J. P., *Real Estate Values in Vancouver*. Vancouver Archives, 1954.

PACIFIC COAST FIRE INSURANCE CO., *Our Fifty Years*. Vancouver, 1940.

ROSS AND CEPERLEY, REAL ESTATE AGENTS, *Vancouver*. Vancouver, 1888.

VANCOUVER ART GALLERY and U. B. C., *People of the Potlatch*. Vancouver, 1956.

VANCOUVER TOURIST ASSOCIATION, *Vancouver, The Sunset Doorway of the Dominion*. Vancouver, Clarke and Stuart, 1905.

PUBLISHED ARTICLES

"The Battle of the Ports," *Toronto Saturday Night*, September 13, 1924.

BOUTILIER, H. R., "Vancouver's Earliest Years," *British Columbia Historical Quarterly* (Note: in subsequent listing, *BCHQ*), Vol. 10, No. 2 (April, 1946).

GORDON, C. L., "Government Services," *British Columbia Magazine* (Note: in subsequent listing, *BCM*), June, 1911.

GORDON, W. R., "Industrial Vancouver," *BCM*, June, 1911.

GRANT, J. H., "Burrard Inlet in Early Times," *BCM*, June, 1911.

HOWAY, F. W., "Early Settlement on Burrard Inlet," *BCHQ*, Vol. 1, No. 2 (April, 1937).

KENVYN, R., "Vancouver's Harbour and Shipping," *BCM*, June, 1911.

KERR, J. B., "Journalism in Vancouver," *BCM*, June, 1911.

LASSERRE, F., "Keeping Pace With Architecture in Vancouver," *Canadian Art*, Vol. 15, p. 84.

"Lots of Work in Vancouver," *BCM*, June, 1911.

MacDonald, Dawn, "Vancouver," *Chatelaine*, October, 1969.
Makovski, L., "The Rise of the Merchant Princes," *BCM*, June, 1911.
Matthews, J. S., "Vancouver Burns," *Vancouver Historical Journal*, No. 3 (January, 1960).
McDougall, P. J., "How Vancouver Gets Snow-water from Mountain Streams," *BCM*, June, 1911.
McGregor, D. A., "The Marvel of Vancouver," *BCM*, June, 1911.
McInnes, T., "The Port of Vancouver," *Canadian Geographical Journal*, April, 1931.
Morse, Eric W., "Some Aspects of the Komagata Maru Affair, 1914." Toronto, *Canadian Historical Association*, University of Toronto Press, 1936.
Paton, J. A., "The Story of Point Grey," *BCM*, June, 1911.
Playfair, W., "Vancouver and the Railways," *BCM*, June, 1911.
Pogue, P., "Outdoor Vancouver," *BCM*, June, 1911.
Pugsley, E. E., "Old Pioneer Passes; the Story of Hastings Mill," *Canadian Magazine*, Vol. 72 (July, 1929), p. 12.
Reid, R. L., "The Inside Story of the 'Komagata Maru,'" *BCHQ*, January, 1941.
Sage, Walter N., "Vancouver: the Rise of a City," *Dalhousie Review*, April 22, 1941.
Somerville, B. S., "Vancouver as a Grain Port," *Toronto Saturday Night*, February 21, 1925.
"Two Cities of the Far West," *Chamber's Journal*, May 26, 1888.
"Vancouver, a City of Beautiful Homes," *BCM*, December, 1911.
"Vancouver's Telephones," *BCM*, June, 1911.
Weston, C., "The City Police," *BCM*, June, 1911.
Weston, Garnet, "The Flame Fighters," *BCM*, June, 1911.
Wilson, Ethel, "Young Vancouver Seen Through the Eyes of Youth," *Habitat*, Central Mortgage and Housing Corp., Ottawa, 1967.

GENERAL REFERENCE

British Columbia Directory, 1882–83.
British Columbia Journals, 1886.
CITY OF VANCOUVER, *Municipal Year Book*, 1969.
Source material for a History of Vancouver. 6 vols. Uncatalogued items from Vancouver newspaper from 1886, Canadian Club of Vancouver.
Vancouver Historical Journal, Archives Society of Vancouver.
Files of the Vancouver *Daily News-Advertiser*.
Files of the Vancouver *Province*.
Files of the Vancouver *Sun*.
Files of the Vancouver *World*.

INDEX

PHOTO CREDITS

1–Provincial Archives, Victoria, British Columbia
2–9, 11–24, 26, 28, 32–35–Vancouver Public Library
10, 25, 27, 29, 30, 31, 36, 37, 40, 43, 44, 45, 47–The Vancouver *Province*
38, 41–Vancouver Visitors Bureau
39–British Columbia Government Photographs
42–Greater Vancouver Tourist Association

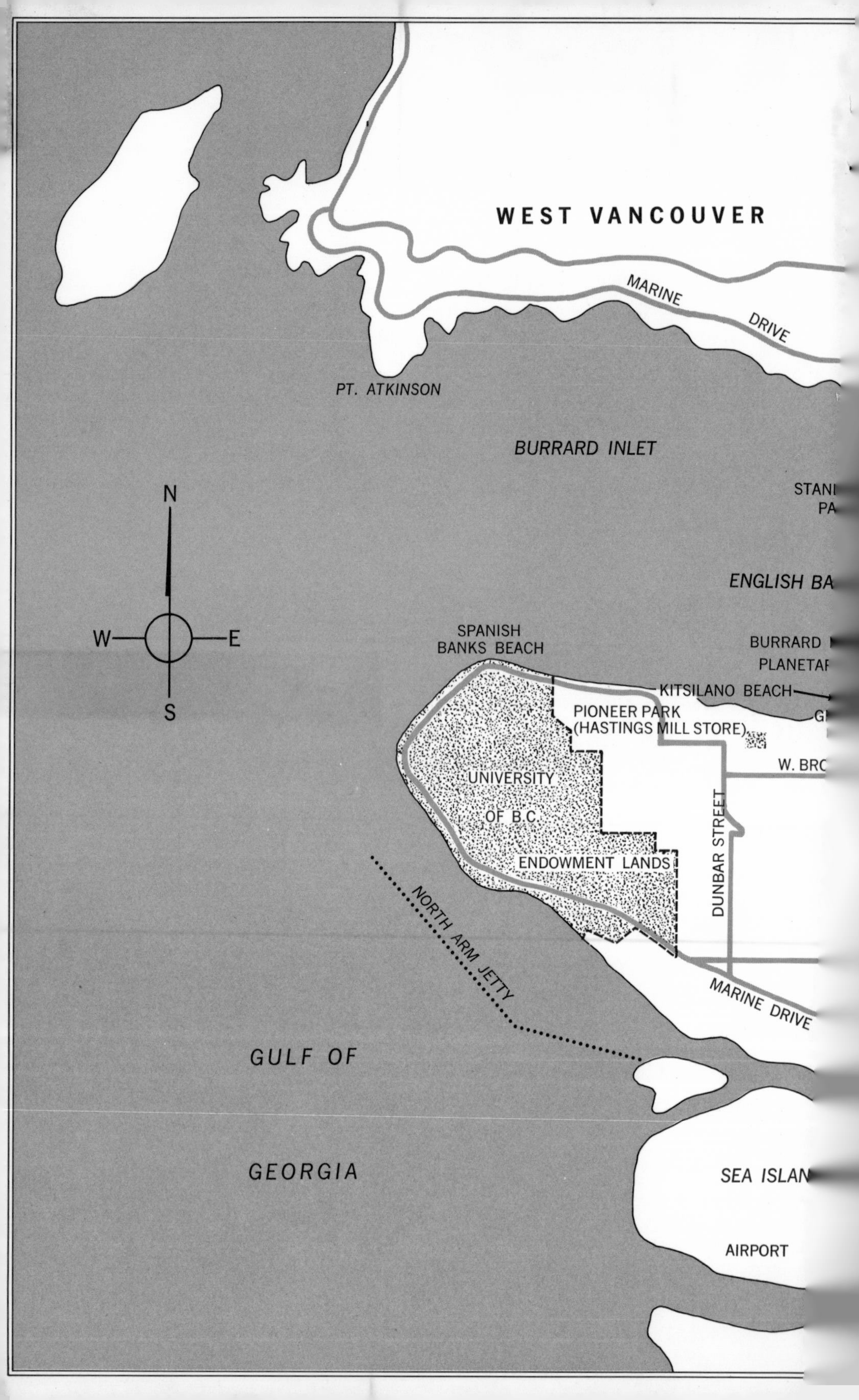
WEST VANCOUVER
MARINE DRIVE
PT. ATKINSON
BURRARD INLET
N
W
E
S
SPANISH BANKS BEACH
KITSILANO BEACH
PIONEER PARK (HASTINGS MILL STORE)
UNIVERSITY OF B.C. ENDOWMENT LANDS
DUNBAR STREET
NORTH ARM JETTY
MARINE DRIVE
GULF OF GEORGIA
AIRPORT